BACKSTAGE PASS

Interviews with Women in Music
by Laura Post

Foreword by Dar Williams

New Victoria Publishers

© Copyright 1997 Laura Post

All rights reserved, worldwide. No part of this work may be reproduced or transmitted in any form by any means, electronic or mechanical, without permission in writing from the publisher.

Published by New Victoria Publishers, Inc., a feminist literary and cultural organization, PO Box 27, Norwich, VT 05055-0027

1 2 3 4 5   2001   2000 1999 1998 1997

Printed and bound in Canada

Cover Design by Claudia McKay
Cover photos are of Ani DiFranco, Deborah Henson-Conant, Gaye Adegbalola, Laura Love, and Joan Osborne.

Library of Congress Cataloging-in Publication Data

Post, Laura.
    Backstage pass : interviews with women in music / by Laura Post; with a foreword by Dar Williams.
      p.   cm.
    ISBN 0-934678-84-7
    1. Women musicians--interviews. 2. Feminism and music.
I. Title.
ML82.P68 1997
780' .092' 273--dc21   97-5011
                                                                         CIP
                                                                         MN

FOREWORD
by Dar Williams

There's a fine line between sharing one's voice and selling one's voice. There are plenty of businesses that would have singer/songwriters conform to safe and easy ways of greasing the big machine. I watched the uncontainable Ani DiFranco on stage, once, accompanied by drummer Andy Stochansky, and thought about all the industrial alterations one could make:

1. Bring in the pants a tad. The "men's pants" thing is OK, but we've got to show off that butt!

2. Lose the male drummer. Get a voluptuous, yet dykey, female replacement. Cash in on any possible intrigue between you.

3. Maintain hairstyles for at least six months at a time, so that we can generate enough publicity around each look.

4. Shine those army boots!

In other words, limit the complexity of the performer, and take the bite out of the message. Of course, Ani resists this packaging, and the result is communication, not commerce. The same goes for everyone else in this book, like Holly Near. In challenging all the hype around lesbianism, she sings, "It's simply love—simply my love for a woman," ("Simply Love", 1980), and women of all persuasions get choked up because it's not often that we venture into a public space and feel such uncompromising gentleness.

Folk singer/agitator/organizer U. Utah Phillips pointed out to me that in many cultures, the unfortunate symbol of power is the control of the natural resources, and that women are seen as a natural resource. Women thus serve as the currency of status, like diamonds and real estate. Hair color, age, and overbite are assessed from the trading floor. When the commercial media get ahold of the hottest commodities, they go crazy. And so do the women who scramble to define themselves as the market does: from the outside in.

At some point, I picked up the nasty habit of defining myself from the outside in. When I was in college, I didn't think I was a real woman. On campus, real women had "lovers" with whom they "talked and cried until three in the morning," after which they had "incredible sex." Or so I thought.

Then I encountered the infamous wall. It was the first stall of the women's bathroom in the campus center. It was a mosaic of scrawl and counter-scribbling. "I bore myself." "I haven't had sex in two years." "I've never had sex." "I never felt like an idiot in Cleveland." "White feminism sucks." All of these had comments attached, "Good for you," or "Call this hotline," or "I wish I'd been celibate. You're lucky. I spent two years with a really bad lover!!!!!" to which was written, "Try women!" and the reply was, "It was a woman!!!!!" I found myself within this wall of voices, because it was simply a diversity of voices. This collection of exceptions proved that there is no rule.

All the women in this book, whether they achieved mainstream or alternative success, have a voice that they've brought to the table. They weren't created for a market. They themselves created pools of recognition, simply by lifting things up and saying, " Hey, look what I've found." Look what I found in this relationship, this region, this field, or just this moment.

This process of recognition renews and perpetuates itself. Every voice that claims its unique ground leads to more voices that render deeper subtleties. Each nuance empowers and gives rise to more voices again. Sometimes, as with Sweet Honey in the Rock, there is an effort to reinvigorate the life-affirming voices of the past, while continuously taking on contemporary issues. Recognizing our hidden histories gives even more depth and strength to this movement, which in essence is not a movement, but just an understanding of "We all…everyone of us."

It's a very exciting time to be making music. There is a growing audience for the rich traditions of music that don't necessarily make it on pop radio, and there are many networks, from cafés to cyberspace, that struggle to uphold the integrity of these diverse musical strains.

I hope that in seeing the artists behind the art, you will find yourself somewhere, and that you, like me, will find springboards of possibility. Verbally and non-verbally defined, we all have a voice. We are making the world better by telling our stories and cross-pollinating with many levels of community. Perhaps this is why I was struck by something Marianne Faithfull said. Laura asked her how she got sober in 1995. Faithful replied, "I think I was actually going to lose my voice. That was the one thing I couldn't bear. I didn't mind losing everything else—my looks, my life, my child…my money, my lover—I didn't mind that. But I was not prepared to lose my voice."

TABLE OF CONTENTS

INTRODUCTION	5
ALIX DOBKIN—the "head lesbian" returns	9
ALTAZOR—feminist "New Song"	11
ANI DIFRANCO—a righteous babe takes on the world	14
AVOTCJA—we hear your song, we need your song, we love your song	19
THE CHENILLE SISTERS—celebrating ten years of harmony and fun	23
CHERYL WHEELER—life and friendship in music	29
CHRISTINE LAVIN –and the Four Bitchin' Babes	34
CRIS WILLIAMSON & TRET FURE—women's music and the folk mainstream	37
DEBORAH HENSON-CONANT—playing jazz and living improvisation	47
FERRON—taking a new step in an old direction	52
HEATHER BISHOP—bringing victories and celebrations on tour	60
HOLLY NEAR— off on a new path, singing show tunes	66
JANIS IAN—society's child breaks silence and takes revenge	69
JOAN OSBORNE—one of us	78
JUDY SMALL—a folksinger's perspective on the U.S. and Australia	82
JUNE MILLINGTON—rocking the feminist way	89
KAY GARDNER—world music	95
LAURA LOVE—she could be your daughter's lover	98
LAURIE LEWIS—fiddlin' around	104
LIBBY RODERICK—ecofeminist singer-songwriter	109
LINDA TILLERY—big voice, solid roots, new spirituals	114
LUCIE BLUE TREMBLAY—folk, women's music, and quebecois charm	120
LYNN LAVNER—the original yentl sings and laughs about growing	126
MARIANNE FAITHFULL—the secret life of sister morphine	131
MARGIE ADAM—feminist musician and cultural interpreter	139
MARY McCASLIN—here's to the new days, your new destiny	145
MIMI FOX—one of very few female jazz guitarists	150
MOE TUCKER—a velvet vagrant or the birth of housewife punk	153
PATTY LARKIN—busker to big time	158
PHRANC—lesbian artist in women's music and the mainstream	162
RHIANNON—jazz storyteller	168
ROBIN FLOWER & LIBBY McLAREN—angels of change	174
RONNIE GILBERT—face to face with the most dangerous woman in America	180
SAFFIRE—uppity blues that sparkles	184
SUE FINK—certified outrageous	189
SWEET HONEY IN THE ROCK—a community voice, singing from their soul	193
TERESA TRULL—educated feminist redneck sings with soul and integrity	197
THE TOPP TWINS—one has bungee-jumped, the other hasn't	204
THROWING MUSES—Kristen Hersh, her writing is as much a curse as a blessing	209
VICKI RANDLE—the most watched, unknown great-voiced musician in America	213

CREDITS

Alix Dobkin—Earlier versions of this article appeared in *Hot Wire: Journal of Women's Music & Culture* (May 1992) and in Chicago *Outlines* (July 1995).

Altazor—An earlier version of this article appeared in *Dykespeak* (August 1994); reprinted with permission.

Ani DiFranco—An earlier version of this article appeared in *Bay Windows* (May, 1993); reprinted with permission.

Avotcja—An earlier version of this article appeared in *Ache* (summer 1993).

Chenilles—An earlier version of this article appeared in *Dirty Linen* (Feb/Mar 1995) and *Acoustic Musician* (Feb 1995)

Christine Lavin—An earlier version of this article appeared in *Bay Windows* (Sept, 1994).

Cris Williamson and Tret Fure—An earlier version of this article appeared in *Sing Out!* (August/September/October 1995); reprinted with permission.

Deborah Henson-Conant—An earlier version of this article appeared in *Bay Windows* (Nov 1994).

Laura Love—An earlier versions of this article appeared in *Sacred River* (November/December 1992) and *B-SIDE* (in press at the time of submission of this manuscript).

Ferron—Earlier versions of this article appeared in *Hot Wire: Journal of Women's Music & Culture* (January 1994) and *Dirty Linen* (April/May 1994).

Heather Bishop—An earlier version of this article appeared in *Acoustic Musician* (in press at the time of manuscript submission).

Holly Near—An earlier version of this article appeared in *Bay Windows* (March 1994).

Janis Ian—An earlier version of this article appeared in *Acoustic Musician* (in press at the time of submission of this manuscript).

Joan Osborne—An earlier version of this article appeared in *B-Side* (in press at the time of submitting this manuscript).

June Millington—An earlier version of this article appeared in *La Gazette* (December 1995). This article was compiled from a series of interviews with and pages of writings by June Millington.

Kay Gardner—An earlier version of this article appeared in *Chicago Outlines* (April, 1994).

Laurie Lewis—An earlier version of this article appeared in *Acoustic Musician*, (Dec. 1995).

Libby Roderick—An earlier version of this article appeared in *Sacred River* (June 1992).

Linda Tillery—An earlier version of this article appeared in *Sojourner* (March 1995).

Lucie Blue Tremblay—An earlier version of this article appeared in *Sing Out!* (August/September/October 1994) reprinted by permission.

Lynn Lavner—An earlier version of this article appeared in *The Letter* (Oct. & Nov. 1994).

Marianne Faithfull—An earlier version of this article appeared in *B-Side* (November/December 1995).

Mary McCaslin—An earlier version of this interview appeared in *Dirty Linen* (Aug./Sept.1994).

Margie Adam—An earlier version of this article appeared in *The Letter* (November, 1995).

Mimi Fox—An earlier version of this article appeared in *The Letter* (April 1995).

Moe Tucker—An earlier version of this article appeared in *B-Side* (July/August 1995).

Patty Larkin—An earlier version of this article appeared in *Bay Windows* (August 1994).

Phranc—An earlier version of this article appeared in *Hot Wire* (September 1991).

Rhiannon—An earlier version of this article appeared in *Hot Wire* (September 1991).

Sweet Honey—An earlier version of this article appeared in *Bay Windows* (November 1994).

Robin Flower and Libby McLaren—An earlier version of this article appeared in *Dirty Linen* (October/November 1994).

Ronnie Gilbert—An earlier version of this article appeared in *Bay Windows* (October 1994).

Saffire—An earlier version of this article appeared in *B-Side* (November/December 1995).

Sue Fink—An earlier version of this article appeared in *Dykespeak* (April 1994).

The Topp Twins—An earlier version of this article appeared in *Deneuve* (Jan./Feb. 1994).

Throwing Muses—An earlier version of this article appeared in *B-Side* (July/August 1995).

INTRODUCTION

Women's Music is a cultural construct, encompassing music and other arts, built upon the foundation of world music, and ultimately connected to the gay and feminist movements. The Women's Music network cultivated my writing sensibilities and confidence and provided a safe environment—through festivals, bookstores, local events, global events, organizations, publications, workshops, and of course, music—in which I could discover myself.

In 1982 I came out as a lesbian. Indisputably, the Women's Music network eased the process. Recognizing philosophies, opinions and longings in sync with mine, I began to accept, respect, question, defend, and define my own culture.

Doing this book has forced me to think critically about the relative meaning and value of Women's Music and Culture in the world. Is Melissa Etheridge in Women's Music because she played at a Women's Music festival before her career got big, even though she'd be labeled mainstream now? Are the Indigo Girls or Tribe 8 Women's Music because they are lesbians, even though they have neither identified publicly with the movement nor performed at Women's Music venues? Is Tracy Chapman in Women's Music because she has such a devoted lesbian following, even though she is not known to be a lesbian nor has she embraced a Women's Music philosophy?

I decided that Women *in* Music is a more enduring and inclusive term, and so have included in this book women musicians whose art has soothed me, helped me to grow and inspired my writing. This book satisfies a dream of giving back: I've been granted hundreds of interviews from which have come articles in nearly two hundred publications. I've had opportunities to meet interesting folks and make lasting friends through networking and documenting Women's Music and Culture.

This book compelled me to define for myself the boundaries of Women's Music. In addition to performance at Women's festivals, I contemplated the idea of Women's Music markets, self-definition by artists, definition by audiences, and roots of the movement. I also thought long and hard about how the false history of Women's Music as a 'white-woman-with-guitar' phenomenon has been perpetuated when many of the original Mothers of the form were women of color and/or played other instruments or in ensembles. One obvious conclusion is that, like the larger music industry and despite its earliest and best efforts to be politically cognizant and culturally correct, Women's Music has harbored its share of bigotry—a reflection of the community-at-large. After reading these interviews perhaps you will come up with definitions of your own.

My wish is that readers who are familiar with some of the artists will be drawn to and turned on by others. A second wish is that readers who know and enjoy the work of one or more of the women included here will learn more about them, perhaps surprisingly so. I do hope to push some readers' limits: whatever your primary sexual identification or cultural orientation.

On a broader scale, I wish that, in the future, this sort of book will not be so rare. Few overview books on music have been written by women (Gillian Gaar's *She's a Rebel: The History of Women in Rock and Roll* is a notable and worthy exception). A small fraction of review books, like those that have been spawned about Rod Stewart, Chuck Berry, or Jimi Hendrix, exist about women; the only one about lesbians in Women's Music is the recent overview volume *Hot Licks*, by Lee Fleming.

I would argue that most current women performers owe a debt to Women's Music artists for starting to develop women audiences, for beginning to define a female performance identity, and for showing that women can play as well as sing. Even if Suzanne Vega and Liz Phair are not aware of Linda Tillery, or if Debbie Harry doesn't know Sue Fink, or if Chrissie Hynde and L7 and Hole and Belly and Bratmobile are unfamiliar with June Millington, their fates have been linked by the fact that female-rich audiences grew, in part, out of female-only audiences which had first assembled to hear music by and about women.

It saddens me that so much talent is unavailable to the general public because of ongoing and unresolved misogynistic biases. (Several of the women included here have won Grammys, and Joan Osborne and Laurie Lewis were nominated in 1996). If "rock'n'roll is a white man's game" (*Time*, Anthony DeCurtis, April 29, 1996), then music in general is the game of heterosexual, European-ancestered men: increasingly less so but still mostly true.

New grassroots-origins (male) outfits like Green Day, Nine-Inch Nails, Smashing Pumpkins, and Hootie and the Blowfish routinely garner concert and album reviews, as well as celebrity dish, when equally innovative (female) groups, like those mentioned above and found in this book, are routinely ignored. Even the flirtations of Madonna and Courtney Love with the contemporary chic of lesbianism gather more coverage than the news item that Cris Williamson, one of the pioneers of Women's Music twenty years ago, is starting her own label. I guess that the world is not ready for a dyke Michael Jackson.

Women's Music allowed me to finish some stages of my personal blossoming, and there are generations of young women who will benefit from the opportunity to see themselves reflected from the stage, on the radio, and in stores.

If I am a good interviewer, then some of the credit goes to formal training. By metier, I am a psychiatrist; the essence of what I do is to find out about people. Before I tried my hand at interviewing artists, I had interviewed countless clients in and out of hospitals and was familiar with the setup. How fortunate I am to have a career in which I am permitted to ask people questions about themselves and about the world! I must state that, though I do know that I possess an indefatigable curiosity about others' inner worlds, I absolutely consider interviewing a privilege and an honor; and I try to maintain a level of integrity equal to its demands.

Over the years, I have injected my own style and techniques into the interviewing itself and into the writing. I have informally dubbed my interviewing approach 'Feminist Interviewing' for several reasons. First, I understand that being a media representative (like being a psychiatrist!) brings with it a modicum of power, and that power should not be used to hurt people. Toward that end, I have always tried to be visible as a person in addition to functioning as an interviewer. I own my origins and don't pretend to be objective but, instead, attempt to be fair and open-minded. In keeping with this tenet, I have encouraged interviewees to review my transcripts prior to publication and made certain that they knew that the power was theirs to terminate, interrupt, or give feedback on any interview not to their liking. I also refuse to tamper with any dialect or accent different from my own to make it sound "correct" or like the King's English (see what Avotcja has to say about the King's English in this book). This position has been difficult to maintain in the face of some editorial recommendations for homogeneity of the written word.

Second, I am almost always aimed at Truth. Thus, I try to aim my questions at vital and valuable answers, revelations and provocations of thought. My hidden agenda is always to pose the unasked question—not the rude or intrusive one—but that which will evoke a torrent of new ideation, an outpouring of genuine emotion, such that my editing is merely a gentle trim, a light-handed guiding of flow which is already present. The bottom line is that I want to know the source of genius and how it can coexist with the banality of everyday existence.

In the writing, I have felt free to interpolate cut-and-dried phrasing with description, fictionalized storytelling, and first-person observation and editorializing. If "traditional" (read: male) interviewing is a journalistic endeavor aimed at facts, dates, and numbers, then Feminist Interviewing is more qualitative than quantitative; every individual's herstory is crucial and relevant, even if she has not won a Grammy or sold a million copies of her recording or played at a stadium holding sixty-thousand fans. Personal quotes are more important than sound bites. If the interviews represent an integration of psychological flexibility with journalistic exactness, then the narrative reflects equal measures of poetic license, Greek chorus, and heartfelt diary musings.

Great appreciation for those editors and mentors who gave me opportunities to refine my writing and thinking and/or helped to shape my prose and formulate my principles: Chris Van Veghten and Elisabeth Mann (*Common Ground*), Toni Armstrong, Jr. (*Hot Wire*), Rudy Kikel (*Bay Windows*), Tracy Baim (*Chicago Outlines*), Rich Kerstetter (*Sing Out!*), Richard Schneider (*Harvard Gay/Lesbian Review*), various editors at *Ms., The Advocate, Deneuve/Curve, Dirty Linen, Sojourner, off our backs, Washington Blade, East Bay Express*, the late Carol Schutzbank (*B-Side*), ReBecca Béguin and Beth Dingman (New Victoria Publishers); and friends at AWMAC (the Association of Women's Music & Culture). A different kind of appreciation to all my editors and former editors who permitted reprinting of updated versions of interviews that had already appeared in their publications.

Deep thanks from the core of my being to the musicians, especially to Dar, for their patience with me and with this process; for their suggestions and corrections; and for the ongoing gifts of their music. I want to acknowledge the warmth I feel for and connection I feel with Eileen Kirby, whose painstaking transcription of many of these interviews has blessed me with copy that is not only clear and accurate but which represents regional and cultural factors in speech as well as any trained linguist could; it has been a pleasure sharing the early treasures of these interviews with her.

Finally, my most humble gratitude to my life partner, Judith, for helping me to see that I needed to do this book and then for reminding me regularly that I also needed to eat, sleep, talk to other people, and have fun.

Photo: June Parlett

ALIX DOBKIN
the "head lesbian" returns

Alix Dobkin has been the most visible lesbian feminist in the Women's Music and Culture community ever since *Lavender Jane Loves Women* (1973) was released, on Dobkin's own Women's Wax Works label. Typically, Dobkin has sought the essence of wimmin's mysteries as they surrounded her, speaking her truths from the stage and in workshops, as well as singing them in performance and on recordings.

From *Living With Lesbians* (1976) to *XX Alix* (1980), to *These Women/Never Been Better* (1986), to the recorded-live-in-Sydney *Yahoo Australia!* (1990), Dobkin has taken listeners through her own relationships, contradictions, and spiritual travels.

In the tradition of Holly Near's live retrospective *Singer in the Storm* and *Best Of...* releases from Olivia Records (Meg Christian, Margie Adam, Cris Williamson), came Alix Dobkin's *Love and Politics: A 30 Year Saga* (1992). However, Dobkin has never been a follower, and her offering—as well as her career thus far—was unique, bold, and quintessentially woman and lesbian affirming, as well as an effective way to meet her, if one had not done so already.

Love and Politics was more than a careful compilation of life work, it was a distillation of herstory between 1962 and 1992, a Coming Out tale visioned true. If the songs are jewels—familiar, lovely, well-worn, each suited to different occasions—then the liner notes are good friends: genuine, revealing about loves past and life present, and mutually enhancing.

Dobkin's songs fall into three categories: those through which we first knew her; those which have transformed language and thinking about our culture; and those which represent her continually growing attempts to refine and represent her international lesbian world view.

In the first category are "The Woman in Your Life" and "View From Gay Head," and "Crushes," all classics easily sung and remembered, vibrant with lesbian meanings.

The second category consists of such favorites as the deceptively singsong "Amazon ABC" and "Yahoo Australia," the latter with its Down Under slang. "Lesbian Code" is a compilation of euphemisms which Dobkin has painstakingly, lovingly collected during her tours through English-speaking nations. It is worth noting that part of how Dobkin has so successfully constructed cultural networks is by remaining conscious of and acknowledging cultural origins: she gives thanks to a Scottish melody for the "Lesbian Code" tune and to the Michigan Womyn's Music Festival for the live version of "If It Wasn't For The Women."

The third grouping may be the most eclectic and surprising, with such entries as the previously unrecorded "My Lesbian Wars" and the topical, questioning "Intimacy."

Dobkin's ideas, even from the 1970s—"Prayers in school to God in

Heaven/Praise the Biggest Prick of all" (Theme from "Getting Ready")—remain fresh, as do her unembellished arrangements and executions. Most importantly, Dobkin can be counted on to make the necessary point: "The more they take, the more they hate you" ("Some Boys").

Dobkin's classic songs are still concert favorites ("Talking Lesbian"), and she has remained a role model for independence, recording all her releases on her own Women's Wax Works label.

She has however, taken time off from the kind of intensive touring that she once did, retreating from center stage to write her memoirs and to pursue personal healing.

Alix Dobkin: I love performing and doing workshops, I love travelling, meeting and singing for lesbians, for women, being welcomed into so many lesbian homes. It's not that I'm tired of doing that, I'm just tired.

One of the main reasons I think I can take time off is that the job I set out to do, helping to set up a women's community network, is done.

I can still perform, I can still get concerts, I can still make a living, my audience is stable, so that's not the point. In fact, I've gotten wonderful support from women, the perfect kind of support which says "We'll really miss you, but go for it" or "You deserve it; good for you!"

Initially, Dobkin expected to do occasional performances, Michigan (Womyn's Music Festival), and other special events and to reap the joys of just staying home most of the time, instead of being on the road seven months of the year: play on the softball team, participate in ongoing projects, go to the women's coffeehouse, connect up with her Catskills community. Another expected benefit was to shed the identities that she has been constructing for thirty-five years: the Performer, the Entertainer and, for the majority of those years, the Lesbian Celebrity.

These days, Dobkin has been making a few more appearances. In concert, her fresh perspective enhances the worthwhile journey through personal moments and associations, accompanied by the gifts of clear thinking; catchy folk riffs; and direct, unequivocal and proud lyrics ("And I'm not ashamed to be a pushy Jewish girl."). The tell-all notes on her recordings are worth the price, but see her live because you'll love the Lesbian energy as well as the music.

Alix Dobkin has recently relocated from her long-time home in Woodstock, NY and currently resides in northern California.

DISCOGRAPHY

Lavender Jane Loves Women (Women's Wax Works, 1973); *Living With Lesbians* (Women's Wax Works, 1976); *Alix Dobkin's Adventures in Women's Music /songbook* (1979); *XX Alix* (Women's Wax Works, 1980); *These Women/ Never Been Better* (Women's Wax Works, 1986); *Yahoo Australia!* (Women's Wax Works, 1990); *Love & Politics* (Women's Wax Works, 1992).

ALTAZOR
feminist "New Song"

Since the 1960s, the New Song (nueva cancion) music of Latin America has melded folk melodies with socially conscious attitudes into a powerful body of protest/survival music. Made popular by artists like Victor Jara and Inti-Illimani, New Song has been largely dominated by male performers. The innovative all-woman quartet Altazor is changing that reality. With ties to Chile, Venezuela, U.S., and Cuba, Alt-azor ("Alta"= high; "azor"= goshawk) challenges stereotypes about women, about Latin American and New Song cultures.

Lichi Fuentes was five when she first experienced the simple power of singing with her siblings in her native Chile. Influenced by the nueva cancion movement, Fuentes came to North America in 1980, when Chile was under the dictatorship of Pinochet.

Vanessa Whang, U.S.-born of Japanese-Korean ancestry, studied classical music, then folk. Irish and Andean tunes led to New Song, and to La Pena Cultural Center, a Latin American gathering/performance space in Berkeley, California, where she met Fuentes and other exiled Chileans.

The early music of Cuban-born Dulce Maria Arguelles centered around family gatherings. At age twelve, she began her studies in classical guitar and initiated a career as a soloist. Arguelles' involvement in the Latin American music scene, following her 1984 arrival in the San Francisco Bay Area, brought her in contact with Fuentes and Whang.

An ensemble of thirteen women musicians, including Arguelles and Whang, emerged from a 1987 La Pena workshop given by Fuentes. Bonded by the politics of New Song, the group exchanged musical knowledge from their own cultural backgrounds and performed for fundraisers. When Fuentes was invited to perform at the Encuentro del Canto Popular she invited Arguelles and Whang to join her. The gig was a success, their mutual interest and commitment clear. The women decided to continue together.

The three women thought that their musical possibilities would be enhanced by a percussionist. Carolyn Brandy gigged with them—then the Lichi Fuentes Band—at the 1988 Michigan Womyn's Music Festival. Later that year, Fuentes, Whang, and Arguelles met up with Venezuelan multi-instrumentalist Jackeline Rago and invited her to do a gig with them. The group named itself Altazor; Rago became the fourth member.

Altazor's repertoire includes songs from Argentina, Chile, Cuba, Puerto Rico, and Venezuela. The singing (all in Spanish) marks daily acts of bravery, chronicles exile, creates solidarity, and celebrates life's triumphs over misfortune.

Altazor lends a feminist sensibility to portrayals of injustice. It offers the irre-

Photo : Irene Young

sistible rhythms and timbres of traditional Latin American instruments and blends them with seamless melodies and rich harmonies. Altazor creates an ambience of community.

Lichi Fuentes: That is what New Song is all about. That is one of the things we have done well. To experience the group on an album is one thing. To experience the group on stage is a lot more. It is a lot more than the music or the words; it is communication between human beings.

(Post) In 1989, Altazor was approached by Redwood Records, the label founded by cultural activist Holly Near. Near commented, "As I travelled around Central and Latin America, I fell in love with the music, but for the most part, not unlike the U.S., the groups were made up of all men, except for a few singers. When I saw/heard Altazor, it was like the promise of a future for women in music. Altazor allows Latin American women to see it, hear it, feel it, believe it. I would love to see someone fund a tour of Latin America for Altazor so all the hidden women musicians, especially the little girls, could witness Altazor's talent and courage."

Their debut release, *Altazor* (1989) showcased traditional music written by other artists. Altazor's album, *Concurrencia* (1993) features their own compositions, including Redwood-commissioned music for the writings of Nicolas Guillen, poet laureate of Cuba.

Altazor is concerned for the future. They would like the beauty of New Song to continue beyond Altazor's tours across the United States, beyond their individual, unique cultures, beyond their eight hands and four mouths. They would like for the ideas of New Song to be available to youth, as an alternative to the soulless and often sexist music which receives radio play.

Fuentes: What we do is not very complicated. It's just work and working together.

DISCOGRAPHY

Altazor (Redwood Records, 1989); *Concurrencia* (Redwood Records, 1993).

ANI DIFRANCO
a righteous babe takes on the world

What does androgynous twentysomething New Wave folk-punk singer Ani DiFranco have in common with feminist author/speaker/activist Gloria Steinem? They both have developed ardent followings through preaching a contemporary common person's gospel; they both are charismatic onstage; they both believe in the power of the Revolution Within.

When first I heard DiFranco live, at a folk club in Berkeley, California, it was clear that she possessed solid confidence, even more solid rhythmic sense, and an infectious aura of the positive. In the usually hushed hall, the typical audience—quietly appreciative—was replaced by a raucous crowd with body piercings, undaunted attitude, and haircuts that would get you fired from the bank: tufted, dyed, and shaved to the scalp. This "Nose Ring Generation" is spunky, dramatic, brimming with awareness, and bursting with social consciousness unimagined by their forebears at the same age.

Ani DiFranco is their inadvertent messiah. Her understated voice powers her unflinching lyrics. She delivers the intensity of Janis Joplin but will never drown in the discontent she stirs. Her songwriting melds the down-home sensibility of Dolly Parton with the biting energy of metal, and the jittery beat of thrash. The beat used to come from her guitar alone; now drummer Andy Stochansky joins her gigs.

DiFranco's genuine warmth takes some of the edge off her righteous rage. The unarguable rightness of her vision and the tunefulness of her compositions temper the harsh details of her vignettes, celebrating, as they do, people who live in their bodies, who fart and bleed and sweat and swear.

Although only in her twenties, DiFranco is an old soul, who points out over and over again how the Emperor has no clothes, is a man, is patriarchal. Ani DiFranco seems a woman whom every progressive person living in the 1990s would want to take home, to shatter the family's stereotypes.

DiFranco's muse hit early; she was certain at nine that she wanted to do something creative.

Ani DiFranco: My parents humored me; they got me this kid's guitar.

(Post) Taking lessons at a guitar shop, she received additional instruction from an older friend.

DiFranco: He was a degenerate folksinger type. He drank lots of coffee, smoked lots of cigarettes, wrote songs, and played in bars.

(Post) DiFranco's grace onstage defies the bristly quality of her songs; dance was something that she enjoyed during her growing up, not the only artistic passion that she pursued. In her native Buffalo, she briefly attended art school, then enrolled in New York City's New School for Social Research.

DiFranco: I had played every bar in Buffalo. I was sixteen. I was discovering myself.

(Post) Like her generational peers, DiFranco's youth had a certain independence.

DiFranco: My family was always nonexistent, in a good way.

(Post) Though followers have cited the 1991 Mariposa Festival as DiFranco's introduction to the world beyond western New York, she disagrees.

DiFranco: I've been touring constantly for years. It's always been a low-level, organic, grueling process; there was never any turning point. I never sat down in a cafe and got discovered.

(Post) Ani describes the progression from playing locally to playing globally in terms of her friends. Initially, in the world according to DiFranco, the few freaks who knew who she was came out to hear her. Then those freaks told their friends, and more and more friends turned into fans. A west-coast live event producer, Tracye Lawson, had brought a relatively unknown DiFranco to Santa Cruz early in 1993; by the time of DiFranco's return engagement, in the fall of the same year, her audience had multiplied incredibly.

Despite the obvious possibilities, DiFranco has not connected with major labels; far from being disappointed, she is delighted.

DiFranco: It's a good feeling to have thwarted all those fat cats. Now that I'm doing well, they want a piece. They ask me to sign with them, and I say, "No thanks, I'm signed with Righteous Babe Records [her own company]."

(Post) DiFranco's independence has proved itself as successful in business dealings as in her art. Following the startling popularity of her self-produced debut recording, *Ani DiFranco* (1990), she generated enough revenue to not only pay off the small debt incurred in the making the record but also sufficient capital to finance a second album.

DiFranco: Since I had the songs, I did the next one.

(Post) Lest someone mistake her for a mellow smooth-voiced folkie, she called it *Not So Soft* (1991). With increasing fiscal and commercial achievement, the mainstream music power players intensified their interest in signing her.

DiFranco: When I first started, I thought that doing music with those people was a goal. Later, I forgot about those goals. Finally, I thought, "Why would you want a boss if you could manage yourself? Why would you want someone to influence you creatively, to control you financially? I don't even like those people."

(Post) The widening circles of name recognition brought another occupational

hazard: face recognition.

DiFranco: I got a wig, a big wig, a Cher wig. People pretty much see me as a bald-headed chick, so they don't recognize me when I have hair. I still have the same goofy smile, though. Even if they do recognize me, they see that I'm undercover, and leave me alone, out of pity or something.

(Post) DiFranco's prolific streak has become a way of life. Every year since she was nineteen she has released an album. Her 1993 album, *Puddle Dive*, which spent ten weeks on the college charts, provided another quantum leap in recognition. On the basis of *Puddle Dive* DiFranco not only played at the prestigious Vancouver Folk Festival, but sold $10,000 worth of product in one weekend to the discriminating audiences there.

Having employed a small posse of session players on *Puddle Dive*, Ani wondered what would happen if she gave the same treatment to some of her older solo material. The result was *Like I Said / Songs*. DiFranco's, *Out of Range*, pleases her because it demonstrates how much she learned about studio production.

DiFranco: I'm just a fucking control freak.

(Post) She seems unfazed by the quantity and universality of her songs.

DiFranco: I agonize now and then. I obsess about writer's block, about never writing again, then it comes back. Stuff happens in my life, I have to process it. I teach myself about my world. I never sit down with an agenda. I do my writing in my head, things working out unconsciously in the back of my brain for days, weeks. By the time I get to paper, the song is pretty much done.

(Post) As far as specific content, DiFranco cites the wisdom of a friend:

DiFranco: You've got to ignore the facts to tell the truth.

(Post) Finding the actual time to write has become more difficult, despite the fact that her lucrative recordings support an office and staff for Righteous Babe Records. DiFranco feels the lack of time in other ways. She misses her friends in Buffalo and in New York, where she has lived since she was eighteen. Her phone bills have sometimes reached $600; even so, she feels that her friends' lives evolve continuously while her connections with them remain frozen while she's away. DiFranco describes the frenetic pace she travels as intensely lonely, fraught with hassles and assholes, even when accompanied by her buddy Andy, the drummer.

DiFranco: We're friends; we like to play together.

(Post) She usually returns home for at least a few days every month. She considers slowing down, patterning her road schedule after that of performers who have a life.

DiFranco: I would like to dance and paint again.

(Post) What I hear in her music is the resolve of a woman who has answers, the joyous purpose of a woman willing to share them. I ask her how she would define the revolution.

DiFranco: I was discussing that just last night with my anarchist friends. There are so many different sides of me that need to revolve. There are so many different sides of people that need to be liberated. I think that the revolution is about the right to self-determination. It's a mental revolution.

I know that sounds so vague and general, so lacking, but it will be about going beyond, going against the law that says you can't be what you want to be, against that something inside yourself that stopped turning over rocks. You know, what we did in childhood? Then we start living that way. First you have to think you can do it. Then you have to do it and, when you don't get shot, you've become an example.

(Post) I observe that she has been pigeonholed as rebellious, confrontational, (clearly her troubadour style is reminiscent of folk, but her taut, clean lines and hyperkinetic playing transcend that definition).

DiFranco: It is much more difficult not to be myself.

(Post) She gives examples of potentially unreceptive or hostile audiences that she has encountered.

DiFranco: Their little buttholes puckering.

(Post) She tries to prove that being herself, laughing at herself, allows her to slip specific messages in undetected, unopposed. She makes clear that she understands that her words must be carefully chosen, so not to alienate anyone from the start.

DiFranco: I also can't go too fast, or I'll derail them.

(Post) There are, she says, always a few during her shows who scream and laugh with her. There is no doubt that Ani DiFranco seeks to relate to her audiences.

DiFranco: Some performers play with their head down. You might as well listen to the album. I try to communicate.

(Post) I ask her what she does when her methods don't win over the crowds the way she wants.

DiFranco: Like this morning. I don't want to get up and go back on the road. That's the work for me.

DISCOGRAPHY

Ani DiFranco (Righteous Babe Records, 1990); *Not So Soft* (R.B.R, 1991); *Imperfectly* (R.B.R., 1992); *Puddle Dive* (R.B R., 1993); *Like I Said/Songs 1990-1991* (R. B.R, 1993); *Out of Range* (R. B. R., 1994); *Not a Pretty Girl* (R.B.R, 1995); *Dilate* (R. B. R, 1996); *More Joy Less Shame* (R.B.R. 1996); Ani Di Franco and Utah Phillips, *The Past Didn't Go Anywhere* (R.B.R 1996); *Living In Clip* (R.B.R., 1997).

AVOTCJA
we hear your song, we need your song, we love your song

Avotcja Jiltonilro is a musician/vocalist/DJ/off-Broadway composer/photographer/storyteller/teacher; an energetic, creative woman who writes and speaks about herself and her life. There's a rhythm to Avotcja's poetry, a jazz looseness to her rap, a Spanglish/island perspective to her Blues; she spins multi-textured joy at the literary, benefit, Third World, revolutionary, and women's events where she performs.

Born in Brooklyn, raised in Spanish Harlem, Avotcja is a Black Puerto Rican who has been influenced by boleros, African, Euro-classical, salsa, calypso, gospel, Blues, jazz as well as by the performing artists in her family. Her many talents and barrier-dissolving manner are evidenced by her wide successes and in the diversity of those with whom she has shared a stage: Diane DiPrima, Linda Tillery, Rachel Bagby, Mary Watkins, Mother Tongue, Women of All Red Nations, Casselberry-Dupree, Dance Brigade.

Avotcja: Even when I was a baby, I was in love with music, I was always crazy about music. When I was fourteen and got a guitar, my mother had dreams of me sounding like Segovia. At that point I wanted to do anything that would get me a guitar, but then I heard the Blues and heard Blind Lemon Jefferson and Leadbelly and Arsenio Rodriguez from Cuba and wanted to play like them. My mother almost had a heart attack, so I left home with my guitar and fifty cents.

(Post) Following the mythology that artists are dope fiends and drunks, Avotcja became a dope fiend and a drunk.

Avotcja: I went to Mexico for a while. Then Canada and the West Coast; the day before I was 16, I wound up in California, "the runaway state." I looked very young, so people that would hire kids for almost nothing would give me horrible jobs, so I wound up as a farm worker. From the way I talked they knew I wasn't quite as young as I looked, and so I got hired at the playground to work with kids who were learning how to read and write in English and Spanish.

(Post) Currently, Avotcja DJs several San Francisco Bay area radio shows at KPFA and KPOO, a mixture of African, calypso, jazz, and salsa.

Avotcja: The last Thursday of the month, I do a Blues program. There's a weird Blues segregation trip out here that nobody wants to talk about; Gorman Lee, Frankie M., Marilyn Fowler, and I are the only Black Blues DJs in the Bay Area. The white Blues programs, they talk about Blues like they talk about folk-lore, like it's dead. Like it died with Howlin' Wolf or Muddy Waters, but it's not dead, it's very much alive. I play that older stuff, but I also play a lot of the stuff that's happening now, and it is happening, big time. Both styles are real popular, and there's room enough for both of them. Blues is poetry; it's storytelling music. Like calypso, bomba, plena, samba, and reggae; it's the story that gives the Blues its power.

(Post) Avotcja was introduced to mainstream lesbian audiences by Pat Parker and then through the West Coast Lesbian Festival (WCLF).

Avotcja: When Pat was alive, the last years of her life, we double-billed together. We were never lovers, only friends, but very close friends. I was clean and sober, and that Pat wasn't was no secret. She liked being around me, and the ultimate show of friendship was that I never saw her drunk, and I know when I was using I could have never done that; that's the highest respect that anybody could ever give.

I was the one who had the in with the black and Latin circuit, the chitlin' and cuchifrito circuit. And she had the in with the lesbian, the white lesbian circuit. And she had been led to believe by the group that she had run with all those years that black folks would not like her, and I was led to believe that white lesbians couldn't stand me, either.

(Post) After she was scheduled to appear at the first West Coast Lesbian Festival by Pat's friend and festival co-producer Marilyn Van Veersen.

Avotcja: I was thinking that it was going to be everybody singing the same three chords and saying, "I am a lesbian. I am a woman. I am a lesbian woman." But then Marilyn started hiring people that I know who are really good artists: Melanie De More, Rashida Oji, June and Jean Millington, Cheryl Harrison from up north, and lots of folks of color who have seen each other in passing over the years. Still, I thought that with the exception of maybe Barbara Macdonald, I would be the oldest woman there, nobody else over forty-five. I also thought that there would be very few people of color, that me and Melanie and Rashida and Cheryl and June and Jean would probably be the only people of color there.

When I got there it was the complete opposite. There were all these seniors and so many people of color who were just being who they were. Nobody was forcing people into being somebody that they weren't; people were dealing with each other on the basis of respect. It felt really good. I guess I was fifty then. There were women there that made me look like a kid, women that were old enough to be my mother, maybe my grandmother, and there weren't just one or two. There was an army of older women, and they weren't just cute little old ladies, I mean these were hellraisers! I loved it!!!

There was every kind of music you could think of. There were not only a lot of seniors, there were a lot of kids there, kids who were doing great and positive things. For me, that's what a festival is supposed to be like. I'm afraid of people who have to have everybody sound the same and look the same. Something about that is real scary. I'd go so far as to say dangerous.

(Post) Avotcja is not only inspiring, but she has the courageous vision to empower

the next generation: *Inside These Walls* is a collection by prisoners and *Ghetto Flowers*, Volumes I and II are the work of her students.

Avotcja: I work in the public school system and in the county jail, teaching creative writing and music, especially getting to people who may not be proficient in the King's English—like anybody wants to talk to the king in the first place! I'm basically getting people, English-speaking people, African-Americans, Native Americans, some Asians, and lots of Latins as well, to realize that they have their own brilliance and to use it. What we call 'switch-hittin', to be able to speak the King's English when it comes time to get a job and then go back to talking whatever they talk, you know, ghetto rap, barrio rap, as soon as you walk away. I've taught a lot of places.

(Post) Avotcja has written three books: *La Voz Boricua*, *Oh Yeah* and *Ache / Power;* one in Spanish, one English, and one bilingual. She has penned a tome which includes poetry, short stories, photography, and historical documentation, *Pura Candela / Pure Fire*.

Avotcja: I'm trying to do the biography of Connie Williams. Connie is the person who was the real founder of Carnival in the Bay Area, even though they've given credit to everyone else. Connie's a Trinidadian who's in her eighties, and it's disgraceful what's happened; it's also a good lesson in what can happen to folks who do what they want to do, and don't kiss people's behinds. They shined her on, and she's now living down in the Tenderloin after supporting everybody, including the Belafontes and Sidney Poitier.

There's a lot of Connie in me, and I've just accepted the fact that may or may not happen. That's the price you pay for doing what you want to do. I know what I could do if I wanted to make sure that will never happen and I'm not willing to do that; I've already had the chance to pant in microphones and sing nonsense. There are already too many boring people; I don't need to add to that number. This country has never had any respect for its seniors or black folks to begin with, but I think life's too short to be worried about being afraid all the time. So, if you want to do something, and what you're doing is not what the mainstream wants, or the media wants, then you should be prepared to pay the price. I guess I've been spending most of my life trying to get ready to pay that price, whatever that price may be.

(Post) Avotcja has multiple sclerosis and wants readers to know that one can have the disease and still be a functioning person. Her poetry and essays have been published in the collections *Arc of Love* and *Skin Deep* and the magazine *Crossroads*. She has been clean and sober since she was twenty-nine; ("I get high on B flat and high C!")

DISCOGRAPHY

Has Anybody Heard My Song? (Self-produced, 1989).

THE CHENILLE SISTERS
celebrating ten years of harmony and fun

It takes a special musical group to be able to deliver the total openness required for children's shows, the precision and sophistication demanded for collaboration with a jazz ensemble, and the congeniality which underlies wacky humor. The Chenille Sisters—soul siblings born to different parents—have excelled at all of the above and more for ten years.

Though the trio's choice of title was intended as a spoof of groups like the Nylons, the Chiffons, and the Four Satins, the Chenille Sisters are made of much stronger stuff than the raggedy bathrobe fabric of the same name.

Cheryl Dawdy began her music career as a folkie, performing in coffee houses. She was also a library assistant, but the mix didn't work because every time she finished performing a number, she would hold her finger to her lips and tell the audience to "Shhh!"

Connie Huber has sung with rock and country-western bands and is an accomplished performer on guitar and drums. Contrary to rumor, she denies being able to play the piano with her toes.

Having studied opera and performed in musicals, Grace Morand has a voice that fills concert halls. In a twist on the old Ella Fitzgerald commercials, one of Morand's goals is to hit a note that will shatter Tupperware.

In concert, the Chenilles consistently leave people uplifted. They have also garnered much praise, having been awarded honors as diverse as the Parents' Choice Gold Award (for their album *1,2,3 For Kids*); the Indie bestowed by the National Association of Independent Record Distributors (NAIRD); and a thirty-minute television special taped by PBS.

More down-to-earth than the Roches, more contemporary than the Andrews, funnier than the McGarrigles, more earthy than the Boswells, yet with harmonies just as taut and delicate as all of those groups, the Chenille Sisters bring scintillating vocals and quirky lyrics to their politics and parodies. Cleverness and costume changes, affability and attitude changes are in the bag of tricks from which the Chenille Sisters draw in order to make listeners want to be kids again.

In the past, the Chenille Sisters have offered "Amazing Grace" sung to the tune of "Gilligan's Island," and they have liberally re-translated "La Bamba" as a mother's plea for her daughter to marry. When sharing the stage with James Dapogny's Chicago Jazz Band, the Chenilles turn their dial to a hot bebop/swing setting. In a different moment, they produce serious, wrenching ballads.

Grace Morand took time out from the Chenilles' tour supporting *True to Life*, their seventh recording on the Red House label, to speak with me about the group. Morand recounts that she had played informally with Dawdy and Huber at an Ann Arbor bar.

Grace Morand: Connie and Cheryl were in a show together, so they had worked together before. Then Connie and I got a band together, purely for fun, with a rhythm section behind us. We did Motown, Bonnie Raitt, all kinds of songs that we liked. We decided that we wanted to do Aretha Franklin's "Respect," but Connie couldn't do the "Sock-it-to-me" part by herself, so we recruited Cheryl.

(Post) Morand and Huber invited Dawdy to join them onstage more and more frequently; their first gig as the Chenille Sisters was on March 17, 1985. How did they selected the trio's name?

Morand: It was a collaborative thing. We thought of a million different names. One of my favorites was the "Singing Wallendas." We ended up deciding that we wanted to be sisters. We felt that we had a natural blend of voices and also shared the same vision. We wanted to be the "'Something' Sisters," and chenille is comfy and down-home and pokes fun at established sister groups.

(Post) A few casual performances followed. Fortuitously, all three women had the sort of day jobs that allowed gigging at night: Huber a graduate student in speech pathology, Morand a hairdresser, and Dawdy a librarian.

Morand: Quite soon, it became clear to us that what we did had a lot of potential and was an exciting thing. The little bar where we were playing would be jam-packed with a line out the door. That feedback got us started.

(Post) The Chenille Sisters' show may seem entirely impromptu, but in fact, their looseness is the result of the chemistry between them, in which their imaginations flourish.

Morand: We tried to take a theatrical approach, to talk between songs and to add humor.

(Post) Clearly, their approach worked well; in their first year, Garrison Keillor invited them to appear on "A Prairie Home Companion," the first of half a dozen such guest spots on Keillor's show.

The Chenille Sisters have been interviewed in *People Magazine;* appeared on "All Things Considered," on ABC's "The Home Show" and CBS's "Nightwatch." They have opened shows for the Smothers Brothers, Phyllis Diller, Andy Williams and, ironically, the Nylons. Yet, Morand lists the first Garrison Keillor appearance among her personal highlights in the group's career.

Morand: It was such a long shot, sending him the tape, a very home-made living room tape. Just to be singing in front of a couple of million people was amazing.

(Post) Doing "Prairie Home Companion" forced the women to clarify their goals. One immediate objective was to record an album, which was accomplished with loans from some investor-friends. The Chenille Sisters' first album was made in the fall of 1986 and released in December of the same year.

Grace Morand
Photo: Ameen Howrani

Cheryl Dawdy

Connie Huber

Morand: We just did it on our own, and we peddled them at our shows. There's a record store here in Ann Arbor where our record sold gangbusters! At the time, Bruce Springsteen was probably the hottest thing, and we outsold his Christmas release!

(Post) Shows at the Ark, a well-known Ann Arbor folk venue, followed, as did opening for the Persuasions at the Ann Arbor Folk Festival. The Chenilles' increased visibility improved record sales, and wider distribution of their music in vinyl led to more important gigs and bigger venues.

The Chenilles' expanding popularity led to more decisions. An ambitious manager, with her sights set on national exposure was a first step. Another step was choosing between the established career niches occupied by each of the three women and their burgeoning fame as the Chenilles; pragmatically, Huber, Dawdy, and Morand were compelled to assess their commitment to doing music professionally as opposed to pursuing it as a sideline.

Morand: Our bosses, who had been really understanding, were starting to roll their eyes because we were really taking a lot of time off. Our bosses would even come hear us play.

(Post) Three years after the birth of the Chenilles, in 1989, all three women quit their jobs.

Morand: We'd saved money for quite a while, and we decided that we had to do it together. If one was able to quit her job, and another wasn't, that might breed resentment; you know, strength in numbers, let's do it together. We also thought that the worst thing that could happen is that we'd have to go back to our day jobs. We gave it a shot, and we've never had to go back.

(Post) Dawdy, Huber, and Morand are equally democratic about working out their singing harmonies.

Morand: It's collaborative. Generally, if you've written a song, and you bring it in, then you sing the melody. The harmony parts, how we stack them, has to do with whether the melody will be the bottom line with two harmonies higher, or should one harmony be higher and one lower. Once we have decided that, then we just willy-nilly our way through.

(Post) Because Huber is the only one of the three women with formal education in music theory, the arrangements are not written down. Morand is lavish in praising Huber's knowledge and Huber's insistence that the group do non-traditional melodies.

Morand: A lot of contemporary singers tend to sing straightforward melodies and harmonies; a lot of the Beatles music does it that way. Connie has us singing more jazzy and other unusual intervals. She was influenced by those early girl groups, and we all gravitate toward those forms now.

(Post) Since 1990 the Chenilles have been supporting themselves entirely with their gigging and product sales. Morand attributes the Chenilles' marketing successes to the foresight of their manager.

Morand: One of the things that Donna [Zajonc] has gotten us to do is diversify, and that's been key in allowing us to do this full-time. We do a children's show, and we have two recordings for kids. We do a show with a symphony orchestra, a pop show, and a couple of years ago, we started doing a kids' symphony pop show.

We also do a jazz show with an eight-piece band with music from the '20s, '30s, and '40s. We have made a recording with that band. Then, we have our own show where we do our own thing. We feel like plate-spinners sometimes because we're changing gears a lot. We'll learn a bunch of jazz tunes, then we have to put that on the back burner while we quick write a bunch of kids' songs, then come back and spiff up—we call it our grown-up show.

(Post) Morand describes what the Chenille Sisters do as akin to a theatrical company's repertoire, with the difference that the Chenilles travel with each of their shows. From Vancouver to Erie, PA, from Oklahoma City to California, and Florida, the Chenilles have been to the corners of the United States.

Morand: We take a theatrical approach in that we feel that the show needs a flow. We have a planned order of songs, and we have kind of decided what we want to say in front of the songs, but there's always room for spontaneity, there's always room if you want to say something in addition.

As a group, we want to keep doing what we are doing but on a much larger scale. We're pleased with what we've accomplished so far, but we'd like our name recognition to be a bit bigger. We'd like to do some television. We wouldn't mind being—I don't want to say a 'household word', I don't think we wanted to be mainstream like Madonna or Michael Jackson—but there is an alternative audience out that who we haven't yet reached, and I think that we can.

We've gone from Connie's living room to being national, and now we'd like to be international. We've done work in Canada, but we'd love to go to Europe and have people say, "Oh, yeah! The Chenilles." The other day, we read something that said: "This is a group that sounds like the Chenilles." We were pleased because, for many years, people have said about us that we sounded like the Roches. Now that other groups are being compared to us, we feel that we're making progress.

DISCOGRAPHY

The Chenille Sisters (Red House Records, 1986); *At Home With The Chenille Sisters* (Red House Records, 1989); *1, 2, 3, For Kids* (Red House Records, 1990); *Mama I Want to Make Rhythm* (Red House Records, 1991); *The Big Picture and Other Songs* (Red House Records, 1992); *Whatcha Gonna Swing Tonight?* (Red House Records, 1992); *True to Life* (Red House Records, 1994); *Haute Chenille* (Red House Records, 1995); *Teaching Hippopotomi to Fly* (Red House Records, 1996).

CHERYL WHEELER
life and friendship in music

There are some acoustic guitarists who use melodies, rhythms, fingerpicking, original lyrics, and voice to recreate the details of a poignant moment so that it becomes viscerally present. Other musicians are entertainers, relying on repartee, wit, insight and humor to smooth the gap between songs, or as the center of their songs. A third group of musical artists will focus on issues of personal or political significance in order to make a point. Cheryl Wheeler does all of these things, does them superbly, and does them in such a way as to create essential bonds between people.

Yet, Wheeler's music is neither saccharin nor exclusively gentle. Some of her more rapid-paced songs are bitingly humorous ("TV," "Don't Forget The Guns," "Makes Good Sense to Me") while others are irately concerned ("The Rivers"). Attesting to Wheeler's remarkable emotional spectrum are the tunes which manifest great intensity ("Does The Future Look Black," "So Far to Fall"), personal revelation ("Is It Peace or Is It Prozac?"), or captivating riffs ("Piper"). "Howl at the Moon," a song about Wheeler's dog, James, can evoke tears. Similarly, the introspective "75 Septembers" awakens aches of missing someone long departed, aches one never imagined would return. Cheryl Wheeler's music does all these things.

Yet, simple deconstruction of Wheeler's craft merely leads to the conclusion that she is a supple and innovative guitar player, a wordsmith of the highest caliber, and a performer comfortable and empathic on stage. Her seemingly stream-of-consciousness banter keeps audiences lightly tickled or roaring with delight.

In a unique way, Wheeler bares her self and her soul, in her songs with scathing honesty. Somehow, she introduces vital themes of caring in so many varieties that listeners feel an immediate kinship with her, and with each other.

Post: How did you learn to play the guitar?

Cheryl Wheeler: There was this man who moved up the street named Mr. Eck. He played guitar, and I used to go up there and hang out all the time. That was certainly where I learned all the basics. I also feel that I've learned from everyone I ever saw playing. I would go up to them and say 'Show me how you did that.' I did that all the time. I was just a little kid so I wasn't shy. I took violin lessons in the second grade which was a total disaster. When we had a recital, the teacher told me not to touch my bow to the string! Then I took piano lessons, and again it was a total disaster because it concentrated on teaching how to read music, not how to play. I couldn't read music, still can't. I always loved playing, but I hated lessons.

When I was in the eleventh grade, my parents wanted me to take guitar lessons. They bought me this twelve-string Martin, which was a big deal. There was no point in arguing with them; my father was a big believer in lessons. I started with guitar lessons with this guy, and—I'll never forget—we never actually played guitar. We practiced sitting down and holding the guitar the right way. I hated it. I couldn't believe it. I went about three times and then didn't go back.

Music lessons never had anything to do with music so they didn't ruin music for me. They were just some other bizarre part of school, just another thing that someone thought up, and you had to do. I still have that twelve-string Martin. Actually, that guitar went through a lot. It was stolen when I was in college and I got it back. It's a beautiful guitar, I love that guitar.

Post: Where and when did you first play and sing in front of people?

Wheeler: At a coffee house in Timonium, in Maryland, called Fifteen Below, when I was about twelve. I thought it was neat. I played "All the Pretty Little Horses" and some other song, maybe "Separation Blues." That was one of my favorite songs then. I remember liking the warm response I got from the audience and also being aware of the fact that I could stand up on stage and play anything. I wasn't fooled into thinking I was some sort of genius or anything; I knew that they would be glad to give it up for any twelve year-old.

Post: What were you going to be when you grew up?

Wheeler: I didn't actually think of doing music as a job until after I quit college. I thought I was going to be a zoologist, or an oceanographer. I used to read all these children's books about whales. Then, I found out that to be a scientist I would have to do division; I decided, "No." I realized that I was going to have to do something; I couldn't just do nothing. In a way, doing music was a way to avoid getting a job. It was unbelievable to me that I could actually get paid to sit around and do what I was going to sit around and do anyway.

Post: When did you first take yourself seriously as a musician?

Wheeler: Maybe when I got the gig playing bass with Jonathan Edwards. I met him in Newport, Rhode Island. I was the opening act for a weekend of shows he was doing. I had been, and still am, a great admirer of him. He's such a great singer. In his dressing room I asked him to sing this song he'd already recorded, "When The Roll Is Called Up Yonder," because it was an old hymn, and I had a great harmony for it. Our voices went together real well, so I did a few songs with him, then I got the call that he wanted to go out on the road. I 'learned' the bass real fast and went out on the road with him.

I say that tongue-in-cheek. I can't play bass. My bass-playing was, on my very best night, barely adequate. Jonathan was looking for a harmony singer who could cover the bass parts in his songs, and he likes very simple bass. The fact that I could sing the high part while I was playing the simple low part got me the gig. He had some actual bass players try out but they weren't singers. I was very lucky that he was more interested in the singing than the playing.

Post: How did you get from there to doing your first recording?

Wheeler: The first one that was on a record label was called *Cheryl Wheeler* (1986) and was on North Star Records. The guy who runs that label, or used to, is named Richard Waterman. He came to see me a couple of times at gigs and said that he was interested in starting a record company and did I want to be one of the projects. I said, "You bet!" The thing that I absolutely love to do is write songs. Then, I also love going out and singing and playing.

Post: How do you write?

Wheeler: I have a hard time answering that question because I don't really know how I write. I also think that it's good that I don't know. There's something that's kind of magical to me, you know, bang, here comes a song. I haven't lately felt the kind of hard-hitting inspirational sparks that I am sometimes fortunate enough to get.

Post: Some songs seem to have some essential wholeness; do some come out all in one piece?

Wheeler: Absolutely. One song called "Northern Girl" came out completely and totally in one piece. I got up out of bed and I looked at my guitar next to my bed, and I picked it up, and went to the sofa, and sang "Northern Girl" from beginning to end. That was amazing to me. I remember starting to think, "God I really like this song. Go get a piece of paper and write it down." This other voice in my head was saying, "Shut up, keep singing," so I sang all the way through it, without even a hesitation.

If the song-writing thing gets me, I can write anywhere. I wrote a song once at a party in a room with rock and roll music blaring. I just sat in the corner and quietly wrote this song. I had the melody in my head and wrote out the lyrics, and there it was. When it's ready to happen, it's like lightning or something; you can't do anything about it.

Post: Since you're gone so much, what do you do to keep yourself centered and your voice in working order?

Wheeler: Absolutely nothing, and I probably should, but I don't know what to do. I wish I knew; I'm awful. There are a few things I very pointedly try not to do. For instance, if I get to go to a ball game this summer, which I love to do, I can't scream or yell. Another thing is a lot of laughing, loud laughing. That's hard, because I laugh a lot. I smoke cigarettes, not all the time, but sometimes. I'm just a total ungrateful lout.

Post: How do you deal with criticism?

Wheeler: Criticism is hard to take; I've talked to other singer-songwriters about it. It's so funny; you can sing to an audience of X number of people, and if there's one person that you can see in that crowd who isn't enjoying it, your whole focus tends to go to that one person. You can't let yourself be drawn in. You have to just do the best job that you can. Of course, everybody's not going to like what you do.

I have to say I've been pretty fortunate. I haven't—I better watch my words here—gotten that many bad reviews. I've read some nasty stuff on the Internet. That hurts my feelings, too, but I would never respond to it. I've also had some constructive criticism on the Internet. These people, (I don't know who they were, a couple, I think, a man and a woman) they said they had gone to one of my shows, and they'd never go to another one. They were totally annoyed because they couldn't hear the ends of any of my phrases. I've had producers whipping on me for that in the studio for dropping the end of a line, and it never did any good. But when I read that comment, I thought to myself, "I'm sorry those people will never come to another one of my shows, but I'm glad they wrote that because I never cared that it bothered a producer but I cared that it was bothering the audience." It is annoying not to be able to understand the words.

Post: Where do you get those ideas for your album covers?

Wheeler: The first two I didn't have anything to do with. *Circles & Arrows* was my original idea for the first album. That came down because North Star had sent me to New York for a photo session. It was one of the most atrocious days of my life. I walk into this loft apartment, and there is this real babe photographer, with makeup and stuff. I looked at her and thought, OK, I have nothing in common with her, and she looked at me, and I know she thought the same thing. There I was in jeans and tee shirt, and she must have been thinking, "I can't take a picture of this!" So, they put all this makeup on me, and then I had to try to look normal when I was miserable. It was a ridiculous day.

Afterwards, I got a call from my label. It was in my contract that I had to approve any photos they used. So, they called me in, and they said "Well, look," like they're real proud. This guy hands me a copy of an 8 x 10 in black and white and says "What do you think?" I thought I looked like one of the Lennon Sisters! I was obviously not as excited as he thought I should have been. I said, "You can use it if you want to, but club owners are going to be pretty pissed off if you send them this picture, and then they get me." The guy handing me the picture was very insulted that I wasn't thrilled with it. He says, "Look at this," and he shows me the original with all the marks on it. Tactful guy, right? The feeling was: "Look, you ugly dog, see how we improved you?" I cracked up and said, "This is an album cover; use the one with the marks on it."

I thought the person in the retouched part should not look totally "other" than the real person; to me, that was the whole hilarious thing. Here's this person who is a singer/songwriter, that's all. There's all this concern that I should have this look about me. What look? I'm not trying to have a look, I'm just trying to write songs!

I have, in the past, had individuals approach and ask why am I not more political, and why aren't I dealing with this issue or that issue, but I've never taken it seriously because you don't go up to somebody and ask them why they're not something else.

Post: What have been some of the highlights for you in your career so far?

Wheeler: Having other people record my songs. That's a big thrill every time it happens. You can write songs, and like anyone else—maybe, especially like women—there's always a voice that's in your head that's ready to tell you that you're an idiot, and that you can't do this. So, naturally I started writing songs and, of course, that voice would pop up and say, "You can't write songs, fool!" Yet there would be a stronger voice saying, "I am writing them."

Sometimes, I would think they were good, and other times I would think they weren't. Then, when Dan Seals recorded "Addicted" and it went to Number One, that blew me away. At that point, I thought "Addicted" must be a good song.

Suzy Boguss did "Aces;" Peter, Paul & Mary just did "75 Septembers;" Bette Midler did "I Know This Town," and Juice Newton did that one, too, but she called it "I'm Only Walking" [Wheeler's original name for the song]; I wonder if that record ever got released?

I know I'm forgetting some, plus there are some in the works that I don't want to talk about in case they don't happen.

Post: You've said certain things on stage that led me to believe that you might be a lesbian.

Wheeler: Yes, I'm gay. I don't understand "lesbian."

Post: Why are you coming out now?

Wheeler: I'm not intending to come out; it's not a big deal one way or another to me. If I'm at the Freight and Salvage [in northern California], I can crack a joke and make a reference there. There are a whole lot of gay people in the audience, so it would be a place where it would be a perfectly appropriate.

Someone said to me that gay people all have something in common. Well, J. Edgar Hoover was gay, and I don't have anything in common with him. It's like saying straight people all have something in common, or all people with hair have something in common. It's not an issue that deserves a lot of time. Not in my life.

There may be people whose sexuality is paramount in their life-style. It's not in my life-style, and point of fact I am more of an old maid than anything. I'm alone. I don't have a lover and haven't for years. I have a friend I live with, and she's leaving, so I really can quite honestly say now, that I'm completely alone and have no desire at this point to change it.

I like reading, riding my bike, hanging out with my dog, and I like traveling. I like my life, generally speaking. I can't even say that I wish anything would be different. I wish my friend wasn't leaving after fourteen years. I'm not looking forward to that.

When I left Alaska (after a recent trip there), I wanted to go live in Alaska, but I'm not going to do that. I like to swim in the warm ocean with one of those little canvas mats that you can ride the waves in. I could do that forever.

Where I grew up in Maryland, the ocean was pretty warm. I go to Ogunquit, Maine in the summer, and there's this great place where the river comes into the ocean; you can walk up the river, and there's this real fast current. You get in and just drift down into the ocean where the ocean is real shallow. It's great!

DISCOGRAPHY

Newport Songs EP (Self-produced, 1983); *Cheryl Wheeler* (North Star, 1986); *Half a Book* (North Star, 1990); *Circles & Arrows* (Capitol 1992; reissued Philo, 1995); *Driving Home* (Philo 1993); *Mrs. Pinocci's Guitar* (Philo, 1996).

CHRISTINE LAVIN
and the Four Bitchin' Babes

"The Four Bitchin' Babes" is a musical revue thought up by energetic singer-songwriter Christine Lavin. Conceived as a show with an ever-changing cast, the Four Babes include veterans McDonough, Fingerett, Lavin and at the time of this interview, Debi Smith. The Babes derived from the *On a Winter's Night* project as a summer touring vehicle for Lavin and some women friends.

Sally Fingerett from the Chicago folk circuit believes that the broad appeal of the Babes is due to their being women musicians who are not just singers but who play their own instruments, write their own songs, arrange their own harmonies, and have each released solo albums.

Fingerett reveals what being in the Babes means to her, exploring the notion that many musicians and other artists feel outside the mainstream activity. "Playing with the Babes was a gift because they saw it the way I saw it, felt it the way I felt it." She pauses contemplatively, "I like to call the Babes the sorority that I was never asked to join."

For one weekend every month, the four babes gather to rehearse, gig, and schmooze; and when they play together onstage, the experience of debuting new songs is a safe one. "We have so much fun on stage together, I want to continue to make records, to tour, and to play," she concludes.

Debi Smith

The Babes have made two recordings, *Buy Me Bring Me Take Me Don't Mess With My Hair...Life According To Four Bitchin' Babes, Volume I* (Philo, 1991) and *Volume II* (Philo, 1993). The first Babes album (which was nominated for a NAIRD award) sported the cast of Lavin, Fingerett, McDonough and Patty Larkin; the second featured Lavin, Fingerett, McDonough and Julie Gold who then retired from touring in order to write another Grammy-winning song.

Christine Lavin recounts her introduction to music with a garrulous humility which typifies her stage charisma. Apparently deterred from pursuit of the piano by a mean teacher ("She would crack you over the knuckles if you made a mistake"). Lavin subsequently settled on the guitar because it was portable, she liked the sound

Sally Fingerett   Meg McDonough   Christine Lavin
Photo: Irene Young

of guitar music she heard on the radio in the early '60s (Judy Collins, Joan Baez, Bob Dylan, Pete Seeger), and because the guitar tunes of the era told stories that were easy to understand and not difficult to learn. She harbored secret hopes of being a professional musician, but instead went to college as a nursing major, fearing her dream was unrealistic.

After graduating in 1974, Lavin traveled and found herself in Florida ("I was sort of a lost soul"), and learned that Lena Spencer, owner of Caffe Lena in Saratoga Springs, needed someone to help out with a sick, elderly man staying with her. Part of the deal included playing at Caffe Lena once in a while ("Lena knew I was a songwriter"). By the time Lavin was ready to work, the man had died but Lavin wound up living at Lena's anyway for six months between October and February, in a room which had no heat, earning $15.00 a week, and being intimidated by the talented artists who came through: Don McLean, Arlo Guthrie, Rosalie Sorrels, Kate Wolf, Utah Phillips. "If these people who are this talented are not really known outside this small following, then there's no hope for someone like me," Lavin admits thinking. "I didn't (I still don't) feel that I have a natural gift that they all have. I have to work very hard at what I do. But I guess that there's something I have that audiences like, so I just stopped questioning it."

One night in 1976, Lavin's luck turned. Early in the evening she played at the Caffe; in the audience was Don McLean's manager. He advised Lavin that if she played the guitar better, she could have a career. That same night Lavin played her song "Ramblin' Waltz"—from *Future Fossils*—for Dave Van Ronk; Van Ronk invited Lavin to New York to study with him.

"It still took me eight years to quit my day job," she clarifies in her easy manner. A secretarial position at Bellevue Hospital, Lavin's last day job, had brought her $25,000 annually; her first year as a full-time performer in 1984, she made $6,000. Soon after, Lavin began releasing albums: *Another Woman's Man, Beau Woes, Good Thing He Can't Read My Mind* and connected with the Rounder/Philo Label.

By 1989, Lavin had achieved her goal of earning sufficient money to pay the rent and moved from the one-room apartment where she has lived since 1976, having tripped one too many times on her guitar case and broken a finger.

Seeking other challenges, she compiled a cassette of songs that she liked: one by her, nineteen by other artists. That undertaking led to several recordings: *When October Goes* (Lavin and "fourteen other contemporary singer-songwriters sing winter make-out music"), then *Big Times in a Small Town: The Vineyard Tapes*, highlights of the second Annual Martha's Vineyard Singer/Songwriters Retreat. Lavin is very sincere in her support of her peers: "It's a real grassroots way of connecting with each other and getting an audience in."

Lavin laughs when describing the origins of the Bitchin' Babes moniker, which she attributes to Allan Pepper, owner of New York's Bottom Line. "'Four women playing and singing about contemporary issues' didn't capture it," she chuckles. "We wanted to show that it would be a fun kind of night."

The Babes have had so much fun that eight women have rotated through the group, including sister Philo artists Kristina Olsen and Cheryl Wheeler; Mary Travers and Janis Ian. Of the latter, Lavin chortles, "I can't believe it! I listened to her when I was growing up even though we're just about the same age."

DISCOGRAPHY

Future Fossils (Philo, 1986); *Another Man's Woman* (Philo, 1987); *Beau Woes* (Philo 1987); *Good Thing He Can't Read My Mind* (Philo, 1988); *Attainable Love* (Philo, 1990); *Live at the Cactus Cafe*, (Philo, 1993); *Please Don't Make Me Too Happy* (Shanachie, 1995); *Shining My Flashlight on the Moon* (Shanachie, 1997).

CRIS WILLIAMSON AND TRET FURE
women's music and the folk mainstream

Cris Williamson is, simply put, an icon in the Women's Music network. Tret Fure is such a multi-talent that, in a Readers' Choice poll of *Hot Wire: The Journal of Women's Music & Culture*, she was voted both Best Guitarist and Best Engineer.

The two women have performed their folk-based music in many venues—the U.S., Australia, and the former U.S.S.R.—and between them have released twenty-five albums. Their recordings include Williamson's *The Changer and The Changed* (1975), one of the world's best-selling albums on an independent label; Williamson's two *Best Of* collections; a Christmas album; ten film/theater scores; a children's album; and Williamson's several live albums—one from Carnegie Hall—and Fure's and Williamson's individual major-label debuts.

For all the adulation they consistently receive at women's gatherings, they are too little appreciated in the folk community. Harold Leventhal, manager of Pete Seeger and Arlo Guthrie, stated, "Arlo and Pete know the names of Cris Williamson and Tret Fure but haven't listened to the music." This is a tragedy, because what Cris Williamson and Tret Fure have contributed to music is grand and beautiful. When the world is ready for women who write and play about caring; when the world is ready for women who sing together as if they have always sung together; when the world is ready for artists who issue a call to trying, then Cris Williamson and Tret Fure will receive the appreciation they deserve.

The Changer and The Changed symbolized a new musical genre: Women's Music. By, for, and about lesbians and other women, *Changer's* sensuous recountings of inner peace and external hope resonated with a crest of feminism and the post-Stonewall gay movement, exploding Williamson into the collective lesbian/feminist consciousness.

When I went to hear Williamson sing I arrived early, in order to procure a good seat. I was surprised to witness Williamson toting her own equipment, and so much of it. No roadies accompanied her or Fure as they lugged guitars, amps, keyboards, monitors, and cables into the club. The amount of equipment didn't fit my idea of a folkie, just as the self-sufficiency didn't match my expectation of a star.

Then, as at other performances, the magnificent sound system, partly assembled by Fure, redefined the boundaries of a musician and her music. Fure's adeptness at compiling a superb aural experience showed how technical mastery enhances the songs, no matter how clear the lyrical content.

Another surprise was Fure's artistry as a musician. She had been billed as an accompanist/opening act, yet her guitar and keyboard accents were evocative and the hooks of her own tunes memorable. After the show I asked Fure how she had kept her concentration during Williamson's "Tsunami," through which Fure had sung, played keyboards, and electric guitar simultaneously. She initially shrugged off the compliment, then flashed a grin at being appreciated.

What I didn't expect from that show was the magic of Williamson's and Fure's collaboration, their individual voices melding, their instrumentations highlighting emotions. Listening to them was, and is, such a transcendent experience that describing it in mere words always falls short.

Williamson's voice is a tornado in touch with the earth, a turbulent tidal wave rising to kiss the sky, hovering at certain improbable notes until the resonance has penetrated into every soul present. Fure's voice has the ring of a mountain lake: deep and crystal pure. Together, Williamson and Fure bring expanse, clarity and harmony with a seamless precision. The moments captured are decisive yet ephemeral; recordings of them do not do justice to the magnitude of their singing together. That concert was in 1984, and nearly ten years would pass before Williamson and Fure would formally join voices for their first collaboration, *Postcards From Paradise* (1993).

Tret Fure's (pronounced fury—the name means "wind in the pines" in Norwegian) musical talents were prominent early. At five, she was picking out tunes on the piano from what she'd heard on the radio; a year later, she started on piano lessons. Fure's progress was cut short by her family's move from Iowa to Illinois.

Tret Fure: Between my father's new job and my being a kid who would just as soon play outdoors as practice, my piano playing was forgotten.

(Post) In fourth grade, Fure learned violin. Two years later, she was first chair in the high school orchestra. Again, Fure's family moved, this time to Michigan, where the musical instruction was not sophisticated and Fure abandoned the violin. Fortunately, Fure's older brother bought a guitar, which revived young Tret's musical focus.

Fure: I decided to drop the violin and pursue a folk career.

(Post) Fure received no further musical training but learned finger-picking and singing by listening to records by Judy Collins and Joan Baez.

Fure: My oldest brother and I became a folk duo. When I was in seventh grade, we were playing at the university because Rob was in college. We were even a trio for a while, with Scot, my youngest brother.

(Post) By sixteen, Fure was being paid enough for serious pocket money, and was touched by the thrill of performing. In 1969, after high school, she went to UC Berkeley, with ambitions to be an astronomer. Though she had been a straight-A student in high school, once Fure got to college, she was suddenly more interested in becoming a musician.

Fure: It was the last year of riots, and my classes were cancelled. After one year I quit college to pursue a musical career, which was what I really wanted. I often regret not finishing my education.

(Post) Cris Williamson, born in Deadwood, South Dakota, with the name Mary Cristine, was surrounded by music from an early age.

Photo: Mary Massara

Cris Williamson: Church choirs, weddings, funerals, Lions Clubs, Kiwanis, everything that's available in a small town I did.

(Post) Like Fure, Williamson started piano lessons in the first grade, then studied voice and, later taught herself guitar. Williamson's Methodist father, a forest ranger, imparted to his daughter the practices of Native Americans, particularly a profound respect for all natural beings. Williamson's mother was a registered nurse; from them, young Cris learned the value of giving.

Williamson: There's something in my music that appeals to women, I don't design it. I write in more universal language because that's what interests me, like the well where we all come to drink the water.

(Post) Williamson's poetic expressionism seems striking, given the context of what she terms the "inarticulateness" of her family. Williamson mentions that, though her brother has musical leanings, her younger sister has had to contend with her elder sibling's fame.

Williamson: People asked her, "Do you play music too?", when she played sports. She—who was gifted with hands that can reach eleven keys, while I got the stubby little short things—hated the piano.

(Post) Williamson goes on to express the limitations of her piano playing, though her observations represent the musings of a perfectionist, not what audiences hear.

Williamson: I was singing Gershwin songs that required an accompanist, so I learned. I can't jam; what I play is sufficient unto myself.

(Post) When I ask about the expertise contained in her songbook, Williamson beams.

Williamson: Yeah, and isn't that amazing! Adrienne [Torf, who did the transcribing] made my music real for me, just like Meg [Christian] did by singing my early songs.

(Post) Williamson's family moved to Sheridan, Wyoming, where young Cris made three records, as well as making local history by starting her professional career at sixteen.

Williamson: The theater where I used to watch movies is now a performance hall. I used to dream, as a little girl, sitting in that theater, of being famous some day and returning. I have returned to play in that theater, but I'm not so famous that anyone treats me any differently. I realize, now, that I didn't want fame so much as I wanted access.

(Post) Through college in Denver, Colorado, Williamson got into a rock band, The Crystal Palace Guard.

Williamson: I was the female lead in the group. It was when Grace Slick and Janis Joplin were making their way in California.

(Post) After receiving her B.A. in English, 1969, Williamson moved to California, with plans to teach. Her early days were rife with struggle and poverty.

Williamson: I've always been an adaptable creature who insisted on being self-sufficient so that I could always perform, no matter what.

(Post) The Ampex label released *Cris Williamson*, in 1971, six months before closing its record division. This was the album which Meg Christian discovered in a cut-out bin, a recording which Christian promoted enthusiastically to the budding women's audience that she was developing in the East.

In 1973, Williamson was invited to be a guest on the "Sophie's Parlor" radio show in Washington, D.C. Interviewed by Christian about women in music, Williamson commented that women in the music industry face many challenges, and that it might be an interesting idea to start a woman's company in order to provide skills and opportunities for advancement. On the basis of her suggestion, Olivia Records was formed.

Olivia's first release was a single featuring Williamson's "If It Weren't for The Music" and Christian's rendition of Carole King's "Lady." A year later, Olivia released *The Changer and The Changed*, which has sold over 250,000 copies.

It is for *Changer* and for her idea about starting a women's record company that Williamson is best known. However, it has long been my perception that Williamson's dogged early solo work, in an era when the industry was difficult for women, is an equally unique legacy, and I tell her so.

Williamson: Thank you. I don't think anybody's ever remarked on that. I traveled by myself, slept on people's floors, was always the stranger in town. Meg busted me out because she recognized my music.

When I first played in D.C., applause broke out. I realized that people knew of me, of my music. It was wonderful and shocking at the same time. It's such a shame to not be on the radio because it would help with the grueling touring that we have to do. The older I get, the more I long for that access. The progress has gone on, not for us, but for the next ones, and isn't that why we did it? But we did it with hopes that we would have the goodies too. Really, we haven't.

(Post) Williamson laments that radio, like much of contemporary music, is based upon commercial trends and not on genuine appreciation.

Williamson: Nobody owns art. We're owned by beauty. I'm happy that people have been seized by my work, and that they had to go on a journey to find it. That's the cool part of what we did. The journey itself taught people many things.

But ofttimes, other people, men, made that journey and sought my work and found signs saying, "You can't have this; it belongs to us." I never wanted that. That attitude has its place, but it's only a step in the women's movement. The word 'movement' indicates motion, but this seems like a room where you lock the door.

For some people, that was heaven. For me, heaven would be some fabulous vibration where all people are welcome, peace is in the world, and everybody gets to do what they want with their power. I can say, "Well, all right, then. Here's another slice over here that will be just for you."

(Post) The balance between desiring folk renown and honoring Women's Music celebrity has been a tricky one to maintain for Williamson, since she has become an unintended figurehead and spokeswoman for Women's Music, whatever it actually is.

Williamson: It's good that you and I can say "whatever it actually is." We mean that Women's Music hasn't been totally defined; there is still room for growth. There is still a movement going on. Like all good water systems, it sometimes sinks below the ground. But, it's feeding the main stream—we continue to use that metaphor—which is often formed of underground rivers. In many ways, though I want to have access, I'm still happy to be an underground artist.

(Post) I point out that *Changer* celebrated its 20th anniversary in 1995, and that the Michigan Womyn's Music Festival, the largest and most diverse of the predominantly lesbian annual gatherings—featuring as many as eight thousand women from around the globe— also had a 20th birthday in 1995.

Williamson: I'm glad that all the festivals serve their function, which is to give a forum for young musicians who want to play Women's Music. When I started, those venues and festivals didn't exist. People don't say it, but Olivia was at the crux. Women's centers, hotlines, all kinds of things happened as a result of our pushing forward. It would have been a different world without Olivia.

(Post) Currently, Williamson is in a position to pass along keys to her creativity: the ultimate fulfillment of her early aspirations to teach. Not only has Williamson led workshops on songwriting at the Omega Institute in New York, but she has bestowed similar gifts on the Institute for the Musical Arts (IMA). IMA is a non-profit, grassroots organization in northern California: close to Williamson's California roots and, perhaps, approximating her initial vision of a women's educational facility in a different way than Olivia Records.
   Williamson sees herself as a teacher; and likens herself looking over the piano to a schoolmarm peering over bifocals.

Williamson: In concert, I come prepared with my lesson plan, but I've learned to keep my sense of humor about me, like the fine patchwork quilt that it is because without it, I am often shot at and hurt.

(Post) I ask Williamson whether her career was winding down.

Williamson: I'm just starting! I think that every day; isn't it the everyday that is reality? I get up for chores, feed the horses, muck the stalls. Isn't that the kind of life that keeps us sane? NO, I'm not done! As long as my heart is beating. Even then, I won't be done because the music is there. That's the value of artists.

(Post) Cris Williamson has been making music for most of her life. *Changer*—remixed and now available on CD—continues to sell.

Williamson: You're kept fluid by what that you do best, and you get better at it.

(Post) While Williamson was beginning to amass a dedicated following in the Women's Music circuit of the early 1970s, Fure moved to the East Coast. En route, Fure met Joni Mitchell, whose kind encouragement touched her. Fure's voice sparkles as she describes her admiration for Mitchell, including positive regard for Mitchell's painting.

Fure: I love to paint, myself, but I don't have the time.

(Post) The predominance of folk clubs drew Fure to the East Coast, but part of the appeal of New York was that Fure's mother had sung there during the Big Band era. Not enjoying the music scene, Fure's mother gave up singing to raise children. Fure is unequivocal that her mother and other family supported her.

Fure: Even though, many times, I wasn't making a living with music, my mother would say, "Are you sure this is what you want?" She didn't like the life and didn't understand why I did, but she did understand that music was my calling.

(Post) Despite gigging at the hootenannies, Fure felt lonely in New York. She relocated to Los Angeles, where she met June Millington. Fure's search for that label, for that deal, for that band continued. She had begun to teach herself electric guitar and was playing regularly in the L.A. rock scene.

Fure's career took a turn for the better when she worked as vocalist and lead guitarist for Spencer Davis, releasing an album, *Mousetrap* (1970) with him. In fact Fure wrote the single, "What's Going to Happen When The Rainy Season Comes?" for that album.

Fure's first album was produced in 1973. Her tours had her opening for such groups as Yes, Poco, and J. Geils. Fure's single, "Catalina," reached the charts. When personnel changes ended the MCA contract, Fure struck a deal with Heritage Music. Fure was their first artist; the album that she recorded with them was never released.

Discouraged, Fure decided to augment her playing and performing experience with a knowledge of engineering and producing. After eighteen months working as second engineer for Randy Nicklaus, Fure became a first engineer and developed her own clientele. Fure is pleased that she has raised engineering to such a standard of perfection, particularly for a performer.

Fure: It's a field that really lends itself to the ears of women and to the sensibilities of women. I was one of the first women engineers in the industry; Leslie Ann Jones was the only other one I knew. It was a struggle, but I learned so much.

(Post) On the heels of the unreleased second album, Fure recorded a third album, which was supposed to be picked up by United Artists, and wasn't: another industry glitch.

Fure: I had been through many managers; many career changes; a lot of identity changes. I had some great successes and a lot of tough failures. But I kept pursuing that record deal. Fortunately, I had my engineering, and I kept myself in business with that.

(Post) Just when a deal with Pasha Records seemed to be the solution, Fure realized that their owner's idea of her conflicted with her own idea of herself.

Fure: He wanted me all dressed in leather. He was so phony and full of himself that I couldn't stand it.

(Post) After declining the Pasha deal, Fure looked up June Millington who, despite Warner albums and fame in the 1970s, was also struggling. Fure and Millington decided to do an album together. The two women would share creative and producing duties while Fure would engineer. The album, *Heartsong* (1981) was eventually sold to Olivia and kindled Fure's link to Women's Music and to Cris Williamson.

Fure: I didn't listen much to Cris' music. I wasn't anywhere near the women's movement in the '70s.

(Post) Eventually, Millington, who was producing Williamson's 1982 release *Lumiere*, invited Fure to engineer it.

Fure: That was how Cris and I met. I was impressed with Cris' handle on the language and with the music she had written. From the moment we started working on that album, we have not been apart.

(Post) Williamson and Fure started collaborating musically in 1982.

Fure: The universe had changed.

Williamson: Suddenly, everything fell into place. My whole personal life and my career. Tret had the keys to all the rooms and information about which I had minimal knowledge, the language of the studios. If you don't know a language, then you're a foreigner. For many years I felt that way, but Tret has a graciousness about her. It's a beautiful quality. I wish I had more of it myself.

(Post) Fure responds by praising Williamson for helping with her singing, detailing how she has learned to be a better stylist. And, through Williamson she finally snagged a deal with a record company that let her do her music: Second Wave, Olivia's rock-oriented subsidiary.

The two women's words then tumble over each other as they explain that similar voice tones and a deep, mutual love for music drew them together. They have a harder time explaining how they decide to arrange the tunes that they perform together, where one dances harmony around the other's melody.

Williamson: It's a talent to blend as one, and I think we manage to do it. It's wonderful to switch parts, to move around each other vocally, because it will make a melody fuller. Even if you can't tell who's singing the melody, the song becomes one voice. It's fun when we're in the right venue, with the right head room and the right sound, and our voices just sail. There's nothing like it.

Fure: We get off the stage, and we're absolutely high. It's the greatest feeling in the world. It's a lot of why we do what we do. It's for ourselves.

Williamson: You can feel the energy go out to the audience. Even if I've been ill, and I don't sing well, a song should fly by itself. Anybody can sing them, we think. I wrote them so they would be accessible; they are bread and water.

Our songs are found in many ceremonies. We've become part of the comings and goings and bondings and blessings; that's great. We know how audiences feel, and we create even more contact by signing autographs after the show. We know what it's like to be lifted beyond your poor feeble spirits into a place of bliss, and then you walk the streets for hours because there hasn't been any resolution. That's why we do "Lullabye" at the end. It's so peaceful, it settles people down. They can drive home. They feel fine, warm and dear.

If one of us has a strong idea, it's not a hassle for us unless the other one has a radical, different idea, then we discuss. It's harder for me because if I get a melody in my head, it's very hard for me to get it out and change my mind. With the bridge of "Dreamboat," I had a chord and Tret thought I should change it. I bucked around the house for a while, then sat down at the piano. She leaned on her chin nearby as I fooled around, and she went, "Uh Huh, there." That's how we work. We smile on each other, shine the light where it's too dark, and help shade where it's too bright. It's a constant balancing.

That's how we are. We're best friends, and we're true life partners. The world came to be a peaceful place for us despite the violence out there. We finish each other's sentences; we don't have to talk a lot of times. We can sit in pure silence, and it's lovely.

(Post) Cris Williamson and Tret Fure have each had formidable solo careers, including touring with other people. Yet, though they love each other's music, and though I have seen each of them backstage with a beatific expression watching the other sing, I have also seen them fret in the wings, when the other was performing, not out of envy or competitiveness but out of sheer longing to be playing with, singing together, side by side.

When *Postcards from Paradise* was released in 1993, it was one of the most anticipated collaborative ventures in Women's Music. Not only did it represent a formal acknowledgment of one of Women's Music's first couples, but it brought together two greatly skilled, inspired, and complementary souls who had been inching toward this project for nearly fifteen years.

Postcards from Paradise offers optimism in its championing of women's history; in its stance against homophobia, and in its presentation of what the two artists find beautiful in their own lives. With its blend of Williamson's and Fure's individual tunes plus two songs they co-wrote, *Postcards* is unflagging in its grace. And, finally, the stunning harmonies are near-perfect.

Williamson's images—interpreted through her soaring, magnificent voice—are stark and wild: fire, shooting stars, flowing water, light, angels, and the endless, sweeping wind. Her archetypal characters stir the collective unconscious: Peter Pan, Dorothy of Oz, Crazy Horse, Calamity Jane. While reflecting a woman's spirit, Williamson's music gives a call to being and loving and finding the way.

Tret Fure's messages, delivered through consistent rock beats, have drawn attention to important issues such as poverty and disillusionment, fear in the nuclear age, and disempowerment. Masquerading as folk ditties about simple topics, Fure's lyrics can be as sweetly intense about failed and foiled love relationships as about the intricacies of relationships between people and the world.

In 1991, they co-founded In The Best Interest of the Children, a non-profit organization which works with hospital and community pediatric AIDS programs to raise awareness and funds for children with HIV disease.

Williamson: In The Best Interest of the Children happened by accident. I had this little idea: we should do a concert for children with AIDS. At the end of the first concert, we'd enjoyed it so much that we knew that we had to continue. I became chairperson, and Tret's a member of the board. This spring will be the fourth year. It's a wonderful feeling instead of that helpless feeling.

(Post) Williamson and Fure have accomplishments which are monumental. In closing, I want to know what has been a highlight for each of them.

Williamson: One that sticks out for me is my solo night at Carnegie Hall. I don't know if it will ever get better than that. I sang everything right, I didn't screw up. My mother was there, the room was full of love. I was totally exhausted at the end, and I was totally amped at the top. I can always say that I did it just like I wanted to. It was awe-inspiring, and I felt every moment of it. I think that being part of creating Olivia is another one for me; my life with Tret is right there at the top of the list.

Fure: I think my high point is still coming. Things just get better for me all the time. The work that Cris and I have been doing, now, is better work than I have ever done. Overall, that's a high point for me.

(Post) The women concur that continuing on their present path would suit them just fine. Fure specifies that she would like to keep writing music which moves people, to continue as an artist.

Williamson: I'd like people to start thinking about the global village. We want everybody to pay attention and to get it, get up, and make it a better world. I hope that somehow, the wheel will turn, and evolution and revolution will become one, that a spirituality will return. You have to put in something and lean into the wheel. I'm not the wheel, but I will be a cheerful driver.

DISCOGRAPHY

Cris Williamson: *Artistry of Cris Williamson* (Avanti, 1964); *A Step at a Time* (Avanti, 1965); *The World Around* (Avanti, 1965); *Cris Williamson* (Ampex, 1971; reissued Olivia Records, 1981); *Cris Williamson* (EP, Kickback, 1972); *The Changer and the Changed* (Olivia Records, 1975); *Live Dream* (Dream Machine, 1978); *Strange Paradise* (Olivia Records, 1980); *Lumiere* (Pacific Cascade Records, 1982); *Blue Rider* (Olivia Records, 1982); *Meg Christian/Cris Williamson Live at Carnegie Hall* (double album, Second Wave/Olivia Records, 1983); *Portrait* (Olivia Records, 1983); *Prairie Fire* (Olivia Records, 1985); *Snow Angel* (Olivia Records, 1985); *The Cris Williamson Songbook* (Songbook, Olivia Records, 1985); *Wolf Moon* (Olivia Records, 1987); *Country Blessed* with Teresa Trull (Second Wave/Olivia Records, 1989); *The Best of Cris Williamson* (Olivia Records, 1990); *Circle of Friends/Cris Williamson Live in Concert* (Olivia Records, 1991), *Between the Covers* (Wolf Moon Records, 1997).

Tret Fure: *Mousetrap* with Spencer Davis (United Artists, 1970); *Tret Fure* (MCA, 1973); *Heartsong* with June Millington, (Fabulous Records, 1981); *Terminal Hold* (Second Wave/Olivia Records, 1984); *Edges of the Heart* (Second Wave/Olivia Records, 1986); *Time Turns the Moon* (Second Wave/Olivia Records, 1990).

Cris Williamson and Tret Fure: *Postcards from Paradise* (Olivia Records, 1993); *Between the Covers* (Wolf Moon Records, 1997).

DEBORAH HENSON-CONANT
playing jazz and living improvisation

When I recently learned about an energetic woman musician who resembles Kim Basinger, dresses in leather miniskirts, and plays jazz harp, I was intrigued. Having spoken with Deborah Henson-Conant, herself, I am as awed by the enthusiasm she displays towards the harp, towards jazz and towards her muse as I am by the music on her CD.

Deborah Henson-Conant grew up surrounded by music and believing that the musical profession was a worthy one.

Deborah Henson-Conant: My grandfather was a junk man who loved to play the piano and dreamed about being Piano Man Sam. My grandmother wanted to be a singer, but she was forbidden by her father. One of my songs, "Anna Bella" (*Caught in the Act*), named after my grandmother, is about them. When I play this song, I can pretend that they really did live their dreams.

(Post) The musical tradition was continued by her mother who was a singer. Even more important was the personal musical legacy from her parents.

Henson-Conant: My parents courted through singing. When they split up, they each communicated with me through music.

(Post) Not only was there a separate set of songs for each parent but Henson-Conant's concept of intimacy revolved around sharing music with somebody. (Henson-Conant's tape for kids, *Songs My Mother Sang*, derived from her mother's repertoire).

After her parents' divorce, young Henson-Conant moved from relative to relative, all of whom had pianos and encouraged her to play.

Henson-Conant: From the age of five, I would make up stories and play the sound tracks that I would compose.

(Post) When Henson-Conant was seven, her mother gave her a ukulele. A series of music instructions on different instruments followed, ostensibly to nurture the budding music lover; however, Henson-Conant did not practice.

Henson-Conant: It wasn't that I didn't like to play music, it was that I didn't like lessons. Why would I want to learn how to play music that anybody had played before? My idea was that you made it up, and it was new.

(Post) Once Henson-Conant arrived in college, in northern California, it became clear that those few lessons she had endured proved useful.

Henson-Conant: The College of Marin needed a harpist and asked if anyone had ever touched a harp. I told them that I could even tune it!

(Post) A stint with the concert band followed, as well as five albums in New Age style, including *Flute and Harp for Christmas*. By that time Henson-Conant was willing to practice and found that she really enjoyed the harp. She was deterred, however, by her sense that the harp was exclusively a classical instrument and that 'real musicians' wore long, black dresses and worked with symphonies.

Henson-Conant: I tried to be that for a year and a half. Suddenly, the other me—the me that loves to improvise, the me that loves to create, the me that loves to do it differently—took over.

(Post) The next few years saw Henson-Conant in transition, gigging in hotel lounges.

Henson-Conant: I was playing a lot of tunes my mother used to sing when I was a kid, but I only knew about ten songs, and I was supposed to play four hours a night. So, I improvised. Because the harp sounds so pretty, I could really get away with a lot of experimentation.

(Post) By 1981 Henson-Conant had learned a lot more tunes and reached the top of her profession.

Henson-Conant: I was at the Waldorf-Astoria, in New York City, plenty of money, in my mid-twenties, and at the pinnacle of my career as a lounge musician. I started thinking, "Where do I go from here?"

(Post) Henson-Conant had envisioned a career in which she could peak at age eighty, not at twenty-seven; she concluded that she must be in the wrong career.

Henson-Conant: I left New York and moved to Boston, where I met Peter Kontrimas, a great bass player who took the time to help me focus my love of improvisation into serious jazz playing. He taught me to play in rhythm, to take solos, and understand jazz forms. In 1983, we asked a drummer to join us and thus was born the Jazz Harp Trio.

(Post) Several recordings followed produced by Kontrimas, and Henson-Conant left hotel lounges forever.

Henson-Conant: I was so lucky to have played in lounges, because it was a chance to learn on the job, to practice, to develop and to get paid for it. I'm very grateful for that. But in 1983, when I played my first public concert, that was the beginning of my real career, and I don't think it could have happened quite like this in any place but Boston.

(Post) Boston supported Henson-Conant from the beginning. She received fellowships and grants for her composing. As she explored her jazz career, she was able to pay her bills by playing private parties. She found countless great players to work with and, once she started touring internationally, she found that Boston had an additional advantage for her, she was able to fly anywhere in the U.S. or Europe from Logan International.

Henson-Conant describes her own compositions as fitting in with jazz because of their improvisational nature but being different from jazz because they don't use traditional forms of theme and variations.

Henson-Conant: A lot of my songs have stories, and I can't tell the story with just theme and variations. My forms are more complex than that, and then they have areas of improvisation.

(Post) It is clear that a story is essential to Henson-Conant's music, even if a tune is part of a story. She points out that "Danger Zone," also from *Naked Music*, was originally part of a suite for harp and string quartet called "Stress Analysis of a Strapless Evening Gown."

Henson-Conant describes the progressive simplification of her music towards its essence, likening her process of composing to that of digging archaeologically for the tunes buried within her. She concludes by saying she knows that when audience members approach her with requests for tunes by their stories ("Are you going to do the one about…?"), she has succeeded in engaging their imagination.

Not surprisingly, Henson-Conant lists among the highlights of her career a favorable Boston Globe review of her first public performance, in 1983.

Henson-Conant: When I read the review, I thought, "Wow, I'm being accepted as a real artist. This music is really getting across to other people."

(Post) The next four years saw a lot of experimentation with recording, which culminated in a self-produced and re-released CD of jazz standards, *Round the Corner*.

Other professional triumphs for Henson-Conant have included her debut as soloist and composer with the Boston Pops; her frequent touring in Europe (she spends three to four months each year touring and recording in Germany, France, Hungary, Switzerland, the U.K., etc.); appearing on national television for the first time in 1988; a three-record deal with GRP Records (*On the Rise* in 1989, *Caught in the Act* in 1990, and *Talking Hands* in 1991) which she described as a fabulous learning experience about artistic control and commercial music-making.

After her contract expired in 1991, Henson-Conant realized she had to reassess her identity.

Henson-Conant: I had to go back to square one, start all over again, find out who is really in the center of me, and look at myself naked in the mirror.

(Post) Hence her '94 release, *Naked Music*, produced for the German Laika label. Henson-Conant's self-search seems to have paid off.

Henson-Conant: *Naked Music* is selling better in Europe than any of the albums I made with GRP.

Photo: David Tucker

(Post) Since then she's completed two more recordings for Laika Records: *Just For You*, a live CD which captures her talent better than any studio album and which marks the first time her live performances have been made available on CD; and a solo Christmas album, *The Gift*, which, she feels, turned out to be one of the most creative projects she'd ever done. For the first time, Laika sent her into a studio on her own terms, encouraging her to find her own voice and to discover the sound that she alone can make with her harp.

I feel compelled to break one of my own rules of interviewing with this next question, but Henson-Conant's stage persona demands it. Why the leather miniskirt? Henson-Conant's rich laugh fills the space between us, and she replies that there are several reasons for her non-traditional stage garb. First, she says, she takes more risks on stage when dressed in daring fashions.

Second, her own development as an artist, leading players more experienced and skilled than she, required her to adopt non-traditional attire in order to assert her strengths as a pathfinder, and as a woman pathfinder to boot.

Third, wanting to break through the mythologies of the harp as an angelic, 'nice-girl's' instrument, wanting to let the audience know immediately that she is different, prompted the unusual clothing.

Finally she offers that leather doesn't wrinkle, and a small miniskirt takes up less room than some other garments might take, a fact crucial on trips overseas with a large instrument. Her leather miniskirt can even be packed between the harp strings for prolonged travel.

Given the size and cost of her harps, I ask whether Henson-Conant has experienced any difficulties in travelling with such a cumbersome, yet delicate instrument.

Henson-Conant: Getting a harp on a plane or into a taxi or up a narrow, winding staircase are all just part of the creative process, like dealing with the inevitable moment when something 'goes wrong' on stage.

(Post) She proceeds to tell a story about breaking a string. Not only did she ask the percussionist to play 'harp-fixing music' while she readied the harp to resume the performance, but she was inspired to leave the amplification on so that the audience could hear the sounds of pulling the broken string out and replacing it with a fresh string.

Henson-Conant: I didn't want to hide from the audience. That's what I mean about improvisation. It's not just jazz improvisation but living with improvisation, being open for those moments when what you didn't plan happens. That's when they really see you, and I love it. That's where the wall breaks down.

DISCOGRAPHY

Songs My Mother Sang (Golden Cage Music, 1985); *Flute and Harp for Christmas* (Heavenly Music, 1986); *Round the Corner* (1987, re-released on Laika, 1994); *On The Rise* (GRP, 1989); *Caught in the Act* (GRP, 1990); *Talking Hands* (GRP, 1991); *Christmas Collection II* (GRP, 1991); *Budapest* (Laika, 1992); *Naked Music* (Laika, 1994); *Just For You* (Laika, 1995, live); *The Gift* (Laika, 1996).

FERRON
taking a new step in an old direction

Ferron is simply one of the best song writers of our time; her songs are like fireflies, connecting us through the darkness of the unknown. She constructs a life, in chains of ideas quick and full, and binds them with undeniable emotions, provocative thoughts, and images which flash and linger.

In listening to Ferron's music, we acknowledge the passage of time, people, memories, and hopes through her poetic metaphors. Her familiar vernacular, her warm, husky voice, and her engaging stage presence have permitted us to identify with her experiences, her struggles and her wisdom.

Born on June 2, 1952, Ferron grew up in a semi-rural suburb of Vancouver, British Columbia, the eldest of seven children in a working-class family. After leaving home at fifteen, she scrambled financially, supporting herself by driving a cab, waitressing, shoveling gravel, and packing five-pound bags of coffee in a factory.

Ferron's first musical audition took place when she was sixteen, her first real gig when she was twenty-three; along the way, she acquired the name Ferron, which loosely translates from the French as "iron and rust." From her basement, she recorded and distributed *Ferron* (1977) and *Ferron Backed Up* (1978). Since both albums are now out-of-print collector's items, Ferron has decided to re-release much of their material on subsequent albums, as she began to do with "Rosalee" and "Who Loses," on *Testimony* (1980) and "White Wing Mercy" on *Phantom Center* (1990).

In 1978, Ferron was "discovered" by Gayle Scott, an American living and working in film production in Vancouver, who became Ferron's first and only manager and business partner. Gayle collaborated with Ferron on her next two studio albums, *Testimony* and *Shadows On A Dime* (1984), on which Ferron continued to convey her polished messages of relationships, questions of identity, and optimism amid fear, through sharply lyrical, soothingly melodic music. Despite a small budget dependent on loans and contributions, and in the absence of organized promotion, *Shadows On A Dime* received wide distribution and praise, garnering a four-star rating from *Rolling Stone*.

In October of 1985, Ferron received a Canada Council Arts Grant, enabling her to take a much-needed year off, ostensibly to write and take voice lessons but also to recover a long-neglected personal life. Recognizing that she would need more than a year to fully heal from the hardships of the road, Ferron remained withdrawn from the spotlight. After the grant money ran out, she earned a living by laboring as a carpenter's assistant, a bartender, and by doing day care.

Having reconnected with her physical and spiritual roots, and having reaffirmed and redefined her own needs, Ferron returned to the studio and the stage with a fresh body of work, manifest in *Phantom Center*.

Post: You returned from five years off, with new music on *Phantom Center* that seems more peaceful, more optimistic.

Ferron: Yeah, right on! You heard that already? You can already feel that? The *Testimony* and *Shadows* era was good for me, but there was a transition after *Shadows*, with people telling me what I was, what I wasn't, what I would never be, what I could have been. I was in my middle thirties and having to sit down and figure out what I cared about, what I absolutely could not live without, what was worth everything.

I wasn't sleeping well, I was always in a different city. How could I get down to finding out what I was doing when everything was changing all the time? There were several people around me who said that it was not a good time for me to stop touring because I was getting attention, and you're supposed to dive after it. Luckily, Gayle, my manager, agreed with me. So, hell or high water, fame, or whatever, I just had to stop doing the music the way we had been because I wanted to know about something else; I wanted to test me, to find out what I was made of.

So I stopped touring for a while, for a year really stopped, and that was interesting. And difficult. I would get an invitation to come down to San Francisco to do a show, and I was ready to go, ready to get away from me and get back into performing full-time. I tried to remember that I was quitting something that wasn't good for me: there was something in the work that had kept me going—a new person, a revelation, a new face—and I just got lost.

Then, I started to calm down. For one thing, I didn't have to pay attention to time six months in advance. I needed to pay attention to my body, to me. Of course, the danger was—and what happened was—that I loved it, and I never wanted to come back again. I had a couple of years of really doubting whether I would come back again. At the time, I thought I could have made a decision not to, but I didn't know what else to do; I don't like anything else as much, and I'm not good at anything else the way I seem to be good at this.

Post: What can you say about what you did during your time off?

Ferron: After deciding that I wanted to have time, I lived on an island in British Columbia; then I went to Santa Fe for a while. What I wanted was to separate from urban life and to have time for me. For a while, I was caught up in myself. I had hidden from a lot of things, and I had to first learn that I was hiding, and, then, I had to figure out what I was hiding from, and whether I wanted to hide any more and what it was going to cost me.

When I was in Santa Fe, I started to see that my actions were really hurting me. It finally hurt so much that I had to change. One of the ways that I was able to experience some kind of discipline in my life was to not consume alcohol anymore. I had been hiding my feelings with alcohol, and that little act of self-love—stopping drinking—opened up a huge door for me. I'm really happy that I have been able to do that, but the stopping drinking is not what's interesting; what's interesting is what led up to stopping drinking.

That had to do with victimization. This probably sounds really contradictory to you. I mean, I'm a writer, I get to go on the stage, I have people who love my work and everything—what kind of victim am I? But, I have my own set of memories and

Photo: Victoria Pearson

I felt that something used to hurt me. When that thing stopped hurting me, I started hurting me. I wanted to stop the process of creating something negative that I was used to. I finally got to a place where I could no longer live with what I knew.

In December, 1985, Gayle invited me to do a meditation. So we went on a ten-day Vipassana meditation where you don't look at each other, you don't talk. In the meditation you do a thing called storming, and I stormed like crazy, and I thought I was having a breakdown. I think it was really the release of negative stuff. I couldn't sleep. I thought I had bugs crawling on me. I mean it was just the worst. I had one rough night. But then it got better and better, and by the time I left there, I was, to quote my friends, a "shimmering love object." When I came out of there, I had been opened; my heart chakra had been opened.

After the meditation, we were driving home in the car, and Crosby, Stills, Nash, and Young singing "Teach Your Children" came on the radio, and I started crying; and I couldn't stop crying, and Gayle kept saying, "What is the matter?" and I didn't know. I knew that there was this whole direction everyone was going in the 1960s, and it was all fucked, and I was crying because I saw the end of a dream.

We did that in December 1985. By May 1986 I was still wild. The world wasn't enough anymore. There was some big new feeling of gratitude, of love; it was so big, and it wasn't in my life. And so then I went to Mexico, and things were beautiful and exotic and hot and the colors of the earth.

I went into my senses, I partied for about six months, and then, it was over. I got hepatitis and had to stop drinking. But what it was that I had wanted with the drinking was the intensity of life that I knew existed, that I, in fact, experienced in the meditation.

Now, I can tell the story to you a whole other way: would you like me to?

Post: Yes, please do.

Ferron: I got worried that I wasn't good enough at anything, and that my life was kind of gray. As a matter of fact, the most intense that that feeling got was through the months of February and March 1986, in Vancouver, when it was raining all the time. I'd stopped touring. I stopped trying to steer my life. Well, when you wait and see what life's going to give you, life can only respond to what's going on inside.

I took a job taking care of kids, working in a group home. These kids were pissed off, and they were kind of a drag to be around. It was very intense. So the next thing I knew, my job had me working out in Richmond, British Columbia, where I grew up, near a house where we had lived that held a lot of bad memories.

After a while I got in my car and I drove toward this house, and I sat in the car, and I looked at the house. I'd look at the address, and I'd look at the house, and I'd get number and number. As I was still working with these disturbed kids, it all started to collide—but I didn't know that. Then someone came up to me and told me that somebody in Jalapa, Mexico, wanted to meet me. I'd never been to a Third World country. I was in rainy Vancouver.

I called up Gayle and said that I wanted to go to Mexico. Well, to tell you the truth, I wanted to go anywhere, but I didn't know that, either: I wasn't knowing, I was living. So Gayle told me that I had a show in Hawaii and that I could go to Mexico afterward. So in a matter of weeks, I was scooped out of the bummer that I was in, I got second-degree burns from the sun because I'd never been in sun, and then I went to Mexico.

I think that, after I meditated, I realized that I had been on a bummer all my life and that life was to be enjoyed and loved and celebrated, and I went too far. I just kept celebrating and celebrating and celebrating. And I see now that it's another kind of celebration.

Now that was three years ago, so it's really steadied out. It's really sweet, I mean I have what I wanted. It is a celebration, but it's a kind of slow celebration. My life's more peaceful now, and everything around me makes sense.

You know, there are people out there who have given me responsibilities; they can't go over the edge, they can't afford to. I think my job is to go a little bit near the edge and come back and talk about it, but I don't have to put myself over the edge. I can just live and it'll be OK. That's what I started to learn and what I wanted to report. I wanted to absolutely try something out and learn how to live a calmer life with juice in it.

I was afraid that there would be no more art, no more music, no more poetry, wit, sarcasm, that there would be nothing good, just an austere life. But that's not true.

I just don't know. It's my life, and I don't want to be on a band wagon. But I'm alive, I'm committed. So on that level, I want to talk about it everywhere. Yay!

I do have a bitch about alcohol, and the bitch is that, as gay people, our love of ourselves is not very developed because of our culture; and then being gay, we have gone into dark rooms. Since I was nineteen years old I have been going into dark rooms with black walls so that I could be with people like myself, and there was always liquid between us.

There's a song on *Phantom Center* called "Stand Up" that talks about taking our pride a step farther and not being burdened down in dark places but coming out and being with ourselves. I don't mean coming out as in, "I'm gay, I'm gay" only, but as we are completely. And so it has occurred to me that not drinking was a revolutionary act.

Post: When did you decide that you were going to make *Phantom Center*?

Ferron: In the kind of work that I do, you don't make a plan about this record or that tour. Things happen, opportunities open. I spent five years being asked for another album. That attention kept me trying, trying to come through in this big relationship. Recording made it real. I didn't make *Phantom Center* because of other people's desire, but that expectation helped.

We learn in affirmative thinking, that, without visualizing in a personal, active way, that things can't come. Last fall before we had even signed with a record company, Gayle and I saw an ad in the Ladyslipper catalogue about my "upcoming album," date unknown, title unknown. I knew then that I would do another album. Some rumor went out, some desire went out. Things happen out of desire, and it was an honor—I was really touched—to hear that desire.

Post: How long did you work on the material for *Phantom Center*?

Ferron: I have been working since 1985.

Post: What is important to you about this album?

Ferron: I think that what has been important is to have the courage to go after what we wanted musically. Gayle and I took a step in a particular direction, and it was a logical next step. You have heard the music, it's a big sound; I need that sound. I want that sound. Recording technology is incredibly different than it was in 1984. Some of these songs have forty tracks. I couldn't do it alone.

I'm excited about this album, and I'm excited to think about people listening to this album and completely accepting that what's on the record I wanted to be there. That I was present.

Phantom Center shows that I am a woman, a gay woman, a cultural survivor, alive and kicking. Women's Music is not only about women opening up, it's about all people opening up to women. When I think of the first Women's Music, I think of the mid-1970s, of early Olivia, of women learning that we could be women together. I wasn't then performing in Women's Music; I was doing folk music up in Vancouver, playing to men and women, some gay, some of them straight.

It makes me feel proud to be gay in the world. I want our sensibilities to be out there. The original thing was that Women's Music was to change consciousness. And it did.

(Post) Ferron has since established her own label, Cherrywood Station. Ferron re-released *Testimony, Shadows On A Dime,* and *Phantom Center* on her own label.

With her partner, Marianne, Ferron has also set up a mail-order from home business distributing her products, an enterprise virtually unheard of for a performer of her renown. Ferron's typical day starts at five-thirty, and includes several disciplined writing stints in her studio, plus answering phone calls, picking up mail, walking her dogs, and checking out the occasional movie with Marianne.

Ferron: Between the two of us, we run the business. Maybe getting a sense of what it is like to just be a regular old person doing your work and hoping for the best.

This is my inclination, to do it on my own label. Let's say that in my life, I've managed to impress three thousand people; that was how many names I had on my mailing list at the time. What's the matter with that? You know, write all these people a letter. Tell them that you've made a record. They love your work. They're not going to hurt you. You're going to give them something and they're going to find a way to be giving back. This is a fair deal. And the people, those three thousand people who got the announcement, they ordered.

Through the last couple of years they've sent me letters, poems, information, photos of their house and children. It's a beautiful place out there, you know. You can also turn on the news and know that there's a kid being shot every day and that there's all this other stuff going on. At the same time I have access to this humanness. And I'm not sure that that isn't where *Driver* came from.

(Post) Ferron's music has also taken several new turns: in 1992, she released two new albums both on Cherrywood Station. *Resting With The Question*, her first instrumental album which wordlessly continued Ferron's moody exploration of the familiar and the unknown, the safety and the shadow. Her first live release, *Not A Still Life*, showcases six lesser-known tunes from *Ferron* and *Ferron Backed Up* plus nine selections from her subsequent releases and also reveals a streak of ingenuous whimsy. Ferron is aware of the increased humor in her more recent work.

Ferron: Well, we do get tired of our burdens, don't we? So, something is starting to be funny; either I'm starting to be funny, or the repetition of patterns is starting to be funny. Sometimes it's funny just how long it takes to let go of something. Once you let it go, you just have to laugh because it was so friggin' heavy.

Post: You have a powerful line in "Girl On A Road," a few words which telegraphically sum up the import of your work, the backdrop against which you create in the present: "My momma was a waitress, my daddy a truckdriver. The thing that kept their power from them slowed me down a while."

Ferron: There was no way to talk about the things that you don't get that you might have wanted as a child. Everybody had a life that didn't turn out somehow. But that's the sentence. When I wrote that sentence down, I started to cry. And I realized that I forgive my parents everything.

Those two lines are so close together about me and about them because I'm born once again out of them, in that sentence. I forgive what I didn't get. Right in the writing what happens is, I forgave. If no one ever heard the song, or ever liked it, it wouldn't matter. The process of it happened right there and I'm—I'm thrilled that you heard that in the first two lines.

The process of it was so incredibly powerful. Everybody lived here in the house. We did this at home. Donny [Benedictson] was my co-producer. After we had recorded it, and I had it on tape and we had to listen and listen, when we were mixing and everything, there'd be moments when we just would look at each other, and everybody's eyes would well up. This is the human experience that life is big and that our hearts are big. And our feelings are big.

There's something we didn't say to somebody, and we're barely able to live with it. There's stuff that happened that we just have to forget about and make a commitment even if our life is an illusion of happiness. You still got to do something. You can't just lay down and die. You want to make something beautiful. You're going to love somebody. Then your life starts coming together. I don't know; I can't tell anybody to do that. But by the time I came to the end of the album, this is what I understood for myself.

Post: There is another line in the song "Girl On A Road" which I found very moving, "Anger upon angry hurt, take me by the hand."

Ferron: It's quite scary, isn't it? I'm crying right now. I don't know what's going on, but I think there's something about – it's kind of like turning towards the thing that maybe you would have run from all your life and it's kind of like joining forces with it.

When were were doing background vocals for this song Donny ran out of the room crying. It's the same cry I'm having now. I don't understand it, and I don't know if you cry, if you cried when you heard this yourself.

Post: I cried when I first heard "Girl On A Road," as did many women at the concert where I first heard the song.

Ferron: There is something that as women, particularly, but anybody who has been violated in some way over a period of time, would cry for. The women at the concert who cried, they're no different from me. We're together. We're all trying to come through something. To make a better place.

I'm not really recovered from doing the work of making this album, it was very hard work. I don't know why other people do music. I don't know why they make records. I don't know what goes on with them, but I don't think I have ever cried so much as making this record. It has been with an incredible joy—I'm not crying because I'm sad. I feel up. I give up to it and to the idea of praying.

By the end of the album, there's some hard knocks and there's loss and there's gain and there's humor. There's some letting go. There's wistfulness. All these things that we do and yet at the end we have, you know, possibly a relationship with the self, a relationship with 'other', a relationship with earth, a relationship with time, and light that is enduring. And the idea that life is an illusion, then, if that be the case, then those are the rules that I'm going to operate by, and here we go.

I don't know if I could ever explain it but when I wrote "Maya," which was the end of January '93, then I knew that I had done the journey.

(Post) In 1995, Ferron licensed both *Driver* and a remix of *Phantom Center* to EarthBeat!/Warner Brothers Records for National Distribution; her back catalog is still available through Cherrywood Station, Vashon, WA. She is currently under a multiple recording agreement with Warner Brothers Records.

The Ferron Fan Club is on the internet: FerronFan @ aol.com and the Web site http://www.ferronweb.com.

DISCOGRAPHY

Ferron (Lucy Records, 1977); *Ferron Backed Up* (Lucy Records, 1978); *Testimony* (Lucy Records, 1980); *Shadows On A Dime* (Lucy Records, 1984); *Phantom Center* (Chameleon, 1990; re-released Warner, 1995); *Not A Still Life* (Cherrywood Station, 1992); *Resting With The Question* (Cherrywood Station, 1992); *Driver* (Cherrywood Station, 1994); *Still Riot* (Warner, 1996).

HEATHER BISHOP
bringing victories and celebrations on tour

For several decades, Heather Bishop has made a career blending an understated seriousness about political issues (child abuse, pollution, oppression) with an unflinchingly personal approach to relationships between people, the elements, and other beings who inhabit the earth. Bishop sensitively addresses life's realities with hopefulness at and appreciation of individual difference and uniqueness. Many admire not only her vocal range and balance, but her consistently good spirits, her quiet sensuality and her witty humor.

Heather Bishop's portrayals of diverse cultures, including her own midwestern Canadian woman-loving one, are easy and unaffected, never strident, but assertive just the same. Her resonant, clear voice carries any message gently to listening ears and hearts, and the relaxed conversation which she offers between songs is equally informative, uplifting, meaningful.

Post: Where did the music come from in your family?

Heather Bishop: I discovered the piano when I was four years old and begged for lessons. I studied piano until I was fifteen—that was in the '60s—and then picked up the guitar because folk music was so big. I had a school friend who was blind and a great guitar player. I would read for him, and he would teach me the guitar. That got me into my adulthood.

Post: Do you remember your first guitar?

Bishop: It was a twelve-string, a Raven or something. It was a cheap one, about sixty dollars, which is usually how you start out, and was hard to play. I'm surprised I didn't give it up.

Post: Was your family supportive?

Bishop: Yeah, especially given how hard it is to have a young person in the house playing the same old boring stuff over and over.

Post: As a child, did you have aspirations to play music professionally?

Bishop: I actually did not; I did music only for personal reasons. I have to say a couple of things, though. One is that, when I was a kid, I was told not to sing, and to mouth the words, because I supposedly didn't have much of a voice. I became a closet singer, in that I would literally go into my room and sing quietly for myself. Second, when I was a teenager, and most people were listening to rock and roll, I discovered Nina Simone and Billie Holiday. I went crazy for that music, and it was a major inspiration for me. I think that singing along helped me to find my voice.

Post: What are your thoughts about what you were initially told about your voice?

Bishop: They were absolutely wrong! In fact, I divide my time, now, almost half and half, between performing for adults and performing for children. One of the reasons I'm so adamant about working with children is because I believe that the message I was given is wrong. I believe that everyone can sing and that if you don't start singing as a child and learn the joy of it, and practice, how do you develop?

The body is an instrument, and you can't just expect to open your mouth and sound wonderful. When I decided I would pursue a professional career, I took vocal training, and I learned that I needed to give my body and my voice the same respect as one would give a guitar or piano.

Post: Your early training was in the Bel Canto style. Can you tell me something about it?

Bishop: For a vocalist, Bel Canto training is like jazz training for an instrumentalist. It gives you the entire spectrum of training on an instrument so that you can sing—or play—anything. Bel Canto develops your entire range: when I started working, I had a range of about an octave and a half, and I ended up having a range of three and a half octaves. I never would have believed for a moment that I had that kind of range.

Post: Can you hold notes and have power all across that range?

Bishop: Yes, it's amazing! My teacher used to say to me that you have to learn to use your body in order to sing well. When people tell me that they want to sing professionally and ask me how they should start in the music business, I tell them to begin with vocal training. It's a part of singing that's often overlooked. People will go and get guitar lessons but imagine that their voice is automatically there. There are two things wrong with those assumptions: one, that you can be a hundred times better at singing with training and the other is that your voice will last a lifetime if you train it. You can look around the music scene and see lots of people who have been forced to drop out altogether because they've wrecked their voices from singing incorrectly.

Post: What do you do currently to keep your voice healthy?

Bishop: I sing so much—I'm always on the road—that my voice stays in shape. Sometimes, I'll get in to do a sound check. You know: get off the plane, drive to the hall, stand onstage and sing. There are always people around, saying, "Wow! How can you sing like that without warming up?" It's because of my training that I use the correct parts of my body to sing.

Post: When you are on the road, do you do anything special to stay in shape, so that your body supports your voice?

Photo: Joanne Hovey

Bishop: I have to stay in excellent physical condition because singing is so physical, and I have to stay emotionally clear. Over the years, I've tried to live a clean life on the road. I'm very careful what I eat, and I'm not one to party after a show. I ask for bottled water, fresh vegetables and fruit backstage. Often, there isn't time, by the time you do your interviews and sound check, to find a good restaurant.

I have to be emotionally and spiritually grounded before I go onstage, so that even if I've had a shitty sound check, or something awful has happened during the day, I somehow leave it in the dressing room. Onstage, that bad energy would seep through the music and affect the audience. I must come from a good space, and what I pray for is clarity and focus, that I can be the vessel that I trained my body to be so that this gift can flow through me.

Post: You seem very comfortable on stage. Have you always been so, or did it come from experience?

Bishop: It came from experience, and it didn't come easily for me. It's been almost twenty years that I've been on the road and only in the last five or so that I've gotten entirely comfortable performing. It took me a long time to get through my head that people were paying money for me to take space so I should take up that space! There seem to be two sorts of performers: performers who are quite shy and who have to work at getting on a stage and filling it up and other people who are always 'on,' whether or not they're on or off the stage.

I'm the first kind. I work hard at the talking part. You see, people are there to hear me sing and also to find out what's going on for me and in our world. It's not just the singing; I'm sort of a traveling minstrel. I bring stories from other places—I just returned from a tour of Australia so, lately, it's Australian stories—and keep us connected with good news. You can pick up the paper or watch the t.v. and get all the bad news. My job is to bring our victories and celebrations.

Post: How did you get started as a professional musician?

Bishop: A friend of mine started a women's dance band, Walpurgis Night, and asked me to play. When she put an ad in the paper, thirty women phoned up and wanted to sing, but hardly any of them could play an instrument. I could play guitar and keyboards so that's what I did. After a year or so, the lead singer quit, and they told me, "You gotta sing." I freaked out and said, "I can't do it." But, I had to do it. We had a gig, and I just started to sing. It taught me a lot.

We sang in halls in small towns all over Saskatchewan: lots of old-time music, a bit of '60s rock and roll. As the night wore on, I'd sing a little blues. As the crowd got drunker, I had to really project. It wasn't until I started thinking about a solo career that I began to pursue vocal training.

Post: Did you think of yourself as a minstrel then?

Bishop: Not at all. I saw it as a blast! I didn't see it as any kind of cultural work. I loved music and I loved watching people get up and have a good time. It seemed a miracle to me that I could be part of this group and get paid, if only twenty-five dollars a night.

Post: How did your solo career start?

Bishop: I wanted to be the kind of solo musician—like Buffy Ste. Marie and others who sang about their oppression—who told the truth because, to me, truth in music makes it all the more powerful. So, I thought my career would last five minutes!

My first big gig was at the Regina Folk Festival. There were about eight hundred people there which, to me, was a huge audience. My parents and grandmother were there, and about three-quarters of the way through my set, I sang a song of Connie Kaldor's, "I Found A Girl," about a lesbian friend of hers. When I finished the set, I got a standing ovation and nearly dropped dead. I couldn't believe it.

Then I had to create places to play; I would phone up rape crisis centers and transition houses and women's centers and ask them if they wanted to put on a concert.

Post: Do you think the women's network developed differently in Canada than in the United States?

Bishop: Oh yes, because in Canada, our population was too small to support a women's circuit separate from the folk circuit. Lesbian and feminist performers either had to be part of the mainstream folk circuit, or we didn't make it. Also with a smaller population, you get noticed more, so the folk festivals did hire performers like Connie, Ferron, and me. Of course, they'd only hire one of us at a time!

There was one occasion, in 1985 or '86, when all three of us played the same Canadian folk festival; it was a big day! In fact, Tom Paxton once told me that one of the things he loved about Canadian folk festivals was that he got to meet the American performers who, in their own country, were performing only in the women's music circuit.

Post: What guitar do you currently use for touring?

Bishop: I have a Linda Manzer guitar that I'm totally in love with. She's a guitar maker out of Toronto who's becoming known all over the world. She makes Pat Metheny's guitars.

Post: On your album, *Day Dream Me Home*, your title track feels solid and smooth. How did you write it?

Bishop: That one I wrote in Boston, on the piano, and it popped out whole. I'd been on the road for weeks, and it was wet and drizzly and a really cold house that I was staying in. I knew that back home [rural Manitoba], there would be snow and Northern Lights, and I was overcome with homesickness. I wrote that song from an emotional place; if I write on the road, it's got to be something strong that I have to express. Otherwise, I don't write on the road because it's so exhausting.

Post: Which music, other than your own, do you listen to, these days?

Bishop: What's in my CD player right now is Judy Small's new album because when I was in Australia she gave it to me; it's great. Roy Forbes [whose music Bishop covered on *Daydream Me Home*] has just recorded a retrospective of old stuff, which I love. If I could pick a guitarist I'd most like to play like, it would be Roy. I'm also a K.T. Oslin fan.

Post: Do you ever see those musicians in concert?

Bishop: No, because I'm on the road eight months of every year. I try not to go more than two weeks at a time—though with Australia, it was a month—so that I can come home in between and have a life. That means I'm gone, with breaks, for most of the year. It's my life, so make it good!

Post: You have received many honors during your career: Canada Council Grant, Juno nomination for Most Promising Artist for *A Taste Of The Blues*; Parents' Choice Gold Award for *A Duck In New York City*; appearances in the U.K., Canada, U.S., Australia and on behalf of numerous progressive organizations and causes. What, for you, has been a highlight?

Bishop: One is playing with large symphonies in Canada. I had a wonderful time with the Vancouver, Winnipeg, and other symphonies. Also, last fall, I did a gig with the Edmonton Vocal Minority which is a seventy-five-voice choir.

Right now, I'm in one of those places where I'm about to make a change in how I present my music; I sort of know what it is but not totally. It's going to have to do with telling more stories, and it's going to be rooted in folk. To me, folk music is the music that preserves people's culture no matter who you are. Folk music is the music that sings about people's issues and what's important in a world out of balance. That's as clear as I can be!

DISCOGRAPHY

Grandmother's Song (Mother of Pearl Records, 1979); *Celebration* (Mother of Pearl Records, 1980); *Bellybutton* for children (Mother of Pearl Records, 1982); *I Love Women Who Laugh* (Mother of Pearl Records, 1982); *Purple People Eater* for children (Mother of Pearl Records, 1985); *A Taste Of The Blues* (Mother of Pearl Records, 1986); *Walk That Edge* (Mother of Pearl Records, 1988); *A Duck In New York City* for children (Mother of Pearl Records, 1989); *Old, New, Borrowed, Blue* (Mother of Pearl Records, 1992); *Daydream Me Home* (Mother of Pearl Records, 1994); *Chickee's on the Run* for children(Mother Of Pearl Records, 1997).

HOLLY NEAR
off on a new path, singing show tunes

Holly Near started out as a small town girl from northern California whose dreams were as big as the redwoods and as wide as the farm valleys. Having ended up as a cultural worker with a feminist attitude and international goals, and more concerned with peace than with hits (though her sixteen albums have sold around two million copies), Near recently gave her audience a new gift: her vibrant, honest autobiography.

In keeping with her multiple talents, Near first unleashed her autobiography in book form (*Fire in the Rain...Singer in the Storm*, William Morrow, 1990), then as a musical show adapted from the book, and finally as the recording from the musical—*Holly Near: Musical Highlights From the Play "Fire in the Rain...Singer in the Storm"* (1991).

Exploring the complex thinking, basic instincts, and occasional ambivalence underlying some of her personal life decisions, the autobiography also documents the corresponding political eras from Near's perspective as a liberal artist/activist attempting to live her politics. One of the core issues addressed—couched behind the self-conscious impossibility of living up to her own expectations—is how grueling, event-filled, and selflessly overextended Near's life has been.

For her singing and songwriting in the name of progressive causes (from Hanoi to Nicaragua and El Salvador to the March on Washington for gay/lesbian rights); for her acting (the film "Dog Fight," an episode of "LA Law"); for her entertaining performances (delicious and moving medleys of song, fervent opinions, and wry humor); for her unflinching portrayal of the process of political awakening (richly revealed in her autobiography); for her persistence in getting her own and others' progressive messages to the world (Near founded Redwood Records in 1973), Holly Near has accumulated a loyal international following and has received many accolades, including being named Woman of the Year by *Ms.Magazine.*

After twenty-two years of uninterrupted touring, speaking, organizing, coalition-building, and weathering difficult and more conservative political times, Holly Near has decided to transform her focus and slow her frenetic pace.

Holly Near: I need to slow down, make some space in my life for new ideas, new songs. I haven't been able to enjoy music lately. I don't respond with excitement to adventure. Even when confronting war, it is necessary for me to feel at peace. I can't be a leader if I don't know where I'm going. I can't be working hard if I've forgotten how to have fun. So, I'm just taking some time to rediscover the elements that made me want to be an artist in the first place.

Photo: Jay Thompson

(Post) For a change of pace, Near has taken pen to hand and is writing fiction.

Near: I'm not sure what the outcome will be, but it's much different than writing nonfiction or a play. The characters just leap in and tell me, each day, what they want to do. I'm not a commercial novelist so I don't have to follow rules about plot and dialogue and narration. I am having fun.

(Post) She declines to discuss the plot, saying, with a hearty laugh, that the characters might be frightened away.

Near's foreseeable future includes a reduced touring schedule, with a choice of material representing something of a change.

Near: I'm grateful that my audience has always been wonderfully curious about what I'm going to do next, whether it's a musical or touring with Inti-Illimani. A typical show would be mostly my songs, with a show tune or two thrown in.

(Post) Near, whose own theatrical career began with musicals, has retained a special fondness for show music from those productions.

Near: I have always loved the music of the '30s and '40s and the early musicals. I have to admit that I stopped listening to musicals after Rogers-and-Hammerstein, Leonard Bernstein, and Comden-and-Green. I'm not fond of the '80s musicals.

(Post) She describes the process by which, through her interpretation in her shows, classic songs retain their period ambiance while simultaneously offering contemporary meaning:

Near: Here's an example. I recently did "Wouldn't It Be Loverly" from My Fair Lady, and, without changing any words, it became a song about homelessness. I didn't have to say a thing. "All Right With Me" also has a wonderful twist, but you'll just have to come and hear it.

(Post) Holly has also released four books: her autobiography, *Fire in the Rain...Singer in the Storm*, two songbooks *Words and Music* and *Singing for Our Lives*; and *The Great Peace March*, for children.

DISCOGRAPHY

Hang In There (Redwood, 1973); *A Live Album* (Redwood, 1975); *You Know All I Am* (Redwood Records, 1976); *Imagine My Surprise* (Redwood, 1978); *Fire In The Rain* (Redwood, 1981); *Speed Of Light* (Redwood, 1982); *Journeys* (Redwood, 1983;) *Lifeline* with Ronnie Gilbert (Redwood, 1984); *Watch Out!* (Redwood, 1984); *Sing To Me The Dream* with Inti-Illimani (Redwood, 1984;); *Harp* with Ronnie Gilbert, Arlo Guthrie, Pete Seeger (Redwood Records, 1985); *Singing With You* with Ronnie Gilbert (Redwood, 1986); *Don't Hold Back* (Redwood, 1987); *Sky Dances* (Redwood, 1989); *Singer In The Storm* (Chameleon, 1990); *Musical Highlights From The Play "Fire In The Rain Singer In The Storm"* (Redwood, 1991); *This Train Still Runs* with Ronnie Gilbert (Redwood, 1996).

JANIS IAN
society's child breaks silence and takes revenge

In 1966, at the age of fifteen, Ian skyrocketed to fame with her song, "Society's Child," about a white mother's reflexive dismissal of her daughter's black boyfriend and the daughter's regretful rejection of the young man. Though her song was more passionate than challenging, more questioning than criticizing, Ian soon experienced the backlash from speaking the truth: she was spat at and called "nigger lover."

Nearly thirty years and a dozen albums later, Ian has become one of the most highly celebrated artists to come out in the mainstream entertainment world. These days, "faggot," "dyke," and "queer" are yelled at her rather than the earlier epithets.

Willing to endure criticism for her actions, clear that she, the individual, is not the behavior ("I've always been puzzled about how people can say they hate me when it's my songs they don't like"), Janis Ian is certain that her personal freedom is worth the taunts. She is a rare artist whose ethics elevate her music to a level of unflinching social observation and for whom being honest is always worth more than a hit album, a moment of entertainment, or idolatry.

Janis Ian is a songwriter's songwriter, so committed to her own material that she has never recorded music composed by another artist, even though that meant turning down "You Light Up My Life" and "Mrs. Robinson," the theme song from the film, "The Graduate."

Ian's 'purist' commitment to record only her own songs has been proven worthy by the durability of her lyrics. For example, I clearly remember the moment when I first heard "At Seventeen," the Top Ten song from Ian's double-Grammy-winning album, *Between The Lines* (1975). I was fifteen, and her lines brought me to tears:

"I learned the truth at seventeen/That love was meant for beauty queens/and high school girls with clear-skinned smiles/who married young, and then retired...And those of us with ravaged faces/lacking in the social graces/desperately remained at home/inventing lovers on the phone."

For the first time in my life, I was not alone in my self-consciousness; and there was at least one songwriter out there who was willing to talk about teen-angst issues other than falling in and out of love. "At Seventeen"remains an enduring testimony to anyone who grew up looking or feeling different.

Post: With your albums *Breaking Silence* (1993) and *Revenge* (1995), you continue to address difficult topics unflinchingly: child abuse, the Holocaust and its survivors, spousal battering, homelessness.

Janis Ian: I seem to be good at writing about things that others are uncomfortable with. I was taught that, if something bad happened to someone, and I didn't do anything to protest or stop it, then I might be next. It's Jewish tradition.

On the liner notes to her album, *Revenge*, Ian has written a moving dedication: "For my parents, Pearl & Victor, who raised me to be a Maccabee and allowed me to become myself." The definition of a Maccabee (traditional): *Of the family of Jewish patriots who revolted against the Syrians and ruled Palestine;* Maccabee (contemporary): *Powerful underdog fighters for the just cause.*

Post: In your song, "Thankyous," from your 1973 album, *Stars*, you wrote: "Papa gave me music/Mama gave me soul/Brother gave me/reaching out to hold/Teacher gave me license/Learning set me free/Schooling gave me nothing/Music showed me how to leave."

Ian: Everybody in my family is pretty musical. My brother could have been a professional flutist or bassoonist; he was wonderful on both. My dad became a music teacher through the G.I. Bill. My mother was an actress when she was young, and both my parents are the children of immigrants from Russia. They brought a respect for folk traditions that they got from my grandparents. I think that for us, as Jews, music was an inherent part of the culture and such a necessary part of the survival of the culture.

I'm not sure any of that would have mattered, ultimately, because when I was two I figured out that pianos made noise, and that I could make the pianos make the noise. From then on that was all I wanted.

Post: When you were first starting to get noticed, after "Society's Child" was released, you were only fifteen.

Ian: I never wanted to be anything but a professional musician. I think that kind of ambition is something you're born with. So, I had taught myself the guitar when I was eleven, and started writing songs when I was twelve. I was surprised, though, that people listened as hard as they did to what I was saying.

(Post) Janis Ian has claimed a public identity for most of her life. Specifically, she has said that she has been 'Janis Ian' since she was fourteen, when she changed her name from Janis Eddy Fink.

Ian: I've been doing what I do publicly, for better or for worse, with public acknowledgment since I was fourteen. There is a difference between how people treat you after you become famous and how they treated you before you were famous.

I've always maintained that it's not the famous person who changes; initially, it's the people around them thereby forcing the famous person to change. Fame, in a lot of ways, is much harder on the people around you than on you because it's something you've been going after.

Post: I imagine that, during adolescence, being in the spotlight and receiving that kind of acclaim would change a person.

Ian: What positive feedback does is that it reinforces that you are doing something valuable, something morally useful to your society or to whatever group you consider yourself part of.

Post: Speaking of groups: in 1975, the lesbian movement was beginning. That year, Olivia Records was formed, and the Michigan Womyn's Music Festival—the largest annual gathering of lesbians in the world—happened for the first time. I am curious about whether you had contact with any of the women who pioneered that movement: Cris Williamson, Meg Christian, Margie Adam.

Ian: No. I've never met any of them that I know of. I knew some people who were connected with Olivia Records, and I played some of those records and was certainly offered a contract by some of those people, but I had a real problem with the concept that I should work with only women whether they were as good as I could get musically or not. I think my driving force has always been music rather than politics, so, for me, as a musician, to exclude anyone from the possibility of playing with me was impossible.

(Post) Janis Joplin reportedly took the younger Janis under her wing in the 1960s, and other women musicians influenced Ian, but Ian is careful to point out that men also taught her.

Ian: When I was a kid, I'd go to hear Nina Simone and Odetta, who were wonderful to me. I would have to say, in fairness, that Dave Van Ronk was also wonderful to me, as was Shadow, my first producer, and Artie Butler, the pianist on my first record. I've always had a good mix of male and female. As a songwriter, though, there weren't any women to look to, in my life, until recently, unless they wrote pop songs…

Post: Like Carole King?

Ian: Yeah. I always looked to Billie Holiday, but she was more of an interpreter than a songwriter, though she did write a couple that were staggering: "God Bless The Child," for one. The main lack of mentors was in the writing because there weren't any women writing songs when I did "Society's Child." There was no female Bob Dylan or Phil Ochs or Tom Paxton or Eric Anderson or John Lennon. That changed in the 1970s; the women's movement probably had something to do with that.

(Post) Janis Ian's early successes, in the 1960s and 1970s, with "Society's Child" and *Between The Lines*, prompted her to relocate from the East Coast to Los Angeles to connect with a thriving music scene. However, Ian walked away from her contract with Columbia Records and from her developing career in 1982.

Ian: It was a combination of three things. First, I'd been on the road for over ten years, and I was exhausted. I'd spent the previous decade knowing exactly where I'd be for the following twelve months; it was always three months a year recording, eight months touring, and the remaining month writing.
  Second, Columbia [with whom Ian had signed in 1973] had changed a lot; it wasn't the company that I'd started with. I wasn't happy with what had happened to it, and

it wasn't a good place for me to be. Third, I didn't like what I was writing. I felt that it was way below my ability, and I didn't see any way to fix it except to stop touring.

(Post) After she left the road, Ian suffered a burst intestine; divorced a psychotic, abusive husband; dealt with Chronic Fatigue Syndrome; had a hysterectomy; lost her savings and home as the result of the negligence of a former business manager. She also spent time studing ballet with Dora Kranning at the Paris Opera Company and script interpretation with Stella Adler, technique with Chao Sheo Lin of the Peking opera company and directing with Jose Quintero. In 1989 she moved to Nashville.

Post: What got you back into recording and touring in the early 1990s?

Ian: I was in Nashville and doing well, starting to get a fair amount of cuts, making a reasonable living, and paying off my debts. I was hanging out at the Bluebird, and people kept saying, "When are you recording, when are you recording?" Ella Fitzgerald had taken me to task, in 1987, for not recording. It had never occurred to me that other performers waited for my work; that was meaningful to me. Then, I started writing songs like "Tattoo," and I felt that I had something to say again. I knew that nobody else would say it. Sort of like when I wrote "Stars." Then, I thought, "Aah! I am a writer and I have the right to be doing this!"

To me, there are so many people, particularly from the '60s, who are out there now, writing songs that are OK but not their best work. Doing decent tours but basically cashing it in. I didn't want to be one of them. I hadn't wanted to do a record until I had enough songs that nobody could point a finger at, including me.

Post: You seem to be aware of the new emotional tone—I call it peacefulness—of your current repertoire.

Ian: It's hard to know whether that comes from just getting older or from losing everything or really realizing how little anything means, or living with the same person (her partner, Pat) for six years, or feeling like it's safe to pull your head out of the sand or living in Nashville.

I notice my changes probably more slowly than anyone else because I'm right in the middle of them. I don't notice peacefulness as much as tenderness and how good it feels to be surprised by joy. I think some people have to learn how to be happy, and I'm one of them. It doesn't come easily to me.

Post: What have you learned, in terms of your own temperament and tolerance, that has resulted in pragmatic changes to your work?

Ian: My schedule is actually not that different, right now, from how it used to be, which is not making me very happy, but there doesn't seem to be much that I can do about it. I have learned how to take vacations, and Pat and I have learned that we have to go somewhere with no phones because people will call. Also that I can't go on vacation right before a tour or an album. We've learned the hard way!

Hopefully, I've got some good people around me, and it's not in their best interest to wear me out. I think I've shown that I will just stop if I get that worn out. I think

Photo: Randee St. Nicholas

that if you take six months off from the road, the world doesn't end. Even a year. Mary Chapin Carpenter just took a year off. Her career certainly didn't end, and her writing was vastly improved afterwards. I've learned that it's an acceptable risk.

Post: I wonder how you keep centered so that your voice stays clear, whether you meditate, for example?

Ian: Oh, I can't meditate. I've never been able to. There's a part of me that does that when I'm doing other things, what I call "the back of my head," and I zone out. I read a junk novel and drift, but it's never worked for me to make it into a discipline. It's too close to writing without being active.

What I really do is try not to talk too much. That's the biggest problem, on the road, in terms of the physical voice. If all I had to do was sing every other night, it wouldn't be so hard. But I do interviews, or get stopped in stores, and that places stress on my throat.

I'm going to take a voice lesson tomorrow, in fact. I need something to fall back on. I don't have a strong voice to begin with, and I'm careful with it.

(Post) I return to the topic of her song, "Tattoo," which conjures images of Nazi concentration camp identity tattoos. Other songs on that album *(Breaking Silence)* deal with tough themes: "What About The Love" about bigotry; "His Hands" looks at battering; "Guess You Had To Be There" reflects disappointment that the '60s didn't cleanse the world; and "Some People's Lives" chronicles the despair from not being loved enough.

Post: Noticing has always been a theme in your songs; witnessing other people's difficulties, singing about them...

Ian: Witnessing. I like that word.

Post: In *Breaking Silence* and *Revenge*, you have continued your witnessing more at a societal level, while, in your earlier albums, the focus was more personal.

Ian: I got less interested in my own life as I got older. It became more mundane to me. Stella Adler [with whom Ian studied acting for four years] whipped that out of me! She used to say, "What is this fantastic 'I' you are always going on about?" When you examine your own life in the light of a Tennessee Williams play, when you look at it in the scope of history, there's not much 'I' there.

Post: Yet, "This Train Still Runs," is about aging and coping, surviving and thriving, and seems to tell your tale.

Ian: That's a show opener, and it's entirely my story. In general, the songs on *Breaking Silence* came in a bunch. "Tattoo," "This House" [about pretending to love somebody] and "Stolen Fire" were written at the end of 1989; "This Train" and "Sacred Ground" [about fleeing the rat race] came in early 1992.

You know, I don't mean to sound snotty or arrogant, but I've hit a point, in the last five or six years, where I don't keep track of whether they are old songs or new songs or how many I've written recently. They're all part and parcel of a body of work, and I turn them in to the publisher.

Post: Your concert selections reflect a mixture of newer directions while honoring your past triumphs.

Ian: I do a blend of new and old songs, but I'm moving away from the old ones. Last tour, it was about a third old, now it's down to a quarter of the show.

All of my songs, the ones that I'm comfortable with, are in my current repertoire: the ones that I feel sound good on my voice. Some songs, "Thankyous," for instance, don't sound good for me to sing. I love that song, but I'm forty-four, and there's a difference between my voice now and my voice of twenty-two years ago.

Post: *Between The Lines* is twenty-years-old this year.

Ian: I think that Columbia Records should send me part of their building! Seriously, I feel that I am coming full circle, which is a very strange feeling. If I had the kind of career where there were big billboard ads all over like they have when they want to shell out hundreds of thousands of bucks to support an artist, it might feel like a special anniversary.

But, no. Next year, it will be thirty years since "Society's Child," but I doubt that will feel important either. It's sort of like birthdays; unless somebody makes a big fuss, they sort of come and go.

Post: How do you do your writing?

Ian: It depends on the song. For "Tattoo" I had the first two lines before anything else. I try to set aside three months a year, which sometimes works and sometimes doesn't. It takes me about two weeks to decompress from whatever I've been doing. After that, I'll book time with other songwriters, to get my wheels oiled.

I was walking in the rain, in Provincetown, and I started singing to myself: 'Take me walking in the rain/Let me be a child again, baby/Let it wipe away the tears/Wash away the years.'

Post: You played at the National Women's Music Festival in the summer of 1995, your first experience at a Women's Music event.

Ian: I played there because they asked me, and it was on a campus, which meant that they couldn't legally exclude men. They were totally together professionally and very well organized and non-exclusionary. That was real important because, obviously, I get asked to do a lot of Women's Music festivals, and I have always turned them down because—as a woman, I understand the desire for a woman-only space, and don't have any problem with it—but, as a musician, I have real problems with exclusionary politics.

Post: Is music truly the key, for you?

Ian: It always has been. As Stella [Adler] would say, the goal is to become a citizen of the world and not to become ghettoized or marginalized or to ghettoize or marginalize your own work. While I can certainly speak out as a gay person or a Jew, I'm not comfortable doing so while excluding another race, or another gender.

Another limiting factor at the women's festival, was that on acoustic guitar I'm limited in that I can only do forty-five or fifty minutes, max. Without my band—who are male—I can't do some of my favorite songs.

Post: It's not only excluding your audience but also excluding yourself?

Ian: Uh huh. That's a problem for me and for many performers, right now. I don't see a solution for it. I know it's discussed among the techies at the festival, and the organizers.

(Post) When *Breaking Silence* was released, and Ian came out publicly, it was big news, and people thought that the theme of the album was going to be her coming out. In fact, Ian now writes a column for *The Advocate* called "Breaking Silence."

Ian: Because I stopped performing and recording in 1981, there was a twelve-year layover. During those twelve years, the gay movement changed totally. It's easier to be out, now; I envy younger lesbians!

In 1989, when I started looking for a record contract, I decided that I was going to come out very loudly. I was talking to Urvashi Vaid, then of NGLTF, [National Gay and Lesbian Task Force] and she started quoting suicide statistics to me and saying that gay teenagers have triple the suicide rate that straight ones do. She asked me to wait for my album release, in order to do the most good. That was a lot of incentive.

Post: Was there was a social purpose to your coming out?

Ian: Yes. To come out as a publicity tool for me would have been humiliating. It's not a good reason.

Post: Has it turned out to be a good decision to be out?

Ian: There wasn't any question about whether it was going to be good or bad. It was always good because I was living with Pat, and there was no way I was going to have her excluded from my daily life. I would have had to hide her, and I'd never done that before. I think that coming out has probably hurt me here and there, but any big decision is bound to have some negative consequences.

If there is anything that comes with age, it's the understanding that there's always a price to pay. The only question is: Are you willing to pay that price? Am I willing to pay the price of being on an independent label in order to do the records I want to do? Fortunately, I seem to be able to do the records I want to do in a mainstream enough way so that I don't get too marginalized. So, it makes it worthwhile for me to do it that way.

(Post) Janis Ian has had a lot of high moments and awards in her career: In 1973,

Roberta Flack had a Top Ten hit from Ian's song, "Jesse," and many other singers have covered her songs: Chet Atkins, Glen Campbell, Stan Getz, Etta James, Nana Mouskouri, Joan Baez, Cher, Nanci Griffith, Kathy Mattea, Cheryl Wheeler, John Cougar Mellencamp, Amy Grant. "Some People's Lives" was the title of Bette Midler's 1990 double platinum album.

Ian has been nominated for nine Grammys and won two; has collaborated with Chick Corea, Giorgio Moroder, Mel Torme, Leonard Cohen, James Brown, Linda Perry, and has written scores for "The Bell Jar" and "Foxes". In 1991, Ian performed in Japan, England, and Ireland, and her experimental album—only available in Holland—went platinum.

Post: What are Janis Ian's hopes for the future?

Ian: I want to play Madison Square Garden and then go off and be a writer; I'd like to do more of the stuff I'm doing for *The Advocate*. I'd like to write that one song that will change the entire world: a "We Shall Overcome."

DISCOGRAPHY

Janis Ian (Verve/Forecast, 1996); *A Song For All The Seasons Of Your Mind* (Verve/Forecast, 1967); *The Secret Life of J. Eddy Fink* (Verve/Forecast, 1968); *Who Really Cares* (Verve/Forecast, 1969); *Present Company* (Capitol, 1970); *Stars* (Columbia, 1973) *Between The Lines* (Columbia, 1975); *Aftertones* (Columbia, 1976); *Miracle Row* (Columbia, 1977); *Janis Ian* (Columbia, 1978); *Night Rains* (Columbia, 1979); *Restless Eyes* (Columbia, 1981); "Days Like These" for the John Cougar Mellencamp film, "Falling From Grace" (Polygram, 1992); *Breaking Silence* (Morgan Creek, 1993); *Revenge* (Beacon, 1995).

JOAN OSBORNE
one of us

If I hadn't known from her vibrant voice, bold topics, and interview poise that Joan Osborne was on her way to the big time, then the profile in the *New York Times* that appeared just after I interviewed her provided ample confirmation.

Joan Osborne always loved singing, whether in the shower or in school choirs and shows, but she never considered it as a career.

Joan Osborne: When I was young, I used to sit by the record player and memorize the records. Singing is not the easiest thing to do, and the chances of succeeding are pretty low. Strangely enough, it took over my life.

(Post) In 1986 Osborne moved to The Big Apple from Kentucky to study film at New York University. While working to afford tuition, she found herself living near a blues bar. One innocent event led to another and a musical career was launched.

Osborne: I went in late one night. The band was finished, but the piano player was still noodling around. The friend I was with asked me, then encouraged me to sing a song. When he finally dared me, I did, and the piano player invited me to the weekly jams.

(Post) In trying to prove a point to her friend, Osborne happened upon a career path which pleased and suited her.

Osborne: I ended up going back to the bar and discovered a whole community of musicians who were doing very roots-oriented, bluesy stuff. It was very scary, at first, to stand in front of people and to be a white girl singing the blues, but then I fell in love with it. Going out and hearing other people's bands and learning a lot of songs became a release and a passion.

(Post) Osborne fronted a series of loose groups, then assembled her own band.

Osborne: It snowballed in a natural way, and I learned by doing. If it were to end tomorrow, I would have really enjoyed doing it up until this point. The reason to keep doing it is not that I'm dreaming of becoming some famous rock star but that it is gratifying to me. My musical career started organically, and that's how it keeps going.

Music is like the ocean; you can swim around, but you're never going to get to the other side; there's always more to learn. At first the challenge was to stand in front of an audience and sing without freaking out or embarrassing myself. At first I couldn't do that: my eyes were closed, I couldn't move around. The next challenge was to get a gig and make a little money; then, the challenge was to write songs.

(Post) When it fell on Osborne to deal with the business end of playing, she became her own manager. Like breaking into the music scene, learning about the pragmatic aspects of the industry came naturally. Though Osborne downplays her achievements in this arena, claiming them as the result of common sense, her successes at keeping herself booked and with musical partners garnered positive media attention and, eventually, concerts in Europe.

Osborne: I was at a job where I had use of the phone and copy machine when nobody was looking!

(Post) By the early 1990s, having convinced a fan to front $10,000, Osborne recorded her first album, live. Audience and commercial response to the record were both positive.

Osborne: It wasn't like we got reviewed in *Rolling Stone*, but I was encouraged. Several successive small steps led to the release of another album, also on her own Womanly Hips label, and a connection with Rick Chertoff, president of Blue Gorilla Records (Mercury). Most recently, Osborne has been favorably reviewed in *Billboard*, *Elle*, *The New Yorker* and, ironically, *Rolling Stone*.

(Post) The making of *Relish* (named for the sensual enjoyment which Osborne derives from singing) was entirely different from her previous recording experiences.

Osborne: The majority of the songs are new—two are from the old days, "Crazy Baby," which I wrote, and "Help Me," by Sonny Williamson—and we spent much more time working on the songs. We took our time with the process, which I was never able to do because I didn't have the money. I was able to explore many new possibilities.

(Post) In covering Bob Dylan's "Man In A Long Black Coat," Osborne forayed into daring territory, but her melding of spirituality and sexuality ("St. Teresa" about a prostitute; "Right Hand Man," which evokes the rush of spending a first night with someone) establishes her as a provocative artist with an unfettered penchant for unusual lyrical associations set in soulful, bluesy, rock tunes.

Osborne is delighted by the album, but her speech warms as she describes an opening for Gloria Steinem at a Planned Parenthood-sponsored convocation for peace at New York's renowned St. John The Divine.

Osborne: It was an incredible ceremony, and singing in that church—it is one of the most acoustically amazing places I've ever sung—was inspiring.

(Post) In a short time span, Osborne has racked up numerous accomplishments, but her vision for the future is not related to those.

Osborne: I want to combine the passion I have for music and take the energy that the music gives to me and try to use it for something that I believe in and that is going to affect the community as a whole and not just for entertainment.

(Post) When Osborne has defined her causes as clearly as she has refined her voice and writing, she will be an unstoppable force. Who knows, she just might make a film.

DISCOGRAPHY

Soul Show (Womanly Hips Music, 1991); *Blue Million Miles* (EP, Womanly Hips Music, 1993); *Relish* (Blue Gorilla/Mercury, 1995); *Early Recordings* (Blue Gorilla/Mercury, 1996).

Photo: Terry Richardson

JUDY SMALL
a folksinger's perspective on the U.S. and Australia

It is sometimes difficult to imagine a time in my life when I was not listening to music every moment, seeking prospective new artists to interview and new tunes to review. However, there was such a time; and it was during that time that I first heard Judy Small. In fact, it was her understated but compelling songs which impelled me to start my career writing about music.

During the spring of 1987 I was driving across the United States. Near the center of the country, I heard a song on the radio—on some local channel I'd flipped to—and there came a distinctive melody interpreted by a rich alto voice of great expressivity and abundance. The subject: Jessie Street, an inspiring Australian woman.

At the next big city, I exited the freeway and sought a music store. I had to know the artist, and I had to hear more of her music.

After a bit of searching in Indianapolis, I found the recording in question: Judy Small's *One Voice In the Crowd*. The song, "A Heroine of Mine," typified what I was to learn about Judy Small. She writes rhyming verses with a fluidity that allows her opinions to unfold as if casually spoken in conversation with a friend. The topics bespeak a fantastic intellectual grasp of ideas great and details small. She designs melodies that effortlessly insert themselves into one's conciousness and which quietly invite singing along. She reflects relevant history in her lyrics, interspersed with the occasional wry self-revelation.

For nearly 2000 miles, I sang and learned. Small's tunes also affected me personally. Her "Alice Martin" reminded me so strongly of a teacher I'd had in high school that I sat down and wrote a letter of reconnection immediately after hearing the tune. My grappling with race and class and privilege issues were so well captured in "One Voice in the Crowd" that it inspired me to write an essay about my own upbringing, with all of its faults and advantages.

When I arrived in California I sought Small's earlier music and listened to it with much eagerness and delight. I couldn't wait for more music from Judy Small.

When her next album was released, less than a year later, I was jazzed. Upon realizing that *Home Front* was every bit as exhilarating and important as the previous work, I began introducing my friends to Small's work. In turn, my friends began showing me reviews of Small's music in industry publications. Reading other's words about Small, I was quickly aware that what I had to say on the subject was not being addressed. Thus, my career in writing about music was initiated.

Judy Small in person is an ordinary, middle class woman who sings about things that interest her. Born in Australia in 1953, she grew up in Coffs Harbor, New South Wales, a once-sleepy fishing village that has since become host to the largest McDonald's in the Southern Hemisphere (that cultural transformation inspired Small to write about "hamburger imperialism" in the song "Golden Arches"). Currently one of Australia's finest contemporary singer-songwriters, Judy Small has successfully integrated wit with words, empathy with politics, and Australian with American perspective.

The folk boom reached Small in her formative years, so when she bought her first guitar at fourteen, it wasn't the Beatles or the Rolling Stones that she hungered to emulate; it was big-voiced women such as Joan Baez and Mary Travers, who sang of real people and significant issues. While those early styles remain evident in Judy Small's craft, her current influences wax topical and eclectic. As a feminist folk singer doing lesbian-affirmative music, she has written music which examines themes as radical as Australian and American colonial assumptions, the painful invisibility of woman-loving-women, and the negative outcomes of engaging in war.

Small started performing, in Australia's clubs and coffeehouses to finance her education: college and a Master's degree in psychology, and, starting in 1980, two-years part-time studying law. Small's first album, *A Natural Selection*, was released at the end of 1982. At that point, her burgeoning singing career forced her to choose between public service and music. She left law school to make singing her living.

Judy Small: I came to the U.S. in 1982 for a holiday. Part of that holiday involved attending the Vancouver Folk Festival. I was not scheduled to play; I was just audience. Eric Bogle, a Scottish-Australian folksinger better known than I and with whom I had previously shared the stage, was also present. He asked if I would sing a couple of songs at his workshop. Ronnie Gilbert was there; I knew of the Weavers but not of modern-day Ronnie. Thus began our eight-year friendship as well as the start of my collaboration with Redwood Records.

And then it sort of just grew from there, my songs preceding me. Priscilla Herdman, a New-York-based folksinger, had performed "Mothers, Daughters, Wives" all over the place and recorded it in 1983 before I ever did a major tour in the United States. By the time I returned to the U.S. in 1984, people were starting to know my music and my concerns, if not me personally. That was a spark; subsequently, my career expanded. Over the next several years I released my second and third albums, *Ladies and Gems (Mothers, Daughters, Wives* in the US) and *One Voice in the Crowd*.

I toured the festival circuit in 1984, and my then partner, Margaret McAllister, and I made a very clear and conscious business decision to invest time and money in building a specifically U.S. career for me. That first tour cost us something like $8,000, but it has paid off. From a promotional perspective, financing a U.S. career for me was crucial since Australia, a country/continent the size of the United States, is inhabited by sixteen million as compared with two hundred-fifty million in the U.S. Effectively, there exist six major Australian cities and maybe another half dozen towns. A reasonable U.S. tour might include thirty cities, without denting the surface of the market. Margret Road-Knight, an Australian folk singer with international touring experience, quips that performers in Australia tread that fine line between overexposure and starvation. In terms of inspirational variety, diversity of feedback, and supply-and-demand strategy, my U.S. career assumed significant importance.

From 1982 to 1987, my study of the law went into abeyance. People would ask me if there were anything that I regretted about going on the road, and I would reply that I had not finished my law degree. Though I had every intention of completing it, one day, that day seemed to get further and further in the future. Then, in 1986, I did a massive, amazing, horrendous tour over the latter six months of the year. I did a performance every one and two-thirds days on three continents and traveled the equivalent of twice around the world. When I finally returned to Australia, my voice was shot, and I was depressed and incredibly burned out. I had experienced being tired of touring, but in early 1987, I truly never wanted to sing again.

It scared the hell out of me, and I realized that I needed some time off. So I went back to law school part-time and started to sing part-time. For the last six months of 1987, I didn't sing at all. I quit singing and went back to the public service to earn a living and kept studying law. I moved out of one relationship and into another and relocated from Sydney to Melbourne to live with my then-new lover, Sue Dyson. And, I went back to law school full-time because it was something I wanted to do, because it was unfinished, because I did not want to sing for a living for the rest of my life.

I had two years of law study remaining, and I made an album in that time, *Home Front* (1988). I don't like the record, particularly, as it reminds me of a despairing period of my life that I would really rather not have to go through again. I did get my law degree in 1989, however.

(Post) The hiatus from performing afforded Judy the opportunity to contemplate her unique position as a cultural missionary.

Small: Though I did not leave Australia for months at a time, I heard all the American news; interestingly, the reverse process does not happen. I had become aware, through my tours, how the U.S. seems to perceive itself as the center of the universe. Australians, I think, understand the entire world as "us;" the United States, particularly politically, sees the world as "us" and "them." I write much of my music about situations different than my own because that is a folk singer's job; many of my songs, however, are in the first person because of how I was brought up and schooled as an Australian. Though there are some topics that I won't write about in the first person, such as aboriginal issues or disability, I feel that I can put myself in the shoes of someone my age and class whose husband went to Vietnam, who is married to an Australian sheep farmer, whose children have been called to war, or is a grandmother.

Australians are very aware of American issues, and this has influenced my songwriting. Australia broadcasts U.S. television programs, music, films, and news, not to mention the availability of McDonalds and the Kentucky Fried Chickens and the Pizza Huts. It is actually a very insidious way to infiltrate culture.

The U.S. has become increasingly isolationist and dangerously right-wing. I don't mean to be presumptuous, but as an Australian—with a broad perspective—while also being quite familiar with U.S. values and issues, I can come to America as a cultural cross-pollinator and commentator. I don't do it consciously; I write about what touches me and what moves me. If those ideas also relate to what people in the U.S. are doing and how the U.S. is thinking, then that's terrific. If I can make a connection between me and my audience, any audience, then that's great, too.

(Post) In 1990 Small released *Snapshot*, her fifth album. This album touches on issues of gender and violence ("Montreal, December '89" describing the senseless massacre of fourteen women in Canada) and gender and injustice ("Evil Angels" calls

Photo: Jacqueline Mitelman

to task those who accused Lindy Chamberlain of murdering her infant). Much of Small's work has addressed the struggles of women: fat oppression ("A Song for the Roly Poly People"), contraception ("The IPD") and social roles ("Mothers, Daughters, Wives" and "From The Lambing to the Wool"). Through specific examination of female relationships, including friendships, idols, and sexual alliances, women's issues take on a broad context and power.

Small: Women's issues and lesbian issues are important to me. From *Snapshot*, the song "No Tears for the Widow" compares my own mother's widowhood with the unnamed bereavement of a lesbian. I have written other songs which address the same issue: "Annie" speaks from the point of view of a lesbian teacher harboring the legitimate fears of rejection and dismissal. And, then, of course, there was "Turn Right, Go Straight."

My own lesbianism is important to me. I see my lesbianism as comparable to my right-handedness. Everything I do in life, I do as a right-handed person, whether or not I am using my hands; similarly, everything I do, I do as a lesbian, whether or not it is to do with women or sexuality. In my music I want to portray the ordinariness of lesbians' lives; we are just folks. When we are treated as 'just folks'—teachers, lovers, widows, workers like everyone else—then, in my opinion, that will be true liberation.

I now have a law degree and a musical career. I hope, one day, to be able to combine them. Although I am interested in criminal law and pro bono work, the most likely arena for me would be, of course, entertainment law, which fascinates me tremendously and of which there is a great dearth in Australia. I want to be the kind of lawyer that I wish had been around when I was starting in this business.

My choices can be directly traced to a promise I made to my father, who died when I was about fourteen. I had bought my first guitar just a month or so before he died and was learning to play. I had been playing these two chords that I knew and singing this song. He called me into his room, and he said that, one day, people would want me to sing and that they would pay money to hear me. He asked me to promise that I would get myself a degree in a profession before I entered show business full-time.

Which was his way of saying that this was a cut-throat business and I would need something solid behind me, to fall back on so that I wouldn't get caught up in the turmoil and competitiveness of it. That was twenty-three years ago, and I remember every word of the conversation. And I kept my promise. I think that there was a time when, if I hadn't made that promise to my father, I would certainly have left the university and gone singing; I'm very glad, now, that I stayed in school and completed my education. My first degree was in psychology and then my first profession was psychology, so I sort of have two possibilities in reserve.

A friend commented to me, when I turned thirty-five, that I had spent the first thirty-five years of my life creating options for myself. She was right; options are freedom. I would not have had the options without choices, and I like the options that I have. The law is nothing more than the study of trivia; the songs that I write also focus on details. I am satisfied by both aspects of what I do; it is an incredibly privileged way I've lived my life. It's an incredibly privileged life, but I have worked very hard at it.

Post: What would you say to a younger person who came up to you and said, "Maybe I have some skills at singing and playing and entertaining and I want to do this. How do I go about it?"

Small: What I would say is: Take lessons. I've had trouble with my voice for a long time; sometimes it works just fine and sometimes it doesn't. I'm sorry I didn't have both guitar and singing lessons sooner because I only play guitar well enough to accompany myself. I'm not a musician as such.

The other thing I'd say is that you have a choice at the beginning; you can go for the big bucks and the fame and you may or may not get there. If you get there you'll have a great career, you'll probably make a lot of money and you'll have a career that might only last five years. You may or may not make enough money in those five years to set you up for the rest of your life, and I hope you do. But don't expect it to be longer than that.

Or, you can choose not to go for the big bucks and the big money and the big fame but to find a niche for yourself in the market. I think Ani DiFranco is the classic example of this. She's found herself a place in the market, she's kept total control of her product, she owns her records. She's been really canny.

I'd say: Have a business plan in the sense of which way to go. Acknowledge that if you take the second road you're not going to be famous, but you're going to get so much out of it, and you'll have a much longer career. Know where you want to go and accept the limitations of which ever way you choose. Be yourself. Don't be someone on stage that you're not off stage because people can tell when you're being phony, and they only respect you if you're not phony.

The rewards of this business, the non-financial rewards are huge. I've made so many friends being in this business, I've had so many contacts with people, however brief, that have been really profound and moving and have enriched my life enormously. If what you want is money and fame I'd say: don't, because you'll lose yourself, and you'll lose control of what you do. The business is very different now than it was when I started. I rode in on a wave that had just begun in the early '80s, and that wave is gone. Now we have people like Alanis Morrissette. The difference between Ani and Alanis is that Alanis describes the problem while Ani gives some answers. Alanis is a pop singer and Ani is a folk singer.

The other thing I'd say is: Take notice of middle-aged folk-singers who think they know everything!

Post: What have been some of the highlights of your career?

Small: There have been a half-dozen. Playing with Ronnie Gilbert has been one of the highlights of my life let alone my career. To be on stage with her is an extraordinary experience. She shines on that stage. The first time I ever played with her was at the Redwood Festival of 1985. I have photos of that, and when I look at those, I can still feel the experience. Since then, I've done two tours of Australia with Ronnie which have been just wonderful; she's also one of my dearest friends.

Being asked to go to Denmark for the weekend to play a concert with Pete Seeger and Arlo Guthrie. They had Pete and Arlo to close the Tonder Festival (which is one of the biggest folk festivals in Europe), and they searched the world for a female folk singer to open up for them, and they chose me. I was incredibly honored.

I sang last year in the United Nations Women's Forum in Beijing, China. To sing my songs to my international sisters was very profound. It was very moving for me and loads of fun.

Every now and then I sing the perfect concert. It doesn't happen often. It happened twice, maybe three times on this whole tour, where I sing and perform as good as it's ever been for me. That is a high I'll remember all my life. There may be ten or fifteen concerts in my life where I've done that so I remember all those.

Having Holly Near sing backing vocals on my second album was pretty cool and just being able to meet the women who inspired me, you know, Holly, Cris Williamson, Frankie Armstrong. To be seen as peers of those women just blows my mind. That's all ego stuff, really; it really is the connections I've made and the letters I get that help me go on.

I remember hearing Ronnie in an interview in Australia. This woman said to her rather incredulously, "Why do you keep doing this?" the implication being 'Why do you keep going?' Ronnie was sixty or so at the time and I expected her to talk about the vast public good and changing the world and the politics of what we do and the honorable tradition. But, she said, "I do it because I can create moments between me and the audience that help us both go on." That's exactly why we do it.

Post: What do you think you're going to do in the future for those moments?

Small: I'm still going to have those moments because I'm not going to give up singing. I think also that those connections can be made in other areas. For instance, if I get a defendant in a discrimination case to say, "Yes I was wrong. I understand what I did now," that might be one of those moments. Those moments can happen everywhere.

DISCOGRAPHY

A Natural Selection (Crafty Maid Music, 1982); *Ladies and Gems* (Crafty Maid Music 1984, released in the U.S. under the title *Mothers, Daughters, Wives* (Redwood Records, 1984); *One Voice In The Crowd* (Redwood Records, 1985); *Home Front* (Redwood Records, 1988); *Snapshot* (Redwood Records, 1990); *The Best of the 80s* (Crafty Maid, 1993); *Second Wind* (Crafty Maid, 1993); *Global Village* (Crafty Maid, 1995).

JUNE MILLINGTON
rocking the feminist way

When I first heard June Millington play, I was reminded of a gorgeous racing dog because her movements were so sleek and consequential. The self-absorbed expressions on her face explained the intense outpouring of music from her electric guitar. Offstage she has always been relaxed, her long hair flowing, her generous smile filling the spaces inside people.

Being a serious woman musician in all-women's rock bands in the 1960s and '70s developed Millington's consciousness.

June Millington: When I first started playing, politics was the last thing on my mind. It was groove, groove, groove and survive, survive, survive. But playing Motown and rock & roll when we did was a political act. My sister Jean and I were young and brown, and no one near our age and color (or gender, for that matter) was doing it. People were both intrigued and threatened by us, and why not? We were independent, doing our own thing, stepping away from the norm.

(Post) Millington took piano lessons between the ages of six and eight. For fun, she started to play music with her younger sister, Jean.

Millington: We would pick pop songs off the radio and play them on the ukulele. Like "Tell Laura I Love Her," songs by Neil Sedaka, Harry Belafonte, Kingston Trio. Even Elvis Presley.

(Post) During seventh grade, Millington had a formative musical experience.

Millington: I remember hearing this beautiful sound coming from down the hallway. I got up as if sleep-walking, and headed for that sound. It was as if I had heard a siren calling. I came upon this girl playing the acoustic guitar. It was an epiphany.

(Post) At that moment, she was convinced that she needed to learn the instrument.

Millington: Before then, I had felt lost. I didn't have many friends. I was deaf in one ear and didn't even know it. I was half-white and half-brown and didn't fit in to any stratum in society. All of a sudden, I knew the guitar was my home.

(Post) Millington—whose Irish ancestry contributes as much to her affable garrulousness as her Filipino ancestry does to her love of island music—conveyed her new-found passion to her mother. Her thirteenth birthday present was a small mother-of-pearl-inlaid guitar.

Millington: I turned thirteen on April 14, 1962, and we moved to the U.S. on June 22 of the same year. I brought that guitar with me on the ship.

(Post) Within a few more years, June and Jean Millington were playing at fraternity parties, YMCA gatherings, even school functions. Though Millington had learned, by then, that she was deaf in one ear, even that challenge was not an obstacle.

Millington: It's actually a blessing because I hear so differently from most people, and I am very specific in terms of what I listen for. Like being an avid reader helps my songwriting in terms of ideas, not hearing on one side is useful to me because I hear strange things in my head and they become songs.

(Post) Once the Millington sisters joined with an ever-changing cast of other female musicians, their opportunities for gigging expanded.

Millington: In 1965 when I turned sixteen, the Svelts [1965-68] started. The first song I wrote was "Angel in White," and the second was "Miss Wallflower." That was the one that had gained us fame at our junior high, and people started to talk to us. That's when I had realized that music was key for us because it gained us social acceptance. At first, we all played acoustic guitars and sang together. Then we sang harmonies: Martha and The Vandellas, The Marvelettes. The Beach Boys had those incredible, layered arrangements; the Beatles had both harmony and guitar playing: think about that first chord in 'Hard Day's Night.' I challenge anybody to find a more stunning opening chord!

(Post) As the Svelts turned into Wild Honey (1968-69) and progressed into harder pop, Millington thought that she wanted to emphasize the subtle contributions of rhythm guitar, and enrolled at U.C. Davis with a minor in music. As she spent less time in formal academic pursuit and more time being blown away by the new music of the era, she changed her mind about her musical focus.

Millington: I saw the very first Buffalo Springfield, all the original guys including Crosby and Stills! I saw the original Grateful Dead, when Pig Pen was still playing keyboards! We would go see Country Joe and the Fish, Janis Joplin!! The first show I saw at Winterland was Albert King and Jimi Hendrix on the same bill!! From then on, I definitely wanted to play with power.

(Post) When Millington quit school to play full-time, Wild Honey relocated to Los Angeles: Fanny was born, the first all-girl outfit to play rock music in the big time. Keyboardist Nickey Barclay joined, as lead guitarist Addie Clement departed, leaving Jean Millington on bass, Alice de Buhr drumming, June Millington, and Barclay.

Millington: All of a sudden, I became lead guitarist, and that was terrifying. I didn't want to be that visible. To be a female lead guitarist, in those days, was to invite speculation about 'can she play?,' with or without the subtext, 'can she play like a guy?'

I decided to do it, but from that moment, I worked day and night to learn how to play lead. I asked everyone I met who was a guitar player to teach me licks.

(Post) It was 1969: Open mics at the legendary Troubadour led to jamming around with the likes of Lowell George. Fanny's debut album was produced by hot-shot Richard Perry, as were their next two recordings (Todd Rundgren would later record and produce Fanny's fourth album). The music spotlight shone brightly on the women rockers of Fanny who were proving that they could sing, write, and play "like men." Millington found that she loved to jam, loved to be part of that wall of sound with a solid rhythm section.

Though Millington mentions, as peers, Ramatam's guitarist April Lawton; Birtha; The Gingerbreads; Helen Hooke and Deadly Nightshade; Patti Quatro of Pleasure Seekers; Tret Fure who was playing with Spencer Davis; and the little-known Bonnie Raitt, she concludes,

Millington: There were few other women out there doing rock. We didn't have many role models.

(Post) Fanny's success was so great that, in 1970, June and Jean Millington backed Barbra Streisand on her hit "Stoney End." But the pressure – the endless misogynist comparisons and put-downs– took its toll. In 1973, Millington stepped away from the spotlight and moved to Woodstock, NY to recover and heal. However, Millington's sabbatical turned into yet another formative musical experience.

Millington: The music scene there was amazing. Dylan had just left. The Band was still there. Orleans was just starting up. The energy was incredible.

I was living with Jackie Robbins. Some woman named Cris Williamson sent Jackie a demo tape of live music that she wanted Jackie to play bass for. I heard it and dug the energy: all those women screaming.

(Post) Unbeknownst to Millington, Williamson was not only one of the emerging leaders in a new cultural genre called Women's Music, but she was a fan of Fanny, and wanted Millington to play on the album that she was recording, tentatively titled *The Changer And The Changed*. Enter Women's Music.

Not only did Millington contribute to Williamson's album, but they toured the album together. Millington was able to re-establish her faith in herself and in music; renew her goals; and redefine her limits; but working with Williamson exploded Millington's political awareness.

Millington: I wanted to return to the mainstream and continue to play with Cris. I didn't know how I was going to do that. What happened was that Jean and I cut an album for United Artists, *Ladies On The Stage*, which was sold to EMI, and, as a consequence, was shelved. I was so disgusted that I flung myself into Women's Music.

(Post) Millington found Women's Music delightful.

Jean Millington　　June Millington

Millington: Going to Hollywood and breaking in with the first all-women's rock group was thrilling but exhausting. Going into Women's Music and playing with Cris was, by comparison, a vacation. There was the joyousness of thousands of women's self-discovery in unison. In Fanny, our breakthroughs were more private and hard-won.

(Post) As Millington experienced the sustaining atmosphere of the Women's Music scene, she had another realization: the mainstream had taken its toll on her because she was a woman, a woman of color, trying to simply be herself in a male-dominated industry. Millington solidified her commitment to providing role modeling for newer women musicians.

Millington: In retrospect, there is no doubt that Women's Music has had a profound effect on all women in music, regardless of genre. Melissa Etheridge, Tracy Chapman, The Indigo Girls have all had a place from which to emerge. From the 1970s on, there was a springboard into mainstream music from the Women's Music audiences.

(Post) In 1981 Millington formed her own label, Fabulous Records, and began to produce her own and other women's music. Five years later she began to actualize her long-term dream of developing a safe space in which women musicians—particularly women of color—could develop their creative talents and receive support for their own individual vision, in the form of education and opportunities. Millington dubbed her new visionary cultural center the Institute for the Musical Arts, or IMA.

IMA's Board of Directors (including Angela Davis) and advisory board (musicians Bonnie Raitt, Linda Tillery, and Cris Williamson; producer Leslie Ann Jones; photographer Irene Young, among others) reflected Millington's emphasis on a genuinely multicultural, broadly grassroots approach.

Initially housed in Oakland, IMA currently finds itself in a bucolic setting, featuring gallery and classroom areas, a large country kitchen, sleeping quarters (for artists-in-residence and guests), and a deliciously intimate, sweetly resonant 100-seat performance chamber. Brainstorming and impromptu jams are not unusual in the middle of the night; all guests are graciously welcomed; and most activities are videotaped for storage in IMA's multimedia archives. Possibly, IMA's greatest gift is providing the emotional safety necessary for women to be able to release their creative power.

Concomitant with the establishment of IMA, which wonderfully straddles the mainstream and Women's Music milieus, Millington, herself, has found a personal balance. Bringing her feminist consciousness to her island roots, she has forged a new musical identity: part hard rocker, part settled soul, part Matriarch of Music. While Millington's pre-Fanny bands more than competently covered old material in a new way (i.e. all-female), Millington can now play her own music for appreciative audiences and groove on the audience's energy without sacrificing herself.

(Post) These days, Millington is content with her life at IMA; even hopeful.

Millington: The networking is incredible, and the truly exciting thing is that there is so much really good, commercially viable music pouring out of so many women. We could exist simply as a recording studio twenty-four hours a day and still not capture it all. It's the early dream of Women's Music become manifest: we're sharing skills, equipment, and information. Those of us who have a lifetime's worth of knowledge are delighted to have a place in which to pass it on; to complete the circle, those who are just coming in are thrilled to have a place to go.

June Millington's production credits include: Mary Watkins's *Something Moving;* Holly Near's *Fire In The Rain;* Cris Williamson's *Strange Paradise;* Cris Williamson's *Lumiere;* Melanie Monsur's *Opus K4;* Pam Hall's *Honey On My Lips;* Rashida Oji's *Big, Big Woman;* Gwen Avery's *Live At IMA;* Kathryn Warner's *Glass House;* Melanie DeMore's *Sing My Song.*

DISCOGRAPHY:

Fanny (Warner Brothers Records, 1969); *Charity Ball* (Warner Brothers, 1970); *Fanny Hill* (Warner Brothers, 1971); *Mother's Pride* (Warner Brothers, 1973); *Ladies On The Stage* (United Artists, 1977); *Heartsong* (Fabulous Records-Olivia Records, 1981); *Running* (Fabulous Records, 1983); *One World, One Heart* (Fabulous Records, 1988); *Ticket To Wonderful* (Fabulous Records, 1994).

KAY GARDNER
world music

An internationally-known composer of healing music and a pioneer in the lesbian/feminist and spirituality movements, Kay Gardner takes the listener on an inspirational journey through the curative and transforming ingredients of music and sound, offering insights into their origins and mysteries and how they may be used in the healing process.

Some of Kay's many albums (e.g *Sounding The Inner Landscape: Guided Meditations And Music*) have featured acoustic instrumentation using the principles of droning, toning, mantra, and chant; Other recordings, such as *A Rainbow Path*, are not only meditative classics, but also delights of flute sounds. Finally—this is what so many people tend to forget—Kay Gardner teamed with Alix Dobkin early in the Women's Music movement and released one of the first overtly lesbian-themed recordings, *Lavender Jane Loves Women*.

Not surprisingly, Kay Gardner grew up around music. Both her parents loved Broadway shows and sang around the house.

Kay Gardner: There was always music around.

(Post) At the tender age of four, Kay started the piano. That same year, she composed her first piece and performed it in public: a chant.

Gardner: It was similar to what I do now, and that's interesting.

(Post) By the age of eight, Kay had taken up the flute. Through high school, Kay's ambition was to be the director of a high school band. Actually, she yearned to conduct an orchestra, but was daunted by the reality that there were no female orchestra conductors. Nevertheless, Kay continued to write music.

Gardner: I was always composing.

(Post) Kay's subsequent history—marriage, two children—diverted her from a primary focus on music.

Gardner: In 1971 I became involved with Alix [Dobkin], musically, and we did *Lavender Jane*. We believed that through the media was the way to get the feminist message out there, and recording was the only branch of media we could get into.

(Post) Parallel to the nascent Olivia collective, Kay and Alix made herstory. Somehow Kay and Alix sensed the possibilities for a future of the feminist cultural network.

Gardner: We knew there was more out there, or could be.

(Post) After Kay and Alix separated, they each did their own thing. Kay's consisted of founding her own record label.

Gardner: I never considered going commercial. It was so important to be myself, and I knew that my stuff was not like other stuff. They wouldn't have known where to put it. In fact, sometimes they still don't know. It's classified sometimes as New Age because it contains meditations. Like women's music, New Age draws from many sources and styles, and has to do, really, with the intent of the musicians.

(Post) Years of research into the healing properties of music, and the wisdom of many workshops she taught at the Omega Institute of Holistic Studies, went into Kay's book, *Sounding the Inner Landscape: Music as Medicine*.

At the time of this interview, Kay was awaiting the premiere of her oratorio Ourobouros.

Gardner: A classical-sounding name for something that really doesn't sound classical at all.

(Post) This work, which featured soloists picked in response to a national call, represents the cycles of women's lives. This premier production also included a one-hundred-voice choir and a forty-piece orchestra.

Kay has spend some time performing on the road with Nurudafina Pili Abena, percussionist extraordinaire, whose debut recording, *Drum Call*, Kay produced.

Kay and Nuru's shows reflect their love of World Music. Nuru has studied percussion with West African and Cuban Masters, and lately learned Persian drumming and percussion from East India. Kay recently travelled to southeast Asia and to the Amazon. Both women are avid collectors of music and instruments from around the world.

Gardner: We have worked as a duo for a while; our duo album, *Onespirit*, was released in January 1993. What we perform is influenced by five continents.

DISCOGRAPHY

Lavendar Jane Loves Women (WWA, 1974); *Mooncircles* (Urana Records/Wise Woman Enterprises, 1975); *Emerging* (Urana/WWE, 1978); *Moods & Rituals* (Even Keel Records, 1981); *A Rainbow Path* (Ladyslipper Records, 1984); *Fishersdaughter* (Even Keel, 1986); *Avalon* (Ladyslipper, 1989); *Garden Of Ecstacy* with Sunwomyn Ensemble (Ladyslipper, 1989); *Journeys: Orchestral Works By American Women* (Leonarda Records, 1989); *Ocean Moon* (Urana/WWE, 1990); *Sounding The Inner Landscape* (Ladyslipper, 1990); *Amazon* (Ladyslipper, 1991); *Onespirit* with Nurudafina Pili Abena (Ladyslipper, 1992); *Ourobouros* (Ladyslipper, 1994); *Drone Zone* (Relaxation Company, 1996).

Photo: Susan Wilson

LAURA LOVE
she could be your daughter's lover

Are you familiar with Laura Love? If not, then you'll want to be. Perhaps, you will recognize the Nebraska native from her stint as the bassist/vocalist for the heavy-rocking Boom Boom G.I. Her name might be known to you in connection with her current incarnations as solo performer or in her duo with Linda Severt, as a player of a funky bass with the clever Seattle-based trio, Venus Envy, or with her mixed-gender Laura Love Band (a quartet). You may recall her all-acoustic 1989 debut release, *Menstrual Hut*, with its telling cover of the traditional "I Never Will Marry" and the sassy "I'm Your Daughter's Lover." Her 1990 release, *Z Therapy*, was a mighty fine follow-up featuring songs like "Fences," about Japanese internments, "Things I've Heard People Say," about the stigmatization of people with AIDS, and an electrifying, a capella rendition of the spiritual "Swing Low, Sweet Chariot."

Laura Love writes intense, personal songs which cut to the heart of vital issues, but her politics don't stop with the music. Laura called her own production company Octoroon Biography to reclaim harsh words from antebellum times; octoroon, she believes, is the category in which she would have been placed, on the basis of her looks, by white plantation owners.

Post: How did you start playing music?

Laura Love: My mother got me a guitar for Christmas when I was about eight years old. It was one of those little plastic ones that comes in a cardboard box and doesn't ever really tune. My mother tried to get the things that were really important in our lives, and music was pretty important. The three of us—my sister, my mother, and I—would sing three-part harmony all the time, complex arrangements of songs like "The Lion Sleeps Tonight" and spirituals sometimes. My mother sang the lowest, my sister was in the middle, and I sang the highest, and it kind of worked out. For all her problems, my mother was an incredible musician; my father was, too, but I didn't meet him until later.

My mother was a gifted singer, and she joined my father's band—the Preston Love Orchestra—in the late '50s. My father had played jazz for Count Basie's band—my father's a jazz saxophonist—and then had his own band. My father was a very prodigious man; he's been married forever, to the same wife, but he's made babies all over the country, and I'm one of them.

What happened was that my mother got into my father's band, they fell in love, and she had my sister. I think they were on the road, and I suspect that she believed my father and she would marry or something, but she told us very little about this. A year and two months later she had me, and then, they fell apart. My mother had terrible bouts with psychoses and depression—all her life, and particularly surrounding this split—so she left my father and she raised us alone, but she raised us all our lives telling us that she had been married to our father and that our father had died in a car accident.

Post: It must have been amazing to meet your father.

Love: When I met him, I was floored, I couldn't believe it. I was sixteen years old, I had an apartment of my own—my mother's failing mental and physical health had made it such that I couldn't live with her any more—I was in high school and I was looking through the newspaper for a movie to go to with a friend of mine, when I saw 'Preston Love, world renowned jazz saxophonist returns to Midwest, playing tonight at…,' and, of course, I beat a hasty path to the club. Since I was sixteen years old, I didn't know exactly how to get in, so I made up a story that my father was expecting me to meet him there, and they let me in and put me in the back room to wait. It was this place called the Zoo Bar in Lincoln, Nebraska, and there was a huge line of people waiting, and they just forgot about me.

I sat through the whole first set, and I was amazed. There was this man that looked like me, his sense of humor was much like mine. I believed my whole life that he was dead, so I was trying to screw up the courage to go and talk to him on his break. I went over to him and I said—this is the stupidest thing I could ever imagine that I could say—"Are you Preston Love?" I mean, he'd been playing all night, but I just couldn't think of anything clever. When he said, "Yes," I asked, "Did you ever know a Winnie Winston?"—that's my mother's name—and when he said yes, I said, "I think I'm your daughter."

He said, "Oh, my goodness, are you Laura or Lisa"' and I said, "Well, I'm Laura," so, he started reciting all these important dates from my life, like my birthday, my sister's birthday, my mother's birthday, to prove that he knew who I was and that he had not forgotten, I guess to sort of absolve him of some guilt for not having been involved at all. He gave me some of his albums, and we've had sort of a loose correspondence. I haven't talked to him in a few years now, but I'm very glad to have met him, because it was just a big gap in my life.

Post: How did you get into performing music?

Love: Well, I think I always had a fantasy about it, when I was a little kid; I remember loading up on the Michael Jackson albums, and I would just sing every single thing. When I was about eleven my sister got really into Laura Nyro and Three Dog Night, so she and I would work out parts to sing. I could play a little bit of guitar, and a lot of the stuff we did was a capella too—my sister has a really good voice and a great sense of pitch and harmony—so she and I were in a duo throughout junior high. I entertained the idea of doing music, but I never knew what was going to really happen.

It turned out my father started visiting Lincoln regularly—he moved back to Omaha—and he would gig and would get me up on stage to sing with him on songs like "Too Much, Too Little, Too Late." My sister went up on one or two of them, but she was not as much into it. She has a family thing now and is pretty sidetracked in that way. She's a nurse, and her life is very anchored and stable.

When I was about fifteen, two musicians came to my high school and asked my glee club teacher if he knew of any good singers they could use. They had a grant to do a gig—one guy was a drummer and the other guy was a guitar player—and they were very well respected in Lincoln and, between the two of them, they did all the gigs in town. My teacher suggested me and introduced me to the two men, and I did my first gig doing Chaka Khan covers at the Nebraska State Penitentiary, and I knew that I wanted to do music.

Post: What happened then?

Love: I ended up being lovers with one of the men and moved to Portland with him when I was nineteen; he wanted to become a jazz player, so I thought I'd become a jazz singer. What ended up was that he became a jazz player and I became a worker in a TV station. I was in a very good funk band, though—the Inner City Funk Band—we were eight pieces, with horns and everything; we never made any money, we'd gig maybe once a month, but it was fun.

When Leroy went off and did his thing, I got into a Top 40 band and started touring all over British Columbia and Alaska, and found that unsatisfying. I met another man, went to visit him in Seattle, and decided to settle there. By this time I was really getting used to big cities! And it was in Seattle that I met a woman that I really hit it off with.

Post: Were you able to support yourself with your music?

Love: Oh no, I always had to do something else to make a living until just recently.

Post: Tell me about the last band that you were in.

Love: The last band I was in was a really loud, obnoxious Seattle kind of blues/grunge band called Boom Boom GI, and this particular band was the one that helped me realize that misogyny is just rampant in rock music. What happened was that I met a guy—by this time, I'm fully a dyke, I'm into it—who admired my motorcycle. It turned out he was a drummer, and I was kind of just starting to play the bass a little bit, and he admitted to not being a very good drummer and I said, "Well, I'm not a very good bass player," and so we found some other musicians who weren't very good—I just really wanted to learn how to play the bass, and I thought if I got in a band, that would really help—and formed a band.

I didn't want to play the bass and sing at the same time, so we had this woman named Faye West singing lead. We didn't really have a PA, and the vocals were going through a guitar amp, and it was obnoxious and awful; for the three months that this band rehearsed I never heard a single lyric because it was so loud. The lead singer decided that she would rather do heroin than be in this band, and I had to sing.

I looked at the lyrics for the first time and thought they were misogynist and pretty bad, but we had a gig coming up, and I made a decision that it didn't matter what I was saying, that it was just rock, that it wasn't a big deal. We actually put out an album with this band, and Gillian Gaar, the reviewer for The Rocket— the local music paper—wrote "How can a woman sing these lyrics which are so offensive to women?" It was at that instant that I realized that I was completely responsible for what I say, that people are going to hear it, and that it is a big deal.

I had known in the back of my mind that the words weren't OK, but at the time, I didn't feel like I had a right to complain, but this woman really turned me around. I wrote her a letter and said, "You're right, I'm going to take this to heart, and I'm not going to sing this any more, this is not what I should be doing. If you're not a part of the solution, you are a part of the problem, I'm gonna take some classes and learn about this stuff."

So then I immediately quit Boom Boom GI and enrolled into the University of Washington and started taking women's studies classes. I got affirmation. I got a sense of exhilaration. As I was nearing the end of my studies—I had two years of college in Nebraska and had to go another two and a half years to complete my BA—the final project for one of my classes was either to write a big, long, huge paper or to perform a concert of original music. Even though I hadn't played the guitar in fifteen years, I thought I could do it, and that was *Menstrual Hut*.

Post: How did your class like *Menstrual Hut*?

Love: They loved it! And my professor asked me to play it for some other women's studies classes. Then I got a gig at the Wild Rose, a women's bar, and realized that I enjoyed performing, that this was it, that I had found a niche. I started Venus Envy, and *Menstrual Hut* was highly recommended by the Ladyslipper catalog; I was flattered and satisfied and realized that I could do what I wanted and didn't need to disavow everything I knew to be true to do it. I decided that no matter what kinds of music I play and bands I do—because I still like rock and other kinds of music—I will never ever say anything that I don't want to say again. I don't have to shut up and sit down any more.

(Post) Love's renown has spread steadily, in keeping with her ethic of hard work and with the boldness of her increasingly emotionally complex music. The successes of *Z Therapy, Pangaea*, and *Helvetica Bold* (self-produced on her own Octoroon Biography label) got Love invited to perform, fall of 1994, at Carnegie Hall, one of twenty-eight artists in Putumayo's First New York Singer-Songwriter Festival.

What happened then is entertainment magic. Though shyly thoughtful when before an audience, Love is a dervish of dance. Her unselfconscious gyrations guilelessly match her funky bass lines, her supple voice singing passionately of pain known and overcome. With red bass and beaded braids, Love is as colorful as Sweet Honey in the Rock rolled into one, a galvanized woman grooving to an Afro-Celtic beat of her own invention. The *New York Times* opined that Love "stole the show."

Though Love's previous performances had centered in the Northwest, many independent grassroots magazines in the know had been proclaiming Love as an undiscovered genius. After Carnegie, *Billboard* called her one of the Top 10 unsigned American talents of 1994. In 1995, Putumayo introduced Love to a national audience by releasing the compilation *Putumayo Presents: The Laura Love Collection*.

Love's catapulting path to stardom has brought changes, but Love is determined to stay grounded.

Photo: Mark Van-S

Love: I want to do what I'm doing now for the rest of my life. If I get to no other level of fame, that's OK. I'm not seeking what k.d. lang and Janet Jackson have, though it may well come to that. I always will want to have time for my cats, my home life.

(Post) Finally, with her new visibility, Love has had to fully face her roots. Though her father is still performing, his relationship with Love has been, at best, strained; at worst, hurtful. Several days following this interview, Love was destined to appear in Omaha, her birth city, where she had not set foot in nearly two decades. Ironically, she was to open for the Temptations (one of her early influences) and for whom Preston Love would be playing saxophone.

Certainly, Love will find a way to deal with that eventuality; even more certainly, the experience will find its way into her lyrics. Though Laura Love has always professed that her intentions are to explore the challenges of coexisting in a society containing different cultures, she is equally clear that she has also gained comfort and self-understanding through her songs.

Love: It's a gift that people have given to me. People have been so sweet, so nice to me. I don't have that feeling that I should just shut up and sit down anymore

DISCOGRAPHY

Menstrual Hut (Octoroon Biography, 1989); *Z Therapy* (Octoroon Biography, 1990); *Pangaea* (Octoroon Biography, 1992;) *Helvetica Bold* (Octoroon Biography, 1994); *Putumaya Presents: The Laura Love Collection* (Putumayo, 1995); *Octoroon* (Mercury, 1997).

LAURIE LEWIS
fiddlin' around

Laurie Lewis, a repeat winner of the California State Women's Fiddle Championships (1970s) and of the International Bluegrass Music Awards Female Vocalist of the Year (1992, 1994), is a writer of melodic, thoughtful songs which evoke strong images and tell moving stories.

Her second solo album, *Love Chooses You* (1989) received the NAIRD award for Best Country Album of the Year (the title track was covered by Kathy Mattea); and Lewis's solo offering, *True Stories* (1993), received Honorable Mention in the same category. Lewis's vocal and instrumental performances are outstanding in their interpretation of traditional forms of acoustic music (folk, blues, country, Cajun) with classical, gospel, honky tonk, and pop spins: New Acoustic/California Bluegrass, perhaps?

Lewis and her band, Grant Street (Tom Rozum/mandolin, Peter McLaughlin/guitar, Jerry Logan/bass) are a current fixture on the country/bluegrass circuit. Lewis has also performed country duets with Kathy Kallick and, in June of 1995 Lewis released, with Grant Street bandmate Rozum, their long-awaited duet album, *The Oak And The Laurel*.

Lewis has appeared on TNN's "The Grand Ole Opry," "The Texas Connection," and "Music City Tonight;" NPR's "A Prairie Home Companion;" and PBS's "Lonesome Pine Specials." Lewis was also featured in Cecilia Tichi's book, *High Lonesome: The American Culture of Country Music*, the accompanying CD includes two of Lewis's songs.

Post: Who in your family, if anyone, was musical?

Laurie Lewis: My father is a flute player who, when I was a baby, played with the Dallas Symphony at the same time as he was going to medical school. He never was planning on playing professionally, though I imagine that he had, at some point, been faced with the decision as to whether to play music seriously.

When I was older, my father would have woodwind quartets with other doctors, and it made an impression on me. They would get together in the living room and play; then, I would have to go to bed. I wouldn't be able to sleep because there would be music going on. I would lie there, listening intently. I was probably ten or eleven at the time.

Post: When did you get involved with music, yourself?

Lewis: I started playing violin when I was twelve. My parents had started me on piano lessons when I was seven. My teacher stopped playing the next lesson's music for me because she found out that I wasn't learning to read music. I would listen to her play the piece and then I would remember and imitate it. When she stopped playing my pieces in advance, I got very frustrated, and it wasn't any fun. They couldn't make me practice, so I quit.

Post: How did the violin become your instrument?

Lewis: It wasn't a choice I made at that time. My parents decided that the violin would be a good instrument for me because I had a good ear and because you have to have a good ear to play the violin. I was a dutiful daughter; I said "OK."

Post: You took to it better than to the piano, though?

Lewis: Yeah, much better! It ended up being a good choice for me. I started a little bit late, in terms of when kids start nowadays: you know, the Suzuki Method at age four! I played in the orchestras through junior high and high school, though I wasn't very good. I had one year when I really improved, though. I went to Casa Dura Music Camp, and we lived music all day. When I got back home, I practiced an hour and a half in the morning and the same in the evening for the whole rest of the summer. When I went back to school I didn't have time to practice so much but the improvement stayed with me.

Post: How did you get into music professionally?

Lewis: I got interested in folk music and taught myself to play the guitar from lesson books and with the help of my friend, Dana Everts. When I was fourteen she and I worked out a whole bunch of songs and sang in the lobby of the Berkeley Student Union with lots of people listening to us.
    A year or so later, Dana and I went to the Cabal Creamery in Berkeley and got up onstage. We got part way through the song, and we forgot the words. We tried again but still couldn't remember them. We tried a third time, and it still didn't come. There were probably only ten people in the audience, but it really scared me.

Post: It didn't scare you away?

Lewis: I love music, and I love singing. That experience didn't scare me away, but it did set me back. Actually, I did quit playing music altogether when I was seventeen, but it wasn't because of that time when we couldn't remember the words; it was because of pressure from my father.
    Anyway, I dropped out of Berkeley to work at this dance studio. I got a hundred dollars a month and all the free lessons I could take. At the time, I could live on that, and it seemed like a good deal to me.
    The director of the dance studio, her husband, Geoff Burn, was into bluegrass music. He went to all these country bars, and played bass and sang. Geoff found out that I played violin, and he flipped because that was his favorite instrument. He told me that it would be easy for me to learn to play the fiddle because I played the violin, and he dragged me to San Francisco to hear live old-time music at Paul's Saloon.

There were fiddle players on stage, and when I heard them, all I wanted to do was play fiddle.

My sister happened to be getting married at the time, and asked me to do music for her wedding. I took out my violin, and I'd had this Chubby Wise album for the longest time. It was a record that I loved, but I'd never imagined that I could learn the waltzes on it.

I did, and it was easy for me. I was excited that I could hear it and play it; I still had a good ear. I got together with Geoff, and he played guitar with me. We played two waltzes at my sister's wedding; after that I was unstoppable. I let my dance career go—that was a way of expressing the artistic side of myself that wasn't music—but what I wanted to do was music. I'd wanted it all my life.

Post: How did the Grant Street String Band gets its name?

Lewis: Three of the four members of the original band lived on Grant Street. Two of the three lived together at this house and then another lived down the street. We were all trying to figure out a name for the band and we decided to call ourselves The Grant Street Band, then The Grant Street String Band. We put out an album called *The Grant Street String Band* (1984), and I kept the name when that band split up.

(Post) After the band split up, Lewis took some time off to work on her first solo album, *Restless Ramblin Heart* (1986). After playing several concerts to promote the album she wanted to start a new band to play her music. Tom Rozum was among the original members of that band.

Post: How did you and Tom Rozum decide to do an album together?

Lewis: We love duet singing, and we get a nice blend together. It's something we've worked on a lot, and it just feels good to sing together. It's my band, and we're doing mostly my material, so we have these other songs—great tunes—but we really weren't finding an outlet for it. We've had the idea to do this duet album for a long time.

Post: How do you keep yourselves centered so that you can sing well?

Lewis: There are a lot of things I do that enable me to sing my best. That's a real priority for me. I make sure that I get enough sleep. I bring my own little water purifier everywhere with me, and I drink water all the time. I can have a beer when I get off the stage if I'm not going to be singing again.

We don't perform in any smoking environment. Also, I don't drink much milk, so avoiding dairy before gigs isn't a big deal. I also try to make sure that I'm stretched and physically ready to sing. I learned that from my dance years. Your body is your instrument when you are a singer, and you have to have it centered in order to use it correctly. I hope to be singing when I'm eighty.

Post: When you laid down tracks for your recording, *The Oak And The Laurel*, what was the process?

Photo: Irene Young

Lewis: It depends who's singing lead. Sometimes Tom's first, and I add my voice; at other times, the reverse is true. Tom was saying that he tries to sound like me; I really try to sound like Tom, following his phrasing. If he's singing lead, I try to be his shadow.

Post: How do you arrange songs with the band?

Lewis: Whoever is singing the lead usually has the first go at it. Sometimes, someone will come to the group with an idea, and the rest of us will think of something else and open up other possibilities. It doesn't have to be negative. We're a growing thing, and each individual song will tend to change over time.

Post: Do either of you give lessons or have other day jobs?

Lewis: We do these week-long intensive teaching programs two or three times a year. I have taught private lessons in the past, but my schedule is such that I don't like to be tied down. You have to talk to four people, every time, about rehearsal schedules, flight schedules, and other transportation. We do have a road manager, Paul Knight. So there are five of us! It's new, and it's taken a big load off me, for sure.

Post: Do you think of yourselves as breaking ground in bluegrass tradition?

Lewis: We might be stretching it a little bit from the inside, pushing the boundaries out in some musical ways and in terms of the style in which we do it.

Post: What music do you listen to? Who would you go hear if you had a free moment?

Lewis: We don't have many free moments! We hear lots of music at festivals, but we did go see a Merle Haggard tribute at the Fillmore the last time we were in town.

Post: What would you like for the future of music, and for your future?

Lewis: Because I started playing music professionally in Berkeley, it wasn't unusual to see women instrumentalists in bands or to have women singing or otherwise involved in music. As I got out into the world, I realized that my experiences were unusual, but it's far less unusual now than then. I would like to see more women playing and being accepted in music. I wouldn't mind winning a Grammy!

DISCOGRAPHY

The Grant Street String Band (Bonita Records, 1984); *Restless Rambling Heart* (Flying Fish, 1986); *Blue Rose* (Sugar Hill Records, 1988); *Love Chooses You* (Flying Fish, 1989); *Singin' my Troubles Away* with Tom Rozum (Flying Fish, 1989); *Together* with Kathy Kallick (Rounder Records, 1991); *True Stories* with Tom Rozum (Rounder Records, 1993); *Live In Austin, TX* with Tom Rozum (VHS Hi-Fi Video Cassette, 1993); *Masters Of The Banjo* (Arhoolie Records, 1994); *The Oak And The Laurel* Laurie Lewis and Tom Rozum (Rounder Records, 1995).

LIBBY RODERICK
ecofeminist singer-songwriter

In her youth, Libby Roderick walked through the tall grasses of her native Anchorage, singing at the top of her lungs. Her awareness of the dramatic and beautiful Alaskan wilderness prompted incisive critiques of American assumptions and formulations of ecofeminist theory while in college. Libby Roderick is a well-loved musician who conveys an appreciation of diversity with an unrelenting call for social justice.

Post: How did music enter your life?

Libby Roderick: My family has always loved music, and I just grew up surrounded by the idea that music was nurturing and good. Though I didn't have much formal training, I was given ukulele lessons as a young child. The year after high school I worked as a page in the Alaska legislature and I taught myself to play the guitar during the long hours sitting in the chambers. The next year, I went to college: my parents valued the Ivy League, and my older sister was at Yale, so that was where I went. She and I played together, once or twice, when we were in college. I wasn't writing music back then, but I did sing. Singing has always been a part of my life, a survival tool, how the emotion was expressed in my life, my particular style of moving through the world. Music for me is my professional life, now, but I didn't start on that path until about 1986.

Post: How did you make that transition to singing as a career?

Roderick: After college I returned to Anchorage for my sister's wedding, and I stayed. Once in a while I liked to sing for my friends. Someone asked me to sing for a rally that we were having about violence against women and children. I agreed, then I was terrified; I shook for three days. Once I did it, though, the feedback was encouraging, even though I didn't sing any original material; I didn't have any of my own material. A few months later, I was asked, with several other women, to open up for a Margie Adam nuclear freeze benefit. We put together two songs and were amazed at the positive response.

For years I sang with my sister and two other women in an acoustic/a capella group called Voices. In the process of playing with that band one of the other women suggested that we write our own songs. I was frightened of the thought—the typical response of a non-performer—then I started doing it, and it was fun; once I started writing it became an easy channel. When the other women moved away, I carried on the singing on my own.

Post: How do you integrate your creative process into the business of your work?

Roderick: I don't even try to write every day. I wait on the right moment. There is a feeling that comes to my body that alerts me to the fact that I have creative energy to channel. I take notes, I try to think in poetry. When that energy is available I make time for it. I do have to be alone, but I don't have to have separate time.

Post: What are your thoughts about the music industry?

Roderick: Like many industries, the music industry is basically an oppressive structure, with artists at the low end of the totem pole. Performers and songwriters supply the product that supports the superstructure. There is also definitely some hard work to be done in educating about the value of art. I see two basic problems: one is capitalism and its assumptions—like the odd idea that something isn't worth doing if it doesn't produce a big profit—which need to be challenged constantly; the other is the assumption that one shouldn't enjoy what one is doing.

The general public doesn't have any way of knowing what it is like to be a working artist. I am considered to be wealthy by a lot of people because my debut release came out on CD, but actually only a small percentage of artists are really succeeding financially in a big way. When people assume that I am making a lot of money, they copy my tape. And that costs me. I am not angry at those people, they just don't know. So, back to education. I think that what is needed is large-scale dissemination of information about the obstacles faced by artists outside the mainstream, particularly politically progressive artists. For example, the impact of the fact that independent artists are basically locked out of commercial radio. Once people learn about the realities of the independent music scene, they think differently about artists and become more supportive. And come to concerts. Which is where the education continues.

Post: Is education how your music fits with your workshops?

Roderick: Logistically, I try to do a workshop the day after a concert. It is often the same people who want both types of events: first to hear music, then to talk. Lately I have been focusing on women's liberation and the environment, i.e. ecofeminism. For me, the ecology movement and the feminist movement need to be melded together and are, in fact, one philosophy. It needs to be recognized that human beings and systems and non-human beings and systems are all interconnected. If we negatively impact one part of the universe, there will be a negative effect on some other part. For example, if humans are treated badly, then the earth will suffer, and it will come around again to damage humans.

Feminists have seen that when one group in society is hurt, everybody is hurt. Ecologists have seen that when one species is interfered with, a piece of the ecosystem is wiped out, which has repercussions on all of us. To put these awarenesses together is what ecofeminism is all about.

Post: How did you come to your present understanding of ecofeminism?

Roderick: This is the work that I did when I was in college, without knowing exactly

what I was getting into. I did a whole thesis on a female-versus-traditional-male view of resources: natural resources, human resources, symbolic resources (such as language and images), and so forth. Even though I didn't understand what I was involved with, it was a big deal to me. It also connected with the whole other era of my life when writing, rather than music, was my primary form of creativity.

Some of that writing was about Alaska, so it was partially autobiographical. Alaska is certainly one of the places where there are still relatively wild areas. I do think that the wild places, the wild creatures, and the indigenous people who are still connected to those places and creatures are currently the keepers of world survival and world sanity. I literally believe that, if they go, we will not be able to make it, because their spirit is the soul of people and the planet.

In terms of my present situation, I definitely see music as an opportunity to communicate the values that I believe in. Many people in Alaska do not share my views; Alaska is the furious battleground of the American culture. A good half of the people in Alaska are interested in developing as much as they possibly can. We do have the Native Cultures, though, and that is a precious thing.

Post: What is your connection with people of other backgrounds such that you have come up with songs like "Grandfather Sun" and "Rosa?"

Roderick: The songs come from deep inside myself. I believe that they are connected with other people's deep inner selves. Native people and African American people have been articulating what we all need to hear: the alive stuff. The people of my European American culture are in serious distress. Anyone who is connected with themselves knows that we are not in a human-supportive culture right now. Not that the people aren't good, but the machinery of the culture has gone astray.

I see Native people connected to the land, connected to their community, dancing together. They sing together, and they speak about their roots. I love it, who wouldn't? Which doesn't mean that I don't carry my share of racism. But I do think that anyone who is connected with her-or himself will get the beauty and spirit of these peoples and their cultures.

Post: What are your favorite songs?

Roderick: Two come to mind. I really like "If You See A Dream" because it feels good when I perform it. It has a pacing, a rhythm, a style which feel like me. It was written at a time when I had gone to hear a singer named Susan Grace. She had come down to Anchorage from Fairbanks to do her show about the Arctic National Wildlife Refuge entitled "Keep It Wild." I went home afterwards and thought about Alaska, and eagles and bears, and that Alaska was my home; that the land was in my bones and that I didn't have a song about it at all.

I sat down and went inside my body and looked for what I had to offer. My first feeling was that it was too hard to write about something that I loved so much, that was so big, that was so close, that was so threatened. My experience was, I think, like many people's around environmentalism: overwhelming. And that is what I wrote from. The beginning of the song has the feeling of a cat in the middle of the road that cannot get up. The song evolved, as I was writing it, into the statement that if you see a dream, do something about it.

The line became the title of the album. If you see a woman you like, who is struggling to really like herself, tell her that you like her. If you see somebody trying to preserve their culture, support them. That is the stuff that we can do; each of us can, and many of us do. So I like the line, and I like the song.

The other song is "How Could Anyone," which has been, by far, the most widely used and best-loved song that I have done. I get mail about that song which encapsulates my feeling about what needs to be said to people in a fairly simple way. The song affirms our inherent wholeness.

DISCOGRAPHY

If You See A Dream (Turtle Island, 1990); *Thinking Like A Mountain* (Turtle Island, 1991); *If The World Were My Lover* (Turtle Island, 1993).

LINDA TILLERY
big voice, solid roots, new spirituals

Linda Tillery arrived for the interview jazzed. She held me spellbound with her description of a show by Philadelphia-based jazz and R&B singer Rachelle Ferelle the preceding evening. This is high praise from Tillery, whose big, flowing alto once blew Janis Joplin off the stage.

After cautioning me that she still felt blissed out, Tillery told about winning an award at the Sister-to-Sister ceremony, three nights earlier in Oakland, an annual tradition which pays tribute to local singers who are primarily, but not exclusively, African-American.

Though Tillery was mildly embarrassed and unbelievably moved by the recognition, it is clear that she deserves it. It is equally clear that gatherings like Sister-to-Sister are more than simply events of formal accolade; they are also informal meeting grounds of mutual visibility, sharing, and respect.

Linda Tillery got into music early when she began imitating singers that she heard on television and radio.

Linda Tillery: My folks, though they weren't musicians, were both music lovers. They bought a hi-fi when I was two and a lot of 78's. My father had Count Basie's original recording of "April in Paris." Do I wish I had that record!

I remember a recording by Dinah Washington called "That's All I Want From You," which was the first song I memorized. This was a little girl playing; no one taught me this music. It seemed inviting. To tell you the truth, I was pretty much a bathroom singer until about thirteen.

(Post) It was no secret that Tillery had natural musical ability, but when she was sent to a piano teacher for formal training, the teacher refused Tillery because of her young age. In junior high Tillery joined the school orchestra and was assigned to the string bass, which she played for six years.

Despite the fact that Tillery's first actual performing experience occurred in the context of culturally foreign European classical music, she found herself thrilled by the harmonizing that she heard in the piece, "The Great Gates of Kiev" and by the drum kit and other instruments with which her teacher allowed her to experiment because she was a superior music student.

Tillery: I was messing around with instruments, like the bassoon, that were in bass clef, because I played the bass. After high school I worked for a year and made an attempt at going to college. My parents always wanted me to be a business major.

(Post) Through an ad in the San Francisco Chronicle, she joined The Loading Zone, a local band which had already signed with RCA Records.

Tillery: That was the beginning of my professional career. Though it was the height of drug-crazed rock era, the members of The Loading Zone had all turned to Transcendental Meditation, were completely clean and sober, and were dealing with political issues that a lot of other musicians wouldn't tackle, like confronting the American Federation of Musicians which was not doing a very good job at providing benefits and protections for musicians. It was the beginning of a journey through consciousness-raising and political development for me.

(Post) Being at the front of an extremely popular and successful band proved overwhelming, however. Having changed labels, Tillery, at twenty, made an unsuccessful record for CBS: *Sweet Linda Divine*.

Tillery: Then my education as a hard-working singer began. I made the choices that I was guided to make; I can't say that they were the wrong choices, but I had to learn certain lessons first before I got back out there into the flow of things. I was what I call a '9-to-5 musician' from '70 to '77. Played with a lot of bands, did a lot of club work, only the hours were 9 to 2.

(Post) I ask her to tell me about opening for Janis Joplin. The story I'd heard has it that after winning over Joplin's audience Tillery was asked, by the Pearl herself, never to appear again on Joplin's bill. Tillery confirms the fabled reality—with the correction that "The Pearl" actually made the statement to people who were backstage.

Tillery: Rock music was a liberating medium for a lot of musicians who wanted to break free of the restraints placed on them by the entertainment industry and was also an opportunity for musicians to write and produce their own songs, to dress however they wanted, to address political issues, to be more free in their creativity. That was a good thing.
 But what also happened was a great deal of plagiarism or cultural appropriation. The Stones, John Mayall, Eric Clapton, all of the so-called white rhythm-and-blues and blues artists were making their name by using material written by established black artists such as Chuck Berry, Muddy Waters, Howling Wolf. The music got out there to the mainstream because the artists were white and had a higher visibility. So you have a generation of people growing up thinking that…

Post: R&B was European music?

Tillery: Yeah, exactly! Which it was not. Then you have someone like Janis who was one of those in-your-face kind of screaming singers who covered R&B. White audiences thought that was rhythm and blues, but when Janis went with her band to Memphis, she played for a black audience, and the audience just sat there and looked; you know, like can we hear Sam and Dave? Therein lies some of the truth. I don't say that I was a better singer than Janis was, it's just that I was able to sing the music from an experiential and cultural context. In other words, I was a Black woman singing Black music.

I was raised in the inner city of San Francisco, I did not grow up listening to folk music. I grew up listening to rhythm and blues, blues, gospel, and jazz. Those are the four idioms that I come from; that music is natural for me, feels like home base. If I had gone out and tried to be a ballady folk singer I'd sound ridiculous because it's...

Post: How Janis sounded to the black audience?

Tillery: Yeah, exactly.

(Post) Tillery connected with Olivia Records in 1975, after the band Be Be K'Roche submitted Tillery's name as a producer for their album. In fact, Tillery has worked on more women's music albums than almost any other person, doing production, singing, and playing. Including approximately thirty women's music credits, Tillery's discography totals nearly fifty. The Olivia experience, which lasted until 1979, was enlightening for Tillery.

Tillery: I was quite happy to be in an environment where I could observe other women in the creative process and also in the administrative process because all of my experience up to that point had been working with men. The Loading Zone was nine: me and eight white men; every other band I was in was me and six men, me and five men, me and four men. I had never worked with any women musicians.

I do remember that when I was about thirteen, I saw Vi Red play live at a picnic in Pittsburg, California. I'll never forget it. I went with a neighbor family out on a picnic. There was a woman who came up to the bandstand with an alto saxophone. She had on a long skirt and a blouse, and she stood up there and she played that saxophone. I remember being mesmerized. I had never seen a woman play an instrument like that, really tearing it up. I didn't understand the importance of Vi Red as a musician then, as I do now, but I knew that I wanted to be able to play whatever instrument I chose. I wanted to sing but not just as a centerpiece. I wanted to be a unique voice.

(Post) I ask Tillery whether she felt alone as a woman musician. She replies that she felt alone as a black woman in women's music and cites her meeting with Olivia's Mary Watkins as crucial.

Tillery: I shared some things in common with her musically, I understand who she is, although we function differently; she's a composer/pianist of many styles, but her roots are in the church. Any time I can sit down and have a conversation about hymns and spirituals, I feel pretty good. Mary can play the standards; I would ask her, "Can you play "Stella by Starlight?" and she'd say "Yea." and I said "OK!"

There were years between the late '70s and mid '80s when I coasted because I didn't know where my focus was. I had a bunch of tunes I could sing, and I did it for money. I don't know that I felt particularly connected to the music in an essential way. But since music is what I do, I had to stay in the game.

(*Post*) It wasn't until 1984 that Tillery began to question her path or her purpose. Soon thereafter, she released *Secrets*, intended to be Southern-based R&B but which turned out pop R&B. Fate brought her into performing with the Zazu Pitts Memorial Orchestra in 1987, while working in a travel agency.

Tillery: Being a "Pitts" member took pressure off me that I didn't understand I'd had before. I was not the leader, I did not have the responsibility of hustling the gigs, making the phone calls. For the first time in a real long time, I got to just be a member and watch. I got to see how a large organization works. I earned a living. I was able to quit my day job.

(Post) Around the same time, Tillery, was hired to be one of the vocalists in the house band at Slim's, and began her reconnection to her roots music.

Tillery: In the Slim's band was a guitarist named Bill Campbell. Bill is from Texas, and knew as much about blues and traditional R&B as a person could know. I wanted to be in that band with him because of the understanding and knowledge he had.

(Post) Tillery began to look at soul music in a whole different way.

Tillery: It was no longer dance music or party music. It was part of this fabric that I was trying to piece together, which I now call my survival fabric. I was already in possession of the contemporary threads but there were pieces missing. I could feel that, but I couldn't put my finger on it quite yet.

(Post) In 1989, Tillery was selected to sing with Voicestra, Bobby McFerrin's voices-only ensemble which recreated a variety of instrumentations and styles.

Tillery: We spent a lot of time together learning who we were personally and musically. It was an incredible journey, like a Jules Verne novel. We worked very hard trying to learn—or unlearn —a lot of old habits. It's like when you're eating an artichoke; all you really care about is the center piece. You have to pull away those leaves and the little fabric hairs. Essentially what happened is that each person was able to find the center of him-or herself. We were encouraged to develop that part and to take on new parts.
Bobby would often start singing a spiritual in the dressing room, and the rest of us would join in. Those old songs served as a connecting point for us. I was having seismic vibrations, and the music in my body started to make sense.

(Post) In 1992, Tillery put together Skin Tight, an all-women Motown band.

Tillery: I was earning money but still searching. One night, I was sitting at home, channel surfing. I found a PBS show with Jessye Norman and Kathleen Battle singing spirituals. I had my VCR and TV hooked up to my speakers so I turned the sound up, and it blew me away, song after song after song.
I was hearing and seeing my life flash before my eyes. I'm thinking about my grandfather; he used to sing hymns in the house. I'm thinking about church services and stories my mother used to tell me about her grandmother. I thought, I gotta do something with this music. I knew that there was a folk-based component to my creative identity, and I had found a piece of it.

Photo: Jan Watson/Sharon Green

(Post) Tillery contacted Bernice Johnson Reagon, who recommended some literature and recordings, but it was Tillery's experience of dubbing a soundtrack for a play, "Letters from A New England Negro" which crystallized her vision.

Tillery: They provided the music. I heard that music and said, "This is it. This is it!" The director told me that the songs were from the Library of Congress. He gave me the address. I got the catalogue and started buying and listening. The songs are recorded and held in public trust. Anybody can get this music. I started ordering like a maniac, just immersed myself in it. Then came the idea to put together a group to perform it.

(Post) Though she felt concerned that she might not be able to find anyone to perform the songs, and worried that people might think her old-fashioned, Tillery persevered. When Boo Price, co-producer of the Michigan Womyn's Music Festival offered a chance to appear on the festival stage, Tillery asked ten women singers from across the U.S., and every woman agreed.

The 1992 Michigan set was such a triumph that Tillery subsequently assembled six Bay Area women to sing and develop together. In November of 1992, Tillery collaborated with Redwood Cultural Work for a Thanksgiving-time New Spirituals Project show. The following November, Tillery's Cultural Heritage Choir was a central part of Yonder Come Day, Redwood's second annual New Spirituals Project show held, appropriately, in an Oakland church.

The New Spirituals Project remains a joint collaboration between Redwood and Tillery. The Cultural Heritage Choir recorded the album, *Good Time, A Good Time*. Tillery wants the Choir's influence to involve spreading tradition as well as beautiful sounds.

Tillery: I want kids, particularly young black people, to hear this music. I want grandmothers who are from the south and people who are interested in celebrating history and culture to hear this music. I want all people who recognize the importance of history and ancestry and family and community to hear it.

It's a healthy exercise for all of us to connect with our cultural past. I believe this music is the foundation for most popular music in the United States. Call-and-response, multi-layered harmonies, poly-rhythms are African.

(Post) Tillery concludes that she is, finally, doing the work that she's been guided to. I asked how being a musician sets her apart from the purely academic students of spirituals culture; Tillery sparkled and replied:

Tillery: Some people can write a dissertation on whistling Dixie, but I can whistle Dixie!

DISCOGRAPHY

The Loading Zone (RCA, 1969); *Sweet Linda Divine* (CBS, 1970); *Linda Tillery* (Olivia, 1978); *Secrets* (Redwood, 1985); *Good Time, A Good Time* with the Cultural Heritage Choir (Tuizer Music, 1995).

LUCIE BLUE TREMBLAY
folk, women's music, and Quebecois charm

Lucie Blue Tremblay embodies many of the noble elements of folk music's hopes and strivings: authentic multiculturalism (Tremblay mixes songs in English with songs from her French Canadian heritage); solid singing (her voice is a mountain lake: clear, deep, pure); passion (her romantic focus on real-life process powers her writing); and the unusual (her stunning whistle is one example).

Icing on the cake is the fact that Tremblay offers herself as a conscious connection between the origins of Women's Music and the folk music present; she is one of the few to consistently evoke the names of Women's Music foremothers from the stage.

Tremblay is making her mark as strongly in the folk network. In the fall of 1992 she fulfilled a dream of playing on stage with James Taylor. On E-Town (a National Public Radio show) they performed "The Water Is Wide" together. Also in 1992, Tremblay played at a Quebecois music festival in Paris, France, and for two weeks in the Canadian Pavilion at the World's Fair in Seville, Spain. She also sang Cris Williamson's "Lullaby" to her mother on a Canadian Broadcasting Corporation Canada Day TV special.

One of the sources of Tremblay's widespread success is an intuitive stage persona which allows her to relate to and draw in different types of audiences. Her presence is both ingenuously warm and self-consciously droll, as she plays upon the American weakness for the French language. Through her sparkling political observations; soulful, first-person anecdotes; and fluency in blues, country, and pop, Lucie Blue Tremblay's music makes people feel good about themselves.

Not surprisingly, Tremblay grew up surrounded by different styles of music, thanks to her accordion-playing mother. In fact, Tremblay's professional start came through her mother's music.

Lucie Blue Tremblay: My mother had a lung operation when I was in grade one. She had a big part of her lung taken out, and she couldn't hold her accordion any more. So she bought an organ, and put together a band.

(Post) Tremblay's mother played every Saturday night at her social club, with Tremblay watching and listening. At the age of twelve, Tremblay took over the drumsticks for her mother's group. Though self-taught, Tremblay's skills kept her playing in that band for four years.

Tremblay: Playing drums on weekends was fun, and it was more than the best allowance I'd ever had.

(Post) Tremblay has kept up with drumming because she loves it, and has offered a drum riff or two during recent performances.

Drums were not an instrument on which she could compose, nor which she could play solo, so Tremblay asked her family for the instrument she really wanted: a guitar. The one she received was red snakeskin. She mostly taught herself through books. So interested was Tremblay in music that she studied it in high school and entered college as a music major.

Tremblay: You had to request a first instrument and a second instrument when you went into music. I wasn't mastering any instrument well enough to get into a music program, but I could sing. I went to the audition; everyone was doing concertos and operas, and I came in with my guitar and sang "Me and Bobby McGee." I sang the song phonetically. My English is good now, but it hasn't always been this way. When I listen to songs in English, now, I have a better idea of what people are saying. In those days it was, "Busted flat in baddinrouve," or, "Bobby thumbed a deezeldawn;" I didn't know what a deezeldawn was. Some of those words, I have to admit I still don't know.

(Post) Tremblay was accepted to Vanier College in Quebec, the only one chosen out of her high school. The Fine Arts Award which accompanied the admission made the process all the more exciting, a harbinger of future honors.

Tremblay: My teacher demanded that I do opera. She didn't want me to use my throat voice, she wanted me to find my operatic voice. After singing "Ave Maria" in German for five months, I left college. It was 1976. I did a lot of jobs. I played in smoky bars and started writing. My favorite job was working for Bell Canada as an overseas telephone operator. It was one of my favorite jobs because I got to connect with people since things weren't so automated.

It was during the war in Lebanon. People in Canada were trying so hard to reach people there. The job turned into a wonderful opportunity to be compassionate. I would try to get to the operator in Lebanon, and there would be no circuits available, or the lines would be cut. I was constantly trying to help, and when I got through it was cool.

I also had a job working as a bus driver. I drove the kids to school, then I could just sit in the bus with my guitar and practice. There were some kids that I would bring home for lunch; I would park my bus and wait for them. They would come back with their lunches and listen to me play.

After a few years working day jobs, I travelled to England, hitchhiking up to Scotland I was a hippie with long, really fuzzy hair.

(Post) When she returned, she found the bar scene frustrating.

Tremblay: People were there for background music, and to consume alcoholic beverages; they weren't there for a concert. I wanted people to hear what I had to say.

(Post) One of the first songs that Tremblay wrote was "Voix d'Enfant," a child's view of incest, drawn from her own experience. A lovely piano composition, squarely addressing an important and delicate topic, "Voix d'Enfant" was to be a defining anthem of Tremblay's personal-is-political feminism for many years, as well as a determinant of career decisions.

Tremblay: I quit my job and decided that I was going to play coffeehouses or wherever people could actually hear me. I was really involved with the women's movement in Montréal, and thought that I might even produce some of the shows.

(Post) Not long thereafter, Lucie Tremblay got the break that launched her face into the living rooms of Canada.

Tremblay: In 1984 I went to this song festival in a town a couple of hours away from Montréal, called Granby. This place had been known to put unknown people into the music scene. It's a French-speaking festival that brings people from all over Canada.

They pick sixty musicians across the country who sing in French. I was picked as one of those people. It was very funny because I had said, "Oh yeah sure, I'll submit my stuff." Some guy in a music store who liked my music had said, "You really should submit your material." And I did. No idea that I might get picked as one of the performers. They asked me to show up at Granby and perform three pieces.

For a whole week, people came and went and voted. We got cut down to ten performers' names. The ten of us went off to do some heavy-duty workshops with mainstream artists and music industry people. All of a sudden, it became a big deal.

People who worked in promotion came to me and said, "We think you're going to take this whole thing." There were serious bands, from New Brunswick to Vancouver. It was very hot. The promoters kept saying, "People are going to remember your name." They said, "There is a mainstream performer in Quebec, Sylvie Tremblay. You need to think about that. How are you going to make your name more catchy?"

(Post) What Tremblay did was to contemplate dropping her surname or altering her given name.

Tremblay: I didn't want to do that because my family is so important to me, and my first name tells you what culture I'm from.

(Post) Finally, she sought inspiration from a favorite book, Petersen's *Field Guide to the Birds*; realizing that the ocean and the throat chakra were all connected by the color blue, she selected "Blue" as her new middle name.

Tremblay learned that the industry and media had chosen her for Granby's Singer-Songwriter and Press awards and audiences voted her Best Performer. No one was more surprised and delighted than Tremblay, who had chosen to play the overtly political "Voix d'Enfant" and "Laissez-Moi Sortir," about women prisoners, in addition to the enchanting "St. Jean Port Joli," replete with her haunting whistle, about a seashore near her home.

The flurry of attention that followed led to Tremblay's being asked to record songs for Quebec's national celebration. Record offers rolled in, people wanting to make her a star. Then she had an insight not unlike that which precipitated her flight

Photo: Irene Young

from smoky bars: mainstream fame had its price, and that too-high price was artistic freedom.

Tremblay's half-sister Helene helped in the financing of a full-length, self-titled album, featuring the three songs which had earned her acclaim at Granby. Half in English, half in French, *Lucie Blue Tremblay* awaited a record deal that felt right.

At a women's music festival in Winnipeg, Olivia-connected photographer Irene Young was amazed by Tremblay's music. One connection led to another and, by the end of 1986, *Lucie Blue Tremblay* was released on the Olivia label.

Tremblay: With the Olivia women, I felt comfortable to sing about what I felt was important. Especially in those days, when I didn't have as many bruises as I do now—I wasn't as tough—it was really important for me to feel that support. I feel that Olivia took someone that nobody in the USA really knew, who sang in French and didn't speak English very well, and did a very good job of getting my name out there.

(Post) In the three years that passed between *Lucie Blue Tremblay* and *Tendresse*, her second Olivia release, Tremblay discovered acoustic music and lush instrumentation. Her sturdy political stance wavered not an iota; *Tendresse* contained "Peaking," about teenage suicide, plus the traditional "The Water is Wide." Tremblay also continued her bi-lingual singing and the mixing of studio and live cuts.

Tremblay's best songs remain her most personal ones: "Tour Song," recalling homesickness while on the road and, Tremblay's favorite, from *Tendresse*, "Daddy's Song," a country tribute to her steel guitar-playing father, who passed away right after Granby.

Tremblay: He didn't even get to see my first album. For me, "Daddy's Song" was really important. When [session player] Rick Haworth was doing the pedal steel lines on top of the track that was not finished, I started to cry, and we knew those were the lines that we wanted to keep. It's important to keep that naive innocence, the purity of where my songs come from.

(Post) Tremblay's next recording was a departure for her. Not only was it a shorter cassingle format, but it focused exclusively on self-identification of gay people. Comprising part of a package which one could use in order to come out gently to loved ones, the cassingle, *I Want You To Know Who I Really Am* (1991), is graceful and catchy, and contains resource references for parents and friends of lesbians and gay men: numbers to call, addresses to write to for information and guidance.

For *Transformations* (1992), Tremblay's third Olivia recording, she recorded without any live tracks. Though Tremblay's writing has clearly matured in nine years, the songs on *Transformations* bring a new peaceful joy to her real-life stories.

Tremblay describes the spiritual process which surrounds her creative process:

Tremblay: The hardest song to write wasn't supposed to be on *Transformations* It was written while we were mixing *Tendresse;* that's when I started to write it. For some reason, I couldn't finish it then. It was this song about how life is really different when you get older. I was really down, and was practically in tears playing it on the piano. I couldn't finish it so I left it alone.

When we worked on *Transformations*, we went to Montréal to do some of the production. While they were mixing—we had finished everything—I was in the same studio as during *Tendresse*. I went back to that same piano, and the first thing I did was to play that song from three years earlier. I got some paper, and started writing out the words. The next thing I knew, I was writing the end. I said, "Excuse me, guess what? We have another song to record!"

(Post) Tremblay has gone through a period during which the touring life and the challenges of independence took their toll. She has had to reevaluate her priorities, and her number-one at the moment is to stay healthy and balanced so that she can play what she loves.

Nearly twenty years after she dropped out of Vanier, Tremblay is contemplating returning to school. A positive workshop experience at the Kerrville Folk Festival convinced her that she could, and wanted to, expand her musical knowledge. She knows that she has mastered the art of getting into her own emotions and writing songs which channel and project those feelings, but Tremblay wants to master the technical aspects of songwriting and production.

Tremblay: Maybe I might be a music therapist.

(Post) Giving voice lessons, years ago, demonstrated her facility with music theory, and her easy ability to convey the logic in charts, notes, and chording. She wants to inspire a generation of students confused by the standard classroom methods. Lucie Blue Tremblay is seeking to reconnect with the essence of folk music, with the grassroots of women's music, to be the troubadour that she was born to be. And though she may go back to study, one thing is certain, she'll still be playing her music and still performing.

DISCOGRAPHY

Lucie Blue Tremblay (Olivia, 1986); *Tendresse* (Olivia, 1989); *I Want You To Know Who I Really Am* cassingle (Demi-Soeurs, 1991); *Transformations* (Olivia, 1992).

LYNN LAVNER
the original yentl sings and laughs about growing

When she strides onstage, all five feet of her, in black leather, Lynn Lavner turns heads and wins hearts. Between her cutting-edge, original songs, Lynn talks about life: as a lesbian in a long-term (seventeen years) relationship, as a co-mother, as a Brooklyn Jew, as a socially conscious woman who uses humor to ease acceptance of herself and of her perspectives.

Her albums draw parallels among oppressed people and bear the responsibility for educating. Onstage, Lynn doesn't omit lesbian material when playing to mainstream audiences; she doesn't leave out Jewish material when playing for the Metropolitan Community Church; she doesn't leave out the leather in an attempt to be politically correct.

In interview, Lynn Lavner is as forthcoming as in concert. Her speech emerges polished, yet with an enduring simplicity. Her insights come rapid-fire, the apparent result of unwaveringly honest self-analysis and relentless global examination.

Born the last child of older parents and a much older sib, Lynn's verbal virtuosity was molded by her family culture.

Lynn Lavner: I had to be articulate and funny to be included in dinner table conversation. When I was a child I didn't want to be a princess or a cowgirl, I wanted to do crossword puzzles. I wanted to read the *New York Times* and know how to fold it.

I tried to keep up with what was educated, adult talk; both my parents were practicing lawyers. I had a brother ten years older. So when I was four, everybody had been to law school, passed the bar, or was at least in high school. And had a sense of humor. I think that cultural East Coast New York City Jewish liberal thing, whatever it is, made humor part of the armor that we all went out with every day.

(Post) Though Lynn's 6th grade graduation album had quoted her as saying she wanted to be a singer or songwriter, her path to those goals was indirect.

Lavner: I had a difficult coming out. We didn't have money. My father died, suddenly, when I was eight, which threw us into a financial and emotional tizzy.

Those early hurts made me embrace my middle class dreams. I did socially acceptable, achieving things; I was not a rebel. Upon graduation from college I became a teacher. But with time, there came a return to what was in my heart: music and comedy, the social awareness as well.

My cultural icons were the people who could turn a phrase or write a melody. I was taken with the immigrant experience, with Gershwin and Irving Berlin and the screen actors, from Lauren Bacall to Kirk Douglas to Paul Muni. People from poor

Brooklyn Jewish backgrounds, or whose native language had not even been English, but who re-invented themselves.

My dream had to do with playing the piano, wearing a tux and singing to women, amusing women, having women respond to me. Maybe at first, all of that showing off was a subtext for doing music and comedy, but it's very hard to separate the two.

I've never felt that I'm good at any of this. I'm not a pianist; I'm not a singer; I'm not a monologist; I'm not a stand-up comic. But there seems to be something I do in the combination of all of those things that really works. It can embarrass me to hear the way that it seems to affect others.

I never know whether my name is going to be known. Yet after a show, a woman might come up and say, "I just want you to know how proud I am that you represent me on stage." It is a responsibility. People look to you for more than what they look for when they channel-change. Those of us who are on the cutting edge, who are doing out material are really—whether we like it or not—being judged as representatives of the whole community. It's the Jackie Robinson syndrome.

We may not choose to be where we are, but I don't respect those who say, "Sure I curse and spit and molest children and beat my wife, I'm just a basketball player; I am not supposed to be a role model." Maybe you didn't set out to be; when you find yourself in such a position by accident of life and circumstance, you have choices about what to do with that position. Now that the spotlight is on me, I would like not to be vulgar or profane. I would not go bare-chested inappropriately. I would like to show the best of my community to my community and to anybody else who's watching. I recognize the power that I have.

(Post) Lynn has never been uncomfortable with her power.

Lavner: I'm happy to have it. The danger that those of us in performance face is believing our own press; I won't be carried away by what is written about me. Early in my career I thought I was hot. Gay men have the right saying: "Get over it."

(Post) Though her own coming out was painful, Lynn has opinions on the gay community.

Lavner: It's a process and a movement; it's not well organized. If every lesbian and gay man came out, if we had a movement in the sense of the 1960s Black Civil Rights movement, and you could name leaders the way you could name Martin Luther King or Malcolm X, we might accomplish more. It's just not in the nature of gay people; we are as argumentative and splintering and divisive as Jews. Worse than that, we are trendy, disloyal, and don't even stay in the same apartment; we can't keep a mailing list.

Our relationships, whether they're linear and we grow from them, or whether they're just stupidly ill-planned and selfishly ill-conceived, don't last. We have no carry over. What I do feel part of is the tide that connects and carries us. Some of us look like everybody else, and are like everybody else, except for being gay; some of us are different from everybody else and have felt ourselves to be special and apart from the time we were three.

My work is as necessary as that of the historian, artist, political leaders, and mainstream stars who come out. All are part of a process that takes us along to the next step.

What I convey on stage has elements of humor, of music, of the articulate English teacher that I used to be. Of the Jew. Of the underdog. Of the little girl who wasn't good at what the boys did. An artist has to be an outsider. You can't be an employee or a cheerleader. And you can't be looking to see where the crowd is going so you can lead them.

It's a funny thing choosing to wear leather on stage, it was meant to be provocative and politically incorrect. Then it was accepted. What I have always meant it to be is a visual reminder that I am not like anybody else. The difference that makes us a community is a sexual one; that embarrasses people. Like the Black people who might say, "We're the same except for the color of our skin." Then how the hell do I know it's Aretha Franklin when I turn on the radio? And why do I understand that there is a Black culture and a drive to survive horrible oppression over centuries? Gay people have that too. We are not the same as straight people except for our sexuality. We are a culture, a consciousness, we are diverse. We're pioneers. We're outlaws. What we do with that definition is what shapes us.

Instinctively I knew it was my role to nourish a sense of incompatibility. When people become smug, they can be put in a category: leather people, lesbians, Jews, whatever. People become rigid in reinforcing their own view.

What I want to do most is to create a new picture of the world. One that has a place for us, with an edge of the uncomfortable. That's what I call cabaret. An art form that started in Germany in the rathskellers and after-hours clubs. It was avant-garde, anti-establishment. What I do is not only a performance. If five of us appeared on the same record label, you would not confuse me with someone else.

(Post) Though she has taken flak for her tenacious politics, and had a few unpleasant stage experiences (things thrown at her, been marched on by Nazis), Lynn recognizes that part of her persona also serves as a natural defense.

Lavner: Nobody dares. I'm adorable. I'm five feet tall and angry. There is something about weighing ninety-eight pounds and being well-intentioned and clever; people are disarmed. I'm like Androcles with the lion: I don't want to club anybody over the head, but I can take the splinters out of their paws and achieve my own end without creating more pain in the process.

An artist is sensitive to what it was to be a child. To be insecure. To have the first achievement. To fall in love. The things I'm working on have more to do with my childhood than with anything that's going on politically now. What it was like growing up in Brooklyn when I grew up, the sights and smells of it. I can take myself back to when I was small; that's universal.

I've passed my fortieth birthday, and I'm starting to think about middle age. The new political correctness is that being middle-aged is wonderful; not everything about being older is wonderful! I'm going to talk about that on stage.

Early experiences shape you in a way that I was always aware of the vagaries of what can happen to you in life. That nothing is fair. That very good people get sick and die young. That sons of bitches inherit tremendous amounts of money or live in lovely places. I accepted that. This is the hand that's been dealt, and it reminds me of something that was said to me at the West Coast Festival. I usually travel with my lover. And I was there without her. Someone who knows us as a couple and knows how much we do for each other said to me, "Well, what's it going to be like to go on, in the evening, on stage, without her; who will provide the emotional support?" And I said, "You need emotional support when you're driving a cab to support seven children. I'm going to go on stage and sing for forty-five minutes, and three thousand women are going to love me." This does not require emotional support. I'm lucky, and I know it.

DISCOGRAPHY

Ladies Don't Spit And Holler (Bent Records, 1981); *Something Different* (Bent Records, 1983); *I'd Rather Be Cute* (Bent Records, 1986); *You Are What You Wear* (Bent Records, 1988); *Butch Fatale* (Bent Records, 1993).

MARIANNE FAITHFULL
the secret life of sister morphine

Bessie Smith. Billie Holliday. Janis Joplin. Kurt Cobain. Marianne Faithfull. All voices of their generations, all victims of prejudice and drugs and their own misfortune. All dead—and too early. Except for Marianne Faithfull.

Born the daughter of an Austrian baroness/dancer/drama queen (Eva von Sacher-Masoch) and a British professor/spy/humanitarian (Glynn Faithfull), Marianne Faithfull grew up amidst the conflicting rules of British decorum and Continental freespiritedness. Inspection of her ancestral names might lead one to conclude, however simple-mindedly, that she was unwitting heir to both sweetness (Sachertorte is a delicious cake) and self-destruction (it was the Masochs from Faithfull's family who coined the term "masochism").

Marianne Faithfull's life has been the stuff of legends and tabloids. More than nearly any other musical woman of the Twentieth Century, Marianne Faithfull has lived her life in the public eye, her ups and downs as carefully chronicled and abundantly analyzed as those of Princess Di. For Marianne Faithfull was a queen in rock's configuration of royalty.

Yet, Marianne Faithfull has also led the life of a modern woman: pressured by the world's expectations and besieged by demands from the male (rock) world that she inhabited. Interspersed with happenings on that elevated plane, Faithfull's life has also been laden with more ordinary blessings: motherhood and grandmotherhood.

Her album, *A Secret Life* (1995), a collaboration with "Twin Peaks" composer Angelo Badalamenti, is lushly ethereal and softer than her previous work. Shadows of rage, bitterness, guilt, and danger remain, but the overarching sentiment is that of peaceful remembrance. Nestled in the middle is a tiny nugget of hope ("The Stars Line Up"): gentle and lovely.

In the end, Marianne Faithfull has proven faithful to herself: breaking free of the labels which have trapped her; triumphing over the drugs which enslaved and threatened to kill her; developing her own style of intensely personal, unflinchingly honest music. In the end, Marianne Faithfull's search for her identity—eschewing along the way the titles of baroness' daughter; rock star's girlfriend; middle class housewife; prissy, virginal Catholic schoolgirl with a thin veneer of sophistication; punker; waif; siren; street addict—has been a forty-eight year quest to be in touch with her own exuberance, fragility, her own muse.

In her current position as rock elder, one of the few women in that role, Marianne Faithfull has contemplated the women who influenced her. Though she acknowledges that there were rocking musical women in her era (Fanny, Tina Turner, Moe Tucker, among others), she admits that she didn't really connect with them.

Marianne Faithfull: I thought that Joan Baez was wonderful, though I didn't get that she had anything to do with me! I think the person I got fascinated with, though she's a bit younger, was Joni Mitchell. I suppose because of how subjective her songs were and that she was writing them herself.

(Post) Given Faithfull's status, I query whether she has ever paid her compliments to Mitchell.

Faithfull: I think she knows. I mean I've tried to tell her. It's so difficult to say these things out loud. I'm trying to remember if I actually said to Joni how much her work has meant to me. I'm sure I have. But, then again, sometimes I just back off, and I can't even explain why.

(Post) A moment later, Faithfull is speculating about her own impact on present generations of women musicians.

Faithfull: I must have done a lot of damage with my morphine and with my whole sort of drug image, though I never meant for that to be. Whatever I was doing looked good to other people. I could have done advertising, I know that. What it's meant, in the end, is that I've had much more power than otherwise. I don't want to think about that much power. I just want to get on with my words, my music, my performances.

Recently, Courtney Love was in New York, and she was trying to get hold of me. I did return her calls but I never got her. I feel very bad about it because if ever a girl might need somebody to talk to, she might. But I knew that this was too much for me, and what I would say to her she wouldn't want to hear. I guess I'll have a lot more to say to her if she gets clean. Though it shouldn't be like that, I don't think I could handle it now.

(Post) Faithfull's career was auspiciously launched in 1964 with the release of her single "As Tears Go By." Written by Mick Jagger and Keith Richards, the song—as interpreted by Faithfull—rose to number nine on the British charts. However, it contained within it seeds of destruction: foreshadowing Faithfull's three and one half year relationship with Jagger (which was to mark her as a musical accessory for many years), hinting at the tearful future tragedy contained within the lyrics.

Faithfull has spent much of her life, and a thematic majority of her autobiography, wrestling with gender issues and with finding her own place along the male-female continuum.

Faithfull: There's a difference between men and women that I did not accept when I was young; I think I saw it like a child would see it. I wanted very much not to be seen as a sexual object and to be taken as a friend. In those days it was impossible, and it's still quite hard. It's gotten much easier for me, and it will get easier as I get older and older and less and less beautiful.

(Post) Faithfull segues easily into discussion of Mick Jagger, as if that past were not so remote.

Faithfull: I have tremendous compassion for Mick because I know he really loved me, and I really loved him, but I obviously loved drugs more. Actually, I've had some wonderful men in my life. Then there's the other thing which is that my mission and my work are more important than my private life which is a very hard thing for men to cope with.

Being thrown into the public eye at such a young age was exactly what I wanted, although I sometimes find it very hard to admit. I don't think I knew what I was asking for when I took the offer up. I think I saw what any artist would see. What was so powerful, what lured me, was the chance to express myself, the chance to create something, the chance to be something, to make myself up, to say something, to do something!

At the bottom of it all is that you want to be loved and you want to be loved by as many people as possible. And then you don't know whether you want to be loved by many people or you want to be loved by one.

(Post) By the age of twenty-three, in 1969, Faithfull had left her first marriage; released the morbid, heavy "Sister Morphine" (though she was not yet fully under heroin's spell) plus a handful of folk albums (her rendition of "Scarborough Fair" pre-dated Simon & Garfunkel's by several years); experienced a miscarriage; uttered the first "fuck" in the history of Britain's silver screen (in 1967's "I'll Never Forget What's 'is Name"); been busted at Keith Richards' now-famous Redlands home; initiated a prodigious acting (film and theater) career; spent thousands on clothes and ornaments; borne emotional witness to the death of Rolling Stones' Brian Jones; and had attempted suicide: the first of many overdoses to come.

By the early 1970s, Faithfull was living on the streets of London. Faithfull turns naturally to her relationship with drugs.

Faithfull: I have one of those metabolisms that could take almost anything and metabolize it into nothing. I've still got that, but I don't test it! I've met a lot of actresses, singers, dancers—people who move athletically—who can take whatever their demon is for quite a long time and it doesn't show and then, of course, eventually it does.

(Post) Over the years, the drugs took their toll on Faithfull's life and career. When I wonder what finally got her sober in 1985 her poignant answer is quick, though hesitant.

Faithfull: I think it was—this is very private in a way—I think I was actually going to lose my voice. That was the one thing I couldn't bear. I didn't mind losing everything else—my looks, my life, my child [she lost custody in 1972], my money, my lover—I didn't mind that. But I was not prepared to lose my voice.

(Post) Faithfull is quick to emphasize that, although she followed the twelve-step program rigidly for many years, she does not adhere as strictly now.

Faithfull: I did it for five and a half years and it was amazingly exactly what I needed. I learned so much, but I didn't feel that I wanted to go on with it like that. I'm very, very cautious and very controlled. I couldn't do it forever. I guess when my mother died [in 1990], that was the limit!

(Post) Clearly, singing has been central to Faithfull's experience of joy in life.

Faithfull: My first singing in public was in church. I felt I was singing in front of God. It was wonderful. I still feel like that when I'm performing. I know that there are people there—and I knew that there were people in the church—but I still feel there was another thing I was singing for.

I loved singing, which I still do. I loved performing, which I still do. But the rest of it didn't really interest me. I liked the kind of normal things a little girl would like. I could fuck about with lipstick and things like that, I enjoyed all that. Now, of course, it's a torment. When I go out, I have to look like Marianne Faithfull; I can't just go out. Sometimes, it's just too much.

(Post) Another negative outcome of having her history so well known has been difficulty in obtaining work visas.

Faithfull: Well, I've had tremendous trouble with that. Can you imagine, with my drug history? I've been very, very patient and very, very obedient, which is what you have to do with immigration authorities. You wouldn't believe the shit I've gone through. I never talk about it. I'm not a naturally obedient person, and that's not easy, not even to this day.

(Post) A recurring theme of Faithfull's songs has been that of death, and I am curious about her relationship to that most final of states.

Faithfull: From my maternal side, there's a whole sort of "Viennese Death Culture connection." I'm always poised, artistically, between the two things that pull me: death and love. What makes it difficult for me to stand in my place is that I mustn't let one pull me further along than the other.

(Post) The topic of Faithfull's wrenching cover of "The Ballad of Lucy Jordan"—about a woman who lost her dreams—bounds into the conversation.

Faithfull: You know that she doesn't die? Everybody thinks that. But she's about to jump and they take her away. Let me tell you exactly why I sing that and why I'm interested in it. First off, it's not just love and death. There's sex and hope and fear and all sorts of things. I suppose that dramatization is what I do. That is a most dramatic song.

(Post) When I ask whether Faithfull ever comes close to the edge in order to impart that aura to her music, she replies forcefully,

Faithfull: No no no. Not literally. What I've had to learn, and what I have learned, is how to play with it so that I'm not in any danger. I'm quite safe, I really am. What I have, as a writer, is a much stronger sense of irony. I can do some of the same things, with my songs, but with a slight smile on my face. I don't put myself into personal danger any more. I owe that to myself as a human being.

(Post) Without enumerating Faithfull's low points, which are examined in her autobiography, I want to know what personal quality allowed her to make the transition to survivor.

Faithfull: I don't know what it was. Occasionally somebody tells me something that rings true and sounds really crazy. The last thing I heard—but it sounds so mad I don't know if you want to print it, but I'll tell you anyway because it's a nice little story—was from the Chieftains. I just did three gigs with them in Boston, Washington, and New York. They're good mates of mine, and I see them quite a bit when I'm at home in Ireland. The guy who plays the aolian harp, Derrick Bell, is a particular friend because he's interested in magic and Rosicrucians which I'm interested in.

He told me, completely seriously, I took him completely seriously: "You know what got you through all this? One of the archangels is looking after you!" I thought, "He's absolutely right!" I told him so, and the reason for it is that, when I was confirmed, I took the name Gabriel as my middle name. To this day, I am Marianne Gabriel Faithfull.

(Post) In 1979, Faithfull stunned the public with her scathing, rough *Broken English*, which sported lyrics such as: "Why'd you do it, she said/Why'd you spit on my snatch/Are we out of love now/Is this just a bad patch?" If 1979 was the year in which Marianne Faithfull began to find her adult voice, broken though it sounded, then it would be six more years before she found her sober voice.

Her 1987 *Strange Weather*—Faithfull's first recording after she got clean—was equally stunning, in an altogether different way, with its moody, moving covers. Significantly, Faithfull re-recorded "As Tears Go By" on this album, with her new crackling singing. She would later comment in her autobiography that she truly understood the song for the first time only in her forties.

By 1990, Faithfull was sufficiently encouraged to do a live show in New York, eventually released as *Blazing Away*; interestingly containing her first recording of "Sister Morphine" in twenty-six years. On her 1994 eponymous retrospective, Faithfull used the 1964 version of "As Tears Go By," sung in her original willowy soprano, highlighting the passages etched into her now-gnarled alto.

In 1991, Faithfull decided to write her autobiography. Compiled over three years of increasingly detailed memory, told to writer David Dalton in daily long-distance phone conversations, Faithfull says that she isn't surprised by how much she remembered from so many years ago. She was surprised that the phone connection was easy for her.

Faithfull: I didn't have to worry what my face said. I could just use my voice and my words.

(Post) Faithfull states that what got her into the book project was simple.

Faithfull: Money. I didn't have any high-minded reasons at all. I did feel—and I learned this in the program—that my story was not the most awful of all. I heard so many stories that were much more fascinating, terrifying, horrendous, moving than mine. It really put me into the scale of things. I realized that, although the details were different, the emotions were the same.

I now see that it was a rather good thing for me, but I didn't know that before. I go on trust, you know, and I hope it will be all right. My great fear was that it would be disappointing. I'm not everybody's cup of tea. I sort of accepted it that I don't have to make everybody love me.

(Post) In this vein, Faithfull seems eager to talk more about her album, *A Secret Life*.

Faithfull: This record is the sort of thing I've been trying to do since Broken English which was so strong and so powerful it stood in the way. What my record company wanted was another one of those; they saw me as an angry and bitter person. I think men like that, but this new particular manifestation of the virago no one was comfortable with except for me. So it took this very special person, Angelo, to be able to understand what I was trying to do and to help me to do it.

The connection between the sacred and the profane is there. There's pure love in a lot of the songs. There is a serious streak of masochism in me—it's not as obvious as some sort of mad S/M, it's not that—but I think I am attracted to people who cause me pain. Or I was. I've not let myself fall in love for a long time because I've had enough of this. In my case, I think it's genetic. It's a very bad way to run a life. I've been very, very careful for a long time. If I feel this part of me is going to resurface, then I don't give a shit about sex.

(Post) Faithfull is a superlative actor, a consummate chameleon, and her ultimate mysteries remain cleverly concealed, woven into the music. Though for decades fans have imagined that they knew Faithfull from her work, *The Secret Life* shows that Marianne Faithfull's life is, in fact, a secret.

If Faithfull has indeed triumphed over the labels formerly applied to her, then it is important to know how she now defines herself. She agrees with my listing of her past 'titles' (supplying "debased sex goddess," herself). Charm permeates her remark that her grandson, Oscar, has come along and saved her reputation.

Faithfull: Then they couldn't put me in the same category as before! My friend, Denny, said to me, after I'd done some pictures with my grandson, that I looked like a granny and that he didn't like it. What he meant, I think, was that he didn't want me to stop trying. I am one that if I can find an excuse, I just might take it. I might just walk away, one day. I suppose the thing that keeps me going is making a living.

(Post) Two other facts are eminently clear: first, rough though her voice may be, it has been enriched by her journey and, second, Marianne Faithfull is whole and healthy.

Faithfull: At this moment, I am very much what I want to be: a working artist. When I was young, I don't think I wanted to be a working artist. I wanted to be a great star and a very powerful person and such a beautiful woman that no one could stand up to me! I think I've had everything I've wanted. There's loads of things I still want. True love, more grandchildren, an education.

Photo: Firooz Zahedi

(Post) Marianne Faithfull left school over thirty years ago, when "As Tears Go By" took off, and is currently considering returning.

Faithfull: I don't regret what happened. I loved it all in an amazing way. I learned how to do it by doing it. I do miss the luxury of being able to try things out in a safe way and taking chances in rehearsal or in school that you can't do when you're in public. A friend of mine went back to school and has been telling me that he needed to practice his mind, to put his mind into a discipline. I can feel that I need that. I think my lot wouldn't mind if I disappeared for a year. When I was younger, I would have been afraid. But I took years out to do drugs and other stupid things.

(Post) I point out that, in 1996, Faithfull will be fifty.

Faithfull: I guess I will. Then I really have earned a sabbatical.

DISCOGRAPHY

"As Tears Go By" (single, Decca, 1964); "Come and Stay With Me" (single, Decca, 1964); *Come My Way* (Decca, 1965); *Go Away From My World* (Decca, 1965); *Marianne Faithfull* (Decca, 1965); *North Country Maid* (Decca, 1966); *Faithfull Forever* (Decca, 1966); *Love in a Mist* (Decca, 1967); "Sister Morphine" (single, Decca, 1967); *The World of Marianne Faithfull* (Decca, 1969); *Greatest Hits* (ABCKO, 1969); *Dreamin' My Dreams* (NEMS, 1977); *Faithless* (NEMS, 1978); *Broken English* (Island, 1979); *Dangerous Acquaintances* (Island, 1981); *As Tears Go By* (hits, Decca, 1981); *A Child's Adventure* (Island, 1983); *Summer Nights* (Decca, 1984); *Rich Kid Blues* (Castle, 1985); *Strange Weather* (Island, 1987); *Blazing Away* (Island, 1990); *Faithfull: A Collection of Her Best Recordings* (Island, 1994); *A Secret Life* (Island, 1995); *20th Century Blues*(RCA Victor, 1997).

BOOK

Faithfull: An Autobiography (Little, Brown, and Co, 1994).

MARGIE ADAM
feminist musician and cultural interpreter

Margie Adam's name conjures up her passionate piano work, strong opinions, personal songs, and the forceful style that she has always brought to bear on issues such as women's self-empowerment, lesbians, love. Newer Women's Music artists (Jamie Anderson, Lucie Blue Tremblay, Ani DiFranco) and the infrastructure of the current lesbian community owe a karmic debt to Margie Adam: she helped to define notions about Women's Music as art, as a political force, and as an industry.

Margie gave not only of herself, but gave all of herself; in 1984, after eleven years of nonstop musical and political effort, that self was depleted. It was only at the end of a hiatus (intended as one year, in actuality seven) that she began to write again. On October 19, 1991, in East Lansing, Michigan, Margie Adam made the most eagerly-awaited comeback in the herstory of the feminist cultural network, subsequently releasing *Another Place* (1993) and *Soon and Again* (1996).

This solo piano release shimmers with wisdom and whole views, demonstrating chordings and progressions more complex and subtle than on any of Adam's previous works. There is also reclaiming happening here, with an instrumental version of Adam's "Tender Lady," first brought to recognition twenty years ago by Cris Williamson.

Post: How did you decide to take a break from performing?

Margie Adam: I belonged to a community of women who were committed to this radical vision of women's culture and the translation of feminist values through music to the world.

Things changed. It became less popular to be a feminist. We moved into a conservative period. Economics got shaky. Women grew older and started to think twice about what it meant to be still sleeping on the floor.

There began to be this ambivalent tone connected with discussions of women's music. Is women's music dead? Where's women's music going? Concerts got to be more about the anti-nuke movement, Central America, animal rights. As audiences heard less of the experience of women loving women from the stage, they began to drift away from women's music events. Ironically, by the time a critical number of influential women performers were ready to expand into the mainstream, Women's Music had been identified as separatist by the media gatekeepers. It was then impossible to convey the truth of our diversity and brilliance as a musical phenomenon because the media relentlessly defined the music as anti-male, folk/protest, and marginal.

What happened for me by 1984 was that I was lonely. Even with sister musicians with whom I still felt a kinship, there was no time to come together; we were all moving so fast from city to city. I felt like the focus had shifted from the original feminist

Photo: Irene Young

vision, and the vision had dimmed. I am reminded of Zimmer Bradley's "The Mists of Avalon:" as people stopped believing in the power of the music, access to that power began to diminish. I would never say that I burned out. I ran out of fuel.

I had been looking for my sisters, feeling more and more isolated. When I came off the road, I was in need of a life beyond my work. I allowed myself to be wrapped up by the comfort of women's arms. I needed to come down from being 'on' all the time. I had lived twenty-four hours a day being vigilant about what needed to be done, what I needed to talk about on stage, what the latest issue was that I needed to incorporate into my performance and speaking.

In 1973, a voice inside me had said, 'Take a year off, focus on the music.' In 1984, the same voice said, 'Get off the road, Marg. Take a year off.' At the end of a year, I had no interest in playing or singing. By the end of the second year, I was saying, 'Until I write new material, I'm not going to perform.'

I let the time play itself out. I have been personally involved in recovery from alcoholism since 1978, so another way of being held in women's arms after I came off the road was to become active in this community. I spent the next years working with other women in recovery. I went back to college to get a counselling credential and, finally, took a job in the field.

Almost immediately, it became clear to me that I did not belong in an office working nine to five. My Muse began to call my name more and more loudly. The wonderful woman with whom I was studying piano at the time talked me into playing in her student recital. My first public performance in six years, and I was terrified as I stumbled through the Gershwin Preludes in front of fifteen sets of parents and their small children.

Then, I turned to the audience and, reflexively, rested my hand up on the piano lid as I introduced my own piece, "Naked Keys." When I made those two movements, something shifted at my core, like a creature waking up after a long sleep. I played "Naked Keys" flawlessly; it's in my molecules. Within the next two months, I wrote my first new song.

Post: How was it to start again with a new style of writing and performing?

Adam: I felt relieved to know that I don't have to be all things to all women. My work in the past was to translate feminist principles into a language that as many people as possible might find accessible so they could find a way into the feminist experience. Today I am not so focused on making my music accessible that I am willing to compromise simple truths about who I am and what I think. So, of course, I'm much more relaxed as a performer; I am simply more myself.

Post: How did you originally connect with the Women's Music scene?

Adam: I was reeled in and organized by the women's community. I was mentored; Jeanne Cordova, who ran The Lesbian Tide and heard me perform at Kate Millett's Women's Festival in Sacramento in 1973, encouraged me to write more of my experience as a woman than just my love life. It was a time where the movement of women at all levels, politically, culturally, socially, was so intense that there was a shimmer everywhere. If you could notice it, you were touched by it and could participate in it.

I fell in love with a woman, several women, who played and sang songs that I could have written. I could never really separate the passion I felt from the music from the passion I felt for women who made that music. That's certainly the story of early Women's Music, that we fell into each other's arms, and we fell into each other's music; it was always a race to see which one was going to happen first.

Post: What happened to that terrific energy and idealism?

Adam: That first wave of Women's Music was a tidal wave. Music was an incredibly attractive force, and we all had at least intuitive feminist politics. Some of us were performers and entertainers; I was initially more of a songwriter. But we all had this spiritual hunger and were pulled along by this higher organizational principle, with a larger vision, which was feminism with an emphasis on woman-loving. We were women playing music together, and for a time we tapped a tremendous kind of collective Women's Musical unconscious.

Despite our passion and determination, we all arrived at this moment from lifetimes surrounded by raging anti-woman sentiment and anti-lesbian attitude. Each of us had been conditioned to the political realities of men, and each of us inherited the legacies of woman-hating, internalized homophobia.

Those of us who were involved in the early Women's Music movement were trying to build a true woman-loving community without ever having seen such a thing, and we couldn't move far enough beyond our conditioned impulses and experiences. We held each other to the standards of our dreams, and our demands of each other carried into our work.

In the past few years, I have looked into the faces of some of my musician sisters, and I have seen heartbreak, bitterness, betrayal, and disappointment. We were expected to heal all the other women, and to be coming from a healed place. There was no room for ambition in the 1970s in Women's Music, and we were ambitious. The truth is that those of us who were lifted up as leaders in Women's Music were way over our heads. We were unfinished human beings, not unworthy failures. Feminist expectations were overlaid upon our struggles with alcohol, drugs, and codependency, upon our greed and cheap motives, upon our petty personality conflicts. We went as far as we could. And given that we started with little more than the passion of loving women, we travelled an extraordinary distance.

Post: You were part of the lesbian revolution. How would you describe the women's lesbian community to which you returned seven years later?

Adam: In general, the activist women's community I knew has disintegrated. Many women who were active seem to be asleep now. And those sisters who aren't asleep don't identify with something called 'Women's Music.'

Straight feminists like Susan Faludi discount feminist lesbian participation and contribution to the movement. At the same time, media creations like Camille Paglia claim to be feminists and completely distort the fundamental truths of feminist theory and practice. Some feminist lesbian activists have chosen to shift their focus to 'gay' politics: I have observed lesbians now focusing on AIDS and gays in the military. I don't see gay men, in general, supporting feminist and lesbian concerns. We have to get real about this and understand that no one is going to carry our issues forward if we don't. No one is going to validate and disseminate our culture if we don't.

There are many newcomers to the Women's Music network, but most of the performers don't relate to Women's Music and don't use the term. I observe that they use the network but simultaneously ridicule it. Other musicians refuse to acknowledge their roots of support in the network once they experience success overground. I am disgusted by this behavior. I'm thinking in particular here of Tracy Chapman, the Indigo Girls, and Melissa Etheridge.

Imagine if these women all said in interviews on MTV and at the Grammy's: 'I'm proud to be associated with the movement and network called "Women's Music" that provided me with tremendous support while I was learning how to be a musician and performer. Thanks to all the women who gave me my first breaks!'

I am unapologetically passionate about the history from which I come. Unfortunately, many women musicians who are newer to the scene have absorbed prevalent misunderstandings of what Women's Music is. They repeat the definition that it is only folk, white, middle class protest music meant for only a particular type of lesbian audience. They have come to believe that 'Women's Music' is something other than what they are doing, something of limited quality and interest. I am sad and angry to witness our history revised and distorted.

What is operating here is persistent misogyny and internalized homophobia. Women and lesbians, in particular, still have difficulty honoring our own accomplishments. If we are not celebrating our own history, no one else will. It is up to those of us in Women's Music to pass the history on to the women who are coming up and who carry those misconceptions.

The untruths discount the quality of who we have been and what we have been doing in Women's Music all along. They feed the status quo version of reality that asserts that women without men don't do it right. Women together do it small. Lesbians have nothing of significance to say to anyone except other lesbians. Those of us who know what women's culture really is have a responsibility to speak up and be insistent that the information gets out.

It is frustrating to me that Women's Music has increasingly been defined by the music and politics of only the three or four more prominent musicians. So many important women have been left out of the story that is being told about Women's Music. This reductive approach to the unwieldiness of our true diversity completely obscures the powerful impact this music has had on feminism and on the music business. Ask yourself who it serves to reduce a nation-wide movement—which included and still includes women of color, working class women, disabled, straight, old women who play and sing jazz, folk pop, rock and roll, classical, punk, international, new age, gospel music—to the careers of four white, middle class, temporarily able-bodied, college-graduated, pop/folk singer-songwriters?

Post: What is Women's Music now?

Adam: The Women's Music that I grew up in, the Women's Music that changed my life, still lives in my heart and in history, but there is a new generation, younger women, and the network has evolved. I find it useful to compare the Women's Music movement and the Civil Rights movement. The Civil Rights movement—as a series of events and personalities—exists in its most concentrated form in a period of time in the 1960s. But the Civil Rights movement did not end after the marches, the boycotts, Martin Luther King's assassination. The movement continues to manifest itself today because the work is not done.

The same is true of Women's Music. As a series of events and personalities that helped change how women felt about themselves, about each other, and about the world, Women's Music appeared in its most intense form during a ten-year period between 1973 and 1983. But the work of the Women's Liberation Movement is not done. So, Women's Music lives on in the artistry and feminist principles of certain women in the business of music.

One of the things that is different about the women's music network today is that there is a higher level of consciousness about how diverse we are. Even though there is so much defensiveness and fear and ridicule associated with this beautiful term 'Women's Music,' producers are still able to pull off events like the National Women's Music Festival and Michigan Womyn's Music Festival which demonstrate to new audiences the extraordinary quality and complexity of Women's Music today. In the 1970s our mistake was in not recognizing how much power resided in the label 'Women's Music.' Instead, too often, the focus was on individual record companies and particular performers.

A bunch of musicians out of Seattle got picked up by a promoter who called what they did 'grunge rock,' and this organizing principle allowed several bands to get national exposure. The term 'Riot Grrrls' also functioned as an organizing principle as well to get media attention and, therefore, access to audiences. We could have an MTV special all to ourselves just like gay comics had on HBO if we were willing to claim the term and the tremendous power sitting there in it.

Women must claim what is unique and central to the power of what we do. It is our continued self-hatred that separates us from that power. Why do people unfamiliar with the music in the category 'Women's Music' get so worked up when I use that phrase to identify what I do? I can't tell you how many people over the years have cautioned me not to 'limit' my career by calling my music 'Women's Music.' What is it about the word "women" that is limiting? Do they mean to suggest men would not enjoy music written and performed by women? Why do they assume that the music is protest-oriented and folk-based simply because it is called 'Women's Music'?

I think the fact that the term 'Women's Music' is still so charged after twenty years suggests we should we waving it over our heads in celebration not stepping away from it in fear. This is a controversial idea as well as an organizing principle—whatever is buried in the phrase gets people going. We need to pay attention to this! If we could harness this charged energy by organizing our promotion of artists' touring and festival productions around it, we could get the music out through and beyond the media gate-keepers and directly to an audience who, I have no doubt, would swoon over the extraordinary beauty and power of the music itself.

DISCOGRAPHY

Songwriter (Pleiades, 1976); *Naked Keys* (Pleiades, 1980); *We Shall Go Forth!* (Pleiades, 1982); *Here is a Love Song* (Pleiades, 1983); *Take Hands* (Watershed Foundation, 1985); *The Best of Margie Adam* (Olivia, 1990); *Another Place* (Pleiades, 1993); *Soon and Again* (Pleiades, 1996).

MARY McCASLIN
here's to the new days, your new destiny

"I just stepped off a ghost train, it's never coming back," sings Mary McCaslin in "Ghost Train," from her stunning album, *Broken Promises* (1992). In the thirteen years since McCaslin last recorded fresh material, admirers of her supple, open-tuning acoustic guitar work and Western-myth-meets-Western-reality focus have mourned and wondered at her absence from touring.

Broken Promises not only answers that question but reestablishes McCaslin—the artist of the 1970s folk circuit and half of the Ringer-McCaslin duo of the same era—as a sage writer, warmly expressive singer, and exquisite player.

Her new stance is one of seeking answers instead of merely observing. Her new role, that of an artist who has loved, lost, and grown, is reflected in *Broken Promises'* titles: "You're Gone;" her cover of Jim Ringer's "If I Don't Miss You," tinged with righteous anger; "The Abyss;" and "The Old Days," with its mid-song transformation into a celebration of The New Days.

The passage of time is also manifest in McCaslin's singing. Always one to make challenging vocal leaps across multiple notes, McCaslin has continued to embrace her upper register, unlike several over-forty female contemporaries. McCaslin's current high end conveys a unique vulnerability, while the alto reaches of her range demonstrate a new authoritative resonance.

Finally, by delving into uncharted introspection, McCaslin allows listeners the pleasure of knowing a life. "Once Again" captures the coexisting exhilaration and tentativeness of love; "Someone Who Looks Like Me" poignantly addresses unresolved concerns about her own adoption.

McCaslin spent her primary years in Indiana, surrounded by the 1940s Swing to which her parents listened. When she was six, her family moved to southern California. McCaslin expected cowboys and ranches; hopeful expanses of open plain; rugged beauty of unexplored and unsullied territory: a culture of courage. What McCaslin got was the "stucco suburb forest" (quote from her early-70s classic, "Way Out West") of Redondo Beach. Those contrasting expectations and realities have influenced all of her work.

Because a child's wisdom generated the images, the West that McCaslin conjures is devoid of evil and untouched by racist, proprietary, or imperialist motives. McCaslin's West is filled with dreams as gentle as the western wind, as fluid as the tall grasses, as colorful and soothing as earth tones, as bright as the stars illuminating the night sky, as free as the "wild flying things" which she evokes in her mid-1970s classic, "Prairie in the Sky." McCaslin acknowledges the enduring echoes of those early expectations.

Mary McCaslin: All the years that Jim and I travelled back East, I think that people believed that we were going to ride up on horseback. I wrote out of frustration because I always wanted to live someplace where I could have horses, and I never did. The songs mainly deal with the fact that I'm disappointed with the West I grew up in. In fact, if I had had a horse as a kid, I probably wouldn't have written all those songs.

(Post) In grade school, McCaslin first heard country tunes: a transforming musical experience.

McCaslin: Marty Robbins came out with "El Paso." It changed my life. It was a great western ballad; "Big Iron" came out after that, and I liked it even better. I remember thinking, "This is great! This song is number one on all the radio stations!" After that, within a year or two, I realized that I wanted to be a musician, that I wanted to sing and play guitar.

(Post) McCaslin identified with the clean, open lines of country until the protest movement gave her another transforming musical experience. When Joan Baez and Peter, Paul, and Mary entered McCaslin's world, she knew that she wanted to play folk.

McCaslin: I'm very guitar oriented. Most country singers just strum the guitar for rhythm; it's almost like a prop. I like playing. I figured that with folk, the guitar parts were more interesting. On "El Paso," what stands out is the session player, Grady Martin, doing those beautiful Spanish licks.

(Post) McCaslin saved her money for her first guitar, bought when she was fifteen ("It was a Stella, and it had terrible action. It retarded my playing for years."). McCaslin taught herself to play from the accompanying instruction book. Then McCaslin had a third transforming musical experience.

McCaslin: Joni Mitchell came along. I was listening to her and listening to her. I'm thinking, "What is she doing?" And I realized, "I know what she's doing. She's in an open G tuning." I realized that I could play in open tunings too. It opened a whole world.

(Post) Although McCaslin's mother had arranged a phone company job for her daughter, capping thirteen years in Catholic school, McCaslin persevered with her music, getting involved in the Los Angeles folk-rock scene. Her first gig, at the age of eighteen, was at a small coffeehouse in Orange County, The Paradox.
    Barnaby Records became interested in McCaslin's music and recorded *Goodnight Everybody* (1969), all covers. She was twenty-two. Though she didn't think of herself as a songwriter, McCaslin's songs began to come. "Way Out West" was her second composition; "The Dealers" came soon thereafter.

McCaslin: Writing songs, for me, is like having a tug of war with an elephant. I am not a natural songwriter at all. The first one I wrote I haven't done in years; I don't remember anything about it.

(Post) A Capitol single followed, then the three Philo albums which built her reputation: *Way Out West* (1973), *Prairie In The Sky* (1975), and *Old Friends* (1977). Clearly, McCaslin had an uncanny ability to frame contemporary dynamics in terms of cowpokes, rounders, ladies, and intriguing, romantic outlaws. The straightforward lyrics set against hypnotic minor-key picked guitar refrains made McCaslin's writing haunting and irresistible.

McCaslin also became quickly known for evocative self-harmony and for tasteful, spare added instrumentation, highlighting her hammers-on, pull-offs, and memorable riffs.

McCaslin: I don't want the guitar drowned out. The other musicians have to follow me. Everything is going to be arranged around my guitar playing. It's very common for me to play chords where I don't use the third note: if it's a C chord, I don't use the E note, only the C and G, the 1 and the 5. Well, then, I don't want someone else to come along and install it for me. It's not there because I don't want it there.

(Post) By the early 1980s, McCaslin's career, intertwined with Jim Ringer's, took a difficult turn. McCaslin and Ringer had toured together for many years, married, played on each other's albums, and done *The Bramble And The Rose* (1978).

McCaslin: Jim was very ill. We were playing music, and we travelled from time to time, but it just fell apart. You can get to a point where it takes too much energy and effort to fight all that you have to fight to get to do something. It becomes not worth it. There was no way to try to keep my career going because his had stopped. During the period from 1981 to 1989, when we split up, I wrote maybe three songs.

(Post) Again solo, McCaslin considered resuming her career.

McCaslin: I thought, maybe I'll give it a try. It has amazed me how long it has taken me to get even partially back to how it was.

(Post) A connection with a friend led McCaslin to an encouraging gig in Santa Cruz. Fans asked her to make her music available on compact disc format; McCaslin thought to reissue *The Best Of Mary McCaslin* (1984) on CD. Rounder had a better idea: release a new compilation. *The Best Of Mary McCaslin/Things We Said Today* (1992), spanning McCaslin's seminal Philo recordings, was the result.

McCaslin: It has been a tremendous help getting me work.

(Post) Even before *Things We Said Today*, McCaslin's muse had returned.

Photo: Stuart Brinin

McCaslin: I had been writing songs, writing songs, writing songs. I wrote the bulk of the songs within a year of when I split up with Jim [who died in 1992]. I knew I wanted to do another album, and I knew I wanted to call it Broken Promises.

(Post) It may be her best recording. From "Baggage Song," the last cut on *Broken Promises:* "It seems I've travelled days and days/To finally reach my journey's end/After all these weeks and hours/I wondered if we'd meet again./The only thing that keeps me going/Is how your love makes me feel whole/And the hope our time together/Will start the healing of my soul."

DISCOGRAPHY

Goodnight Everybody (Barnaby Records, 1969); *Way Out West* (Philo, 1973); *Prairie In The Sky* (Philo, 1975); *Old Friends* (Philo, 1977); *The Bramble And The Rose* with Jim Ringer (Philo, 1978); *Sunny California* (Mercury, 1979); *A Life And A Time* (Flying Fish, 1981); *The Best Of Mary McCaslin/The Things We Said Today* (Rounder/Philo, 1992); *Broken Promises* (Philo, 1992).

MIMI FOX
one of very few female jazz guitarists

Mimi "Fast Fingers" Fox is one of a very few established female jazz guitarists (Emily Remler, Mary Osborne are two others). Though Fox has developed a wide following in the Women's Music circuit, her passion and technical excellence have also graced the albums and performances of mainstream jazz luminaries such as Linda Tillery, Faye Carol, Bruce Forman, and Herb Ellis.

Primarily self-taught, Fox focused early on folk styles until she heard John Coltrane's seminal *Giant Steps* at age fourteen.

Mimi Fox: It transformed my life. I discovered a whole other world of improvisational music called jazz.

(Post) Fox cites a plethora of early influences: Aretha Franklin, Dixieland, jazz traditionals. Some of those traditions emerge in Fox's evocative interpretations of jazz with swing stylings, blues, Latin, and her forte, bebop.

Formerly best known as the nimble-fingered bebop guitarist who played on Robin Flower's *Green Sneakers* and on June Millington's *One World, One Heart*, Fox also offers original work as compelling as her fine interpretations. After performing in the San Francisco Bay Area jazz scene for a decade, Fox finally succumbed to requests for an album, releasing *Against The Grain*, to great acclaim in 1987.

One of the strengths of that album is its ability to make jazz accessible. Even for listeners who believe that they don't like jazz, or for listeners who aren't familiar with the standards and language of jazz, *Against The Grain* would be an excellent introduction. It features piercing guitar work, inspired orchestration, and a delightful vocal duet with Rhiannon.

Against The Grain established Fox's playful mastery of standards and medleys, convincing jazz lovers, awing younger fans ("They like it when you play fast"), even winning some pop listeners.

Fox: One of the things I love about jazz is how it cuts across all barriers.

(Post) Fox followed up with *Live* (1991), which took a different turn. Unlike *Against The Grain*, which featured Fox solo with her guitar, *Live* brought together a taut quintet to highlight and interact with Fox's guitar lines and riffs.

Though her interpretation of Cole Porter's "Night and Day" is solid, it is Fox's inspired originals which sparkle most brightly on *Live*. "Judy's Song" is sweetly intimate; "Blues for Les" has a captivating central riff. Throughout, Fox's guitar sings so proudly that she can surrender to the supporting musicians while never losing her

central message. *Live* shows the explosive power of an improvisational approach by a confident artist surrounded by empathic players.

Fox: I love the incredible interchange with a live audience, in a flesh-and-blood, do-or-die performance. Even if I play standards, or my own pieces five hundred times times, they are never the same.

(Post) Most summers, Fox can be found teaching at the National Guitar Workshop in Los Angeles, where she is usually the only woman. This year, she'll be spending some time doing what mainstream jazz artists commonly do: performing in Europe. Having met a faculty member of the University in Freiburg, Germany, Fox's recordings impressed their committee sufficiently that her application to be artist-in-residence during the academic year 1995-1996 was accepted.

Fox: It's great. I'll get to teach two days a week, have free room and board, and be set up to do a concert tour through France and Switzerland.

DISCOGRAPHY

Against The Grain (Catero Records, 1987); *Live* (TuSco, 1991); *Turtle Logic* (Monarch, 1995).

MOE TUCKER
a velvet vagrant or the birth of housewife punk

Crude defiance; droning, dissonant rhythms; horror stories of drugs, sado-masochism, obsession. The inevitable netherworld conjured by the Velvet Underground has persisted musically and in personal legend long after the band's dissolution; the tortured theatre has found burned-out mellowness in the contemporary work of Lou Reed and John Cale. Surprise: it is the drummer who has infused the themes of the quintessential pre-grunge grunge with a truly human element.

Through all the Velvets' extremes, Maureen ("Moe") Tucker provided the beat; some would say also the steadiness:

Moe Tucker: I was the least crazy.

(Post) Though she contributed writing and some singing to *The Velvet Underground and Nico* (1967), *White Light White Heat* (1968), *The Velvet Underground* (1969) and *Loaded* (1971), Tucker's face does not appear on any of those album covers, and devotees of the Velvets and of the Velvets' numerous musical spawn don't recall any woman other than Nico, who split after the first record.

Despite the counterculture interest roused during the band's heyday and the establishment accolades accorded more recently, Tucker did not consider herself a musician until two years ago. Tucker was unaware of other women drummers playing when she started with Velvet Underground, though she readily cites Bo Diddley's guitarist, a woman, as her peer, but assures me that she never felt misogynous treatment any time during her career.

Tucker's drumming: intentionally primal, the reviewers said; untutored, Tucker would say. When she was nineteen, Moe Tucker loved the drumming of Charlie Watts so much that she bought a single snare: all she could afford. Soon after, Mrs. Tucker added to her daughter's kit with a bass drum, floor tom, and cymbals from the local Pennysaver.

Tucker: They looked like they had been run over with a truck.

(Post) When Tucker's childhood friend Sterling Morrison went to Syracuse University and met Lou Reed, Moe was brought into the fledgling group as a temporary fill-in. Through the band's rise and fall, Tucker was the only one who consistently worked a day job, and was also not consistently paid.

Tucker: I was living at home and I didn't need rent money. All I really needed was cigarettes.

(Post) Though she admits she cadged the occasional five dollars from Andy Warhol for gas, Moe Tucker wanted to quit after John Cale and Lou Reed left.

Tucker: It was no longer the Velvet Underground.

(Post) However, she stayed for an already-booked European tour out of concern that the audience would be disappointed to have so few original members.

Tucker: I thought that was kind of shitty so I went on the tour and quit when it was over.

(Post) Tucker continued to work day jobs until her marriage in '75 or '76—she is unclear about the date—then tended an ever-growing brood. In 1981 she was inadvertently launched back into music: When a tune previously recorded with Jonathan Richman was about to be released, Tucker did "Around and Around" for the B-side. Enjoying the process, on her home 4-track, Tucker decided to release her own single, recording "Will You Still Love Me Tomorrow?" for the A-side.

Tucker couldn't give up music; in between diapers and housework, she recorded *Playin' Possum* in her living room, the same year. Following her divorce, Tucker found herself penniless and with five children; relocating to Georgia, where her mother had retired, seemed a logical temporary option. Tucker still lives in that small town, and bemoans the smallness, the heat.

Tucker: They don't know anything about the Velvets. I don't mind the town; what I mind is that it's too far from anything.

(Post) In 1985, Tucker released an ep, *Moejadkatebarry*, then *Life in Exile After Abdication* two years later. In 1989, able to tour again, Tucker left her offspring in the care of their grandmother.

Tucker: I realized that I could make more doing a six-week tour in Europe than all year at WalMart.

(Post) It turned out that six weeks was too long to be apart from her children and too long for Tucker's mother to babysit; recent tours have been limited to four weeks. When Tucker returned home it was impossible for her to resume at WalMart; small towns don't take kindly to comings and goings. Tucker has since supported herself with royalties and tour earnings.

Since Tucker had toured as the opening band for Lou Reed in 1989 and with Reed's band the following year, she was able to call upon him, Cale, and Sterling Morrison to add good noise (her phrase) to her two most recent releases. "It worked out," was how she put it; her life seems to do that.

In 1991, Tucker released *I Spent A Week There The Other Night*, featuring observations that the world is crazy ("stayin' put"), that work sucks ("that's bad" and "s.o.s."), and that drugs are bad for children ("fired up"). With Morrison's sinuous 12-string, Reed's sharp lead guitar, and Cale's punchy viola and synthesizer, the songs are musically reminiscent of the Velvet Underground but create an entirely different

Photo: Kristine Larsen

ambiance, a melding of Velvet motifs and the gritty reality of the common person's everyday life.

Like her drumming—which Tucker did not do on this album or on *Dogs*—Tucker's lyrics are clean and compelling—"Why the hell would I clean the tub?" — and her songs filled with surprising revelations ("too shy").

Most recently, Tucker released *Dogs Under Stress*, intense and even more personal, reprising similar topics. Throughout, Tucker is aware of the unpleasant necessity of working.

Tucker: The message is that everybody works and it really sucks because you never get enough money to do what you want, or even need.

(Post) Elsewhere, it is clear that Tucker's discomfort with her town transcends the weather or geography. "Saturday night" pokes fun at the weekend habits of her neighbors spending all their money at the Dairy Queen. Another tune, "me myself and i" is about hypocrites, Tucker explains:

Tucker: The people I see rush to church every Sunday, the rest of the week they're calling people "niggers."

(Post) I ask her why she doesn't move away; she would love to, she answers, she misses her native New York, but she wouldn't be able to support her family there.

Some of the songs in this album reveal Tucker's most personal concerns. In "i don't understand," Tucker tries to explain the realities of armed children and senseless violence, and is unable to. One solution is escape: in "train," a trip to ny (her spelling) sets Tucker free; in "i wanna," Tucker acknowledges her own fear and, perhaps, some of the difficulties of being a woman in this world: "i wanna run, but first i gotta walk/i wanna pitch, but they always call a balk/i wanna paddle, but there aren't any oars/i wanna ride but i'm afraid of the horse."

I ask Tucker if she is pleased with *Dogs*.

Tucker: I like it very much, but I don't try to do anything but be honest. It's ten songs, that's all.

(Post) Though Moe Tucker is best known for her drumming and occasional electric bass work for the Velvets, her recent recordings have featured her on rhythm guitar, which she plays fast and, well, rhythmically, like drums. Along the way, Tucker also taught herself the alto saxophone, though she shrugs off my praise of her musicality just as she shies away from bearing the labels of avant-garde pioneer, woman role model, or even solid citizen for having raised five children and not shirked from parental and other responsibilities. Disparaging of her own singing, resistant to my attempts to find metaphors in her lyrics and titles (I tried to make a point of the fact that *Playin'Possum* is the only one of her albums to have been recorded during her marriage), Tucker concludes:

Tucker: It's always my best effort. I just learned it as I went along.

(Post) No nonsense, no games, no narcissism. She seems pleased when I tell her that her drumming reminds me of Watts': simple, unpretentious, riveting, even soulful. She seems sincere in her praise for Watts' successes, for the successes of her former bandmates.

Tucker has just turned fifty, and she acknowledges this as a turning point, though into what she is uncertain. She is looking forward to producing more of other people's albums. For fun, she says, she goes on tour, then her voice softens as she describes the tactics employed by her children to accompany her: "Ma, can I come and sell T-shirts?," she imitates. The tour is too tightly budgeted and too financially important to support the needs of even one small additional member, so Tucker goes alone.

Moe Tucker got started in drumming because it was fun for her; she wonders why more women don't play music, though acknowledges that more women are playing than in the late '60s. She is gratified that her current fans are young; years ago, she thought to herself, "If they had turned out to be forty-year-old farts who are there to see this aging Velvet, then I guess this will be my last tour."

DISCOGRAPHY

With The Velvet Underground: *The Velvet Underground And Nico* (1967); *White Light White Heat* (1968); *The Velvet Underground* (1969); *Loaded* (1971).

Maureen Tucker: *Playin' Possum* (Trash Records, 1981); *Moejadkatebarry* (50 Skidillion Watts, 1985); *Life In Exile After Abdication* (50 Skidillion Watts, 1987); *I Spent A Week There The Other Night* (Rough Trade, 1991); *Dogs Under Stress* (Sky Records, 1994).

For further recordings, see Moe Tucker's web page at http://members.aol.com/olandem/tucker.html

PATTY LARKIN
busker to big time

Patty Larkin could be accurately described as a folk philosopher, a serious songwriter with a sense of humor, a topical ironic poet. Apt though it would be, such a description would not pay tribute to the finesse of her guitar work (acoustic, electric, and slide) or to her ultimate optimism amid ruthless observation and relentless questioning. Patty Larkin is a songwriter; one who pays as much attention to the detail of her riffs as to the detail of her lyrics.

Patty Larkin was born in Iowa, raised in Wisconsin.

Patty Larkin: It makes a difference; there's more water in Wisconsin!

(Post) – and cut her folk teeth in Oregon, her jazz teeth in Boston. Though her sister Kathleen played classical piano, and Larkin took four years of piano lessons, her family produced a guitar for young Patty when it was hinted that such an instrument would be welcomed.

Larkin: My uncle brought it back from Mexico. It was a pretty cheap little thing.

(Post) Unhindered by the techno-poor instrumental origins of her music, Larkin devoted many a teenage hour to honing her craft in the solace of her bedroom. Moreover, since Larkin's mother was a painter, her father an amateur player, and both of her grandmothers keyboardists, Larkin received much positive reinforcement.

Larkin: I was encouraged to want to be musical, and I was encouraged to be musical.

(Post) Despite her early inclinations toward and encouragement in music, Larkin did not imagine that she would grow up to play music professionally, or to be able to support herself with her playing, as she has done for the past twelve years.

Larkin: I wanted to be a nun.

(Post) At a small college in the midwest, advised that the school did not offer a Guitar major, Larkin was discouraged from pursuing music seriously.

Larkin: I really wanted to know how to approach studying music, and this guy laughed and said that, if I had talent, I could study with Segovia, and, if I had money, I could study at Berklee.

(Post) Larkin, following an interlude studying in Oregon, eventually wound up in Boston, busking in Harvard Square, teaching at Cambridge Music and building up her chops at the Berklee College of Music.

Larkin's first gig netted her five dollars. What she remembers is that she wanted to give it back. What she also remembers, equally painfully, is how nervous she felt.

Larkin: I had to write everything down that I was going to say between songs. Even after that, whenever I had a gig, I couldn't practice all week.

(Post) My first experience of Patty Larkin's music was at a Boston women's bar in the early 1980s, when she had already begun to implement the witty, intellectual humor which she currently brings to her stage performances. Her intros and patter are such an effective complement to Larkin's serious musicianship that the diva of comic-serious songs, Christine Lavin, asked Larkin to tour with the "Buy Me, Take Me, Don't Mess My Hair" Tour (also including Sally Fingerett and Megan McDonough). Larkin asserts how much she gets from touring with other musicians/songwriters, as she has also done with On A Winter's Night, another of Lavin's projects.

On live performances:

Larkin: I still get scared, and I think that's healthy about live performance. The best thing I can do is to be in the present, to focus on the songs, to breathe and to have air in them.

(Post) Her idea of the most difficult audiences: peer musicians.

Larkin: You know that they know if it's bullshit.

(Post) It was through the smoky, noisy rock clubs, though, that Larkin learned about stage charisma.

Larkin: Those audiences weren't drinking espresso and listening to the finer points of my lyrics. I wanted someone to listen to the finer points of my lyrics, but those gigs did give me confidence. Then, I went back to acoustic music.

(Post) The folk label Philo/Rounder appreciated Larkin's multiple gifts and signed her. *Step Into The Light* (1985), *I'm Fine* (1987), and *Live In The Square* (1990) soon followed. With the backing of Philo/Rounder, Larkin's popularity spread rapidly through New England.

Larkin's more recent releases *Tango*, (1991) and *Angels Running* (1993) have received wider distribution, thanks to the extensive marketing base of her new label, High Street/Windham Hill. Larkin is fortunate that the new AAA radio format (Adult Alternative Album) provides a nice fit with her musicality and that her original audience has grown with her.

Larkin has performed at the Michigan Womyn's Music Festival, though she is much more a multi-audience, mainstream performer who is open to women audiences.

Larkin: My goal was to develop as a songwriter and to get more airplay. I have done that.

Photo: Jana Leon

(Post) These days Larkin is trying, gently, to whittle down the number of gigs per year from the super-busy one hundred-thirty-plus to a more manageable schedule.

Larkin: It's a matter of my sanity. It's my choice.

(Post) Larkin seems startled when I tell her that she is considered by many in the music industry to be one of the most hard-working performers around, in all genres, both genders.

Larkin: Actually, I enjoying playing; it's my job.

(Post) Patty Larkin is talented and famous. No one would dispute her technical expertise in folk, rock, or jazz modes. Few would challenge her ability as a songwriter. Yet, Larkin remains somehow unaffected by the aggrandizing media furor surrounding her career. About her skill playing electric guitar, she comments:

Larkin: I consider that I am still working on the electric guitar. I am still trying to understand tonal differences and what I like. It gives me a new place to go, musically, and I am just beginning to use it solo.

(Post) About her multi-instrumental virtuosity (she plays accordion and mandolin, in addition to guitar), Larkin states, casually:

Larkin: I picked up the mandolin in an Irish band that I was in, and I like how many different cultures make use of the accordion.

(Post) Her dream: to study the accordion in the Balkans. On the topic of her songwriting, Larkin asserts that she is not the type to seek out other performers in need of a cut for their upcoming record and try to write for that category.

Larkin: That's not what I do. I have a sense of what is truth for me.

(Post) She does set aside time in which to complete what she calls the "drudgery of writing: looking for ideas and writing bad songs," though, she says, she likes it when the lyrics and music come quickly. She does ask for feedback on her songs from people who matter to her. She approaches what turn out to be her best songs with a feeling of what she wants to create, a stylistic sense of where she wants to go. When it works…

Larkin: It is the best feeling in the world.

(Post) Maybe playing live is a close second.

DISCOGRAPHY

Step Into The Light (Philo, 1985); *I'm Fine* (Philo, 1987); *Live In The Square* (Philo, 1990); *Tango* (High Street, 1991); *Angels Running* (High Street, 1993); *Strangers World* (High Street, 1995).

PHRANC
lesbian artist in women's music and the mainstream

Born in 1959 in Southern California, a young Jewish woman attends thirteen years of Hebrew School and has her entire childhood dotingly documented on 8-mm film by her parents, Jackie and Stan. Who knew that little pigtailed Suzy Gottlieb who fooled around with the guitar at age nine was to come out as a lesbian separatist, then a punk rocker, then a radical folksinger named Phranc, one of the few lesbian solo artist to perform out to mainstream audiences?

Always feeling that her given name had never suited her, partly because of 'boy-named-Sue' jokes, she took on the moniker Franc at a Lesbian History Exploration that she attended at the age of seventeen. Having met Alix Dobkin—the original all-American, Jewish lesbian folksinger—there and experienced Liza Cowan's slide show on the fashion of the well-dressed dyke (in which Liza shaves her head), the newly-christened Franc remembers:

Phranc: On the day I returned home from the Lesbian History Exploration, I went straight to the barbershop and had all my hair buzzed, completely off, not bald, but about a quarter-inch. I went to show a friend of mine my new haircut and tell her my new name, and she thought it all was great. She told me that she had something for me and went and got a blue baseball cap with a "P" on it. She put the cap on my head, and she said, "Phranc, PH." So that was how I got my name.

(Post) Having dropped out of Venice High School, moved away from home, and started hanging out with feminist lesbians, Phranc was finding acceptance and identity among her woman-loving friends. Initially, Phranc's family did not understand her changes, but she has won them over, as she has won over potentially hostile audiences. Currently, Phranc's parents help with the merchandising of Phranc T-shirts and the screening of press reviews, and Stan Gottlieb has been known to proudly remark, "Have you heard of Phranc, the Jewish lesbian folksinger? She's my daughter!"

Tracing her lyrical roots to Allan Sherman (she has listened to "My Son The Folksinger" since age five), Phranc made music with several members of her family, including her maternal grandfather who played guitar and paternal grandfather on the violin. Phranc also received support from her two grandmothers, to whom she pays loving tribute with "Myriam and Esther," from *I Enjoy Being A Girl* (Island Records, 1989). Though traditionally an independent musical craftswoman who has shunned the dry booklearning of music and avoided hierarchal student relationships, Phranc is currently involved with several collaborations which, she says, are expanding her compositional, technical, and songwriting abilities.

Finding her life niche early, Phranc attended editorial meetings of *The Lesbian Tide*, did graphic work, and listened to and participated in discussions of articles and issues. Contributing also to *Sister Magazine*, a feminist newspaper, she remained focused on only women for several years.

Drawn by the promise of the San Francisco Bay Area women's community, Phranc relocated from southern to northern California but was not able to immediately connect with other lesbians. An offset printer at the time, Phranc found herself moving in with an eclectic flat of roommates, that included a straight leather woman, a straight B-movie starlet, a gay actor, and a straight male speed freak, all with ties to punk.

Phranc: There I was, a Jewish lesbian separatist who had not spoken to a man in years, accustomed to a safe, peaceful feminist intellectual community, suddenly in the midst of an angry, male-dominated musical environment. Never having had friends my own age and with my own unanswered burden of anger, I was very drawn to their energy. And, there were not a lot of rules; in Los Angeles the women had taken care of me. I had slept on a lot of floors and couches and other people's beds. I had not always had a job. So, living in San Francisco taught me that I liked punk style—sleek, handsome, stark, true, bare—but that affection and responsibility were not to be taken for granted.

After an unsatisfying stint of nude modeling at the San Francisco Institute of Art—my gay-actor-roommate and I would take the leatherwoman's toys to pose with—I returned to L.A. where I knew only lesbians but hungered to be in a punk band. I didn't know a soul in L.A. punk, but I would get dressed up and try to look real cool and hope that someone would ask me to be in their band. And, one day, someone did.

(Post) Thus, Phranc debuted in Nervous Gender, equipped with an electric guitar she did not play much.

Phranc: Nobody was a musician then; people couldn't play their instruments, which was one great aspect of punk. If one wanted badly enough to be in a band, it was O.K. to just go for it. It was all very passionate, similar in many ways to folk in that the music was simple and often political and most of the time told a story. Nervous Gender was principally synthesizers—Godawful noise made by three gay men with me singing some unbelievable words.

(Post) Phranc subsequently appeared in another band, Catholic Discipline (from 1979-1980), in which she did play electric rhythm guitar. Tiring of being the only female, however, Phranc next turned to a group of intense women, Castration Squad:

Phranc: Junkies singing weird doom-gloom lyrics, all of us wearing light paint on our faces and red arm bands.

(Post) In 1981, supporting herself as an aquatics instructor, Phranc went solo. Phranc became an acoustic artist the night that she realized that she carried a message that she wanted people to hear. Deciding to sing protest songs to a hard core, slam dancing audience (she wrote "Take Off Your Swastika" in that context), she returned to her first love, folk music. For many years, she did her own booking and managing, producing her first record—*Folksinger* (1985), on Rhino Records—with $1500 that she had saved from teaching swimming. It was through Stiff Records, the album's UK distributors, that Morrissey of the Smiths encountered Phranc, thus inaugurating her career as warmup artist extraordinaire and fostering her abilities to tear down preconceived notions with warmth, firmness, and genuineness.

Rhino Records shunned subsequent record contract talks with Phranc, and, despite multitudes of genuine offers from major labels, no deal transpired. Through the uncertainty, Phranc went ahead and made the also self-financed *I Enjoy Being A Girl*, which was eventually picked up by Island Records, in 1989.

Phranc is always able to bring her truest self to her work and transcend stereotypes and expectations.

Phranc: I've always been out as a lesbian with all of my friends, men as well as women, everyone I've known through the music, all these years; there's a lot of mutual respect. I have never been in the closet, and I've always kind of done what I wanted, musically and otherwise. There is so much good women's music, but there are so few lesbians out in the mainstream to take their music to young women who don't get to hear the word lesbian when they go to a regular concert. I have made this job for myself. I'm not judgmental of anyone else or what they do; this is what I have chosen to do. It is important to me and sometimes not easy but very gratifying. I find it exciting in that I am kept on my toes. It's a challenge for me—and it is just beginning to happen—playing a show at which people are there to see me. What I have been doing for over ten years has been opening for other performers. That has meant that I have largely played for an audience that doesn't really give a shit about my act and only wants to see the headlining group. So, my job has been to win those crowds over as my audience.

I always come out on stage as me, as a lesbian, and then try to get them to laugh. Because if they laugh, then they loosen up and are open to whatever idea or concept or fact I might want to give them. Humor is a very strong tool in the work that I do. Not that some of my songs aren't really angry or sad, but humor is a big key to unlocking people's minds and heightening their receptiveness to new information. I play large shows, to mixed audiences. Often, the audience sees me come out on stage and they don't know what I am or who I am. And they become frightened. They aren't necessarily hostile or unenlightened, they are simply unaware of what I do. Many times, they go crazy and love me from the beginning.

Other times, I need to put some strategy into action, such as tossing out tampons for dramatic emphasis during my rendition of "I Enjoy Being A Girl." My experiences have been very good. I have very few horrendous, or even negative, stories to tell; it has been terrific at least ninety-eight percent of the time.

Interestingly, some of the most difficult shows have been to lesbian audiences: they have seemed to expect and want a certain type of attitude and have been tougher to relax and draw out. I remember that nearly-judgmental seriousness from my collective days, but it is nonetheless startling to me that the mixed audiences have more commonly been willing to go with my mood. On the flip side, some women-only shows have given me a great deal of energy and amazing happiness.

Photo: Ken Seino

I want to talk about the some of the positive experiences I have had. Once, when on tour with the Smiths, the age of the audience was junior high school. I walked on stage, and they cheered. Since then, I have had young women come up to me and tell me that they were fifteen years old when they heard my show opening for the Smiths and that I was the first lesbian they had ever known; some of them have even come out themselves as lesbians. Such scenes are touching to me. Similarly, there are the shows when I have received kudos from parents.

I recall one show when parents brought their kids backstage afterwards; one of the their daughters wanted me to sign something. She must have been eleven or twelve, and she had her Amazon button on. She was enthusiastic, the whole family was very nice. The dad asked me to sign a poster for their other daughter who had not been able to attend the show. The mother told me that she appreciated my being such a good role model for their daughters.

There are the times, however, when sometimes I do feel really lost, and I wonder what I am doing, I feel so alone, why don't more lesbians come out? There are times when I feel sad or directionless, pointless. What keeps me going when I get into that kind of thinking rut is having some positive reinforcement, such as reading a letter that someone sent me or remembering those times when I realize that my songs and my being real in public are meaningful and important to many people. Then my work becomes important to me again.

Even my worst experiences are positive because, as hard as it has been for me to deal with my frustration and isolation, the audiences have had to deal with me. It has been helpful and useful for me to have been in that position: uncompromisingly out as a lesbian, not leaving the stage or telling them to fuck off but trying to work with them. I have wanted to still say what I have to say; I have mostly succeeded in this.

A few negative incidents have occurred, very few, most notably during a tour that I did with the Pogues who, themselves, were thoughtful, wonderful guys who were really good to me. Once in Toronto—an exciting town where I had experienced no trouble in prior tours—the Pogues and I were playing two sold-out nights in a row. The audience was there to see the Pogues; I came out on stage, and they started yelling at me. Yelling the sorts of things that I had not heard in a long time: things like faggot, dyke, asshole, nonstop, for twenty minutes. My response to them was to cut out the slow songs and to cut out the sensitive songs. I played only the fastest and the angriest tunes. After about twenty minutes I stopped and I said, "Let's talk a little bit about tolerance and acceptance here now." I then played "Take Off Your Swastika," I dedicated it to the audience, and they shut up. I did the most vehement, burning version that I'd ever done—my veins were bulging. And they stayed quiet; when I left the stage, they went nuts, cheering, but I would not return to the stage.

(Post) Phranc credits the strong foundation of her lesbian youth with allowing her to make the transition between radical separatist and affirmative lesbian missionary. Experiencing consistent, positive role models; living and working within a disciplined, politically thoughtful collective; and being shown personal tolerance all cultivated the inner reserve and confidence necessary for confronting and thriving within the straight world. Phranc's early path often was unproductive, sometimes wild, and occasionally self-destructive. Nonetheless, she retained a firm commitment to coming out and staying out with her own opinions as well as with her lesbian identity.

Phranc: I was still in high school and I thought that I was the only lesbian in the world. Though most of the lesbians were ten years older than I, I dove in head first; I did not enter the singles/bar scene, I got involved politically, and I grew to love those women. I hope that who I am, in my shows, will offer the young women of today, who are searching for lesbian peers and influences, some of what I finally found during my own adolescence.

(Post) Phranc continues to team up with a variety of musicians and musical genres: mainstream, lesbian, punk, folk, her own unique blend. Her topics span the outrageous dykey "Amazons" and "M-A-R-T-I-N-A;" "Bloodbath," a scathing antiapartheid elegy; "Toy Time," a paean to healthy escapism; a campy cover of "I Enjoy Being A Girl" (from "Flower Drum Song"); the p.c. "Handicapped;" and the no-explanation-needed "Lifelover" and "Individuality."

Staying close to her support system, often by transcontinental telephone, Phranc tours solo, which means that she, herself, totes her guitar and uniform: six white tee shirts, six pair of underwear, six white socks and two pair of Levis with her boots. Still reverential about the magnitude of Alix Dobkin's ongoing effect on her own process, Phranc listens to the likes of Cocteau Twins, 2 Nice Girls, and Jennifer Warnes, is thrilled to have come out in *People Magazine* (August 14, 1989), collects dollhouse toys and vintage GI Joes, swims, and maintains exuberance about the future.

DISCOGRAPHY

Folksinger (Island, 1985); *I Enjoy Being A Girl* (Island, 1989); *Positively Phranc* (Island, 1991); *Bulldagger Swagger* (Kill Rock Stars, 1994); *Goofyfoot* (Kill Rock Stars, 1995).

For further recordings see Phranc's web page
http://www.rahul.net/hrmusic/discos/pdisc.html

RHIANNON
jazz storyteller

Rhiannon, best known through her ten years as vocalist with the jazz group ALIVE!, believes that she has always been in the 'mainstream' of music. Born into the plainness and homogeneity of South Dakota, she grew up with parents who encouraged artistic pursuits which punctuated the harsh farm days. Rhiannon found music early: in her autobiographical performance piece, "Toward Home," she describes how "the cows let me sing to them."

Recently, she has sung in Bobby McFerrin's multicultural a cappella group Voicestra; in the spinoff group, SoVoSo; in an improvisational quartet with Bobby McFerrin called Hard Choral; and has been busy leading retreats and classes for singers of all levels.

Years before this article was even dreamed of, I had the good fortune to attend a Rhiannon-led voice workshop. Like her concerts, her program was rich and sensitive, professional yet relaxed: stories were told and beauty shared. Though I have long harbored severe fear of singing in public, I found myself, as a result of the trust developed, participating relatively easily in various forms of improvisation. Many years after that experience I still retain the unselfconscious enthusiasm generated then, and still do, on occasion, challenge myself with Rhiannon's heartfelt advice: sing always—in the shower, in the car, in the supermarket.

Post: When did you start singing seriously?

Rhiannon: When I was eighteen, I sang some Barbra Streisand in high school and pop tunes, whoever came by that I could hear, but it wasn't right. It wasn't the music that I really wanted to sing. At some point I realized that it was worse for me to sing music that I didn't believe in than not to sing at all, so I quit singing altogether. When I got to college I was in one musical show and transferred my major and went into the theater.

Post: What had been your major before then?

Rhiannon: Nursing. I took biology and chemistry the first semester and flunked them both; I called my mom and said, "This isn't working." I was much happier in theater—it was where I belonged—and dove right into dramatic things. I didn't even tell people that I sang.

Post: What did you do after college?

Rhiannon: I went to the East Coast and taught for a couple of years, taught theater and directed plays. This was the '60s, the very turbulent and wonderful times, in a mostly Black high school on Long Island. That's where I got my real education because I had come from a very monocultural upbringing. As soon as I got to New York I started to hear jazz: being around Black students opened many doors. I got not afraid to have a Black boyfriend, then I got not afraid to go to all the Black clubs; then I got not afraid to really listen to the music. I was still intimidated to try to sing it—I felt it wasn't OK because I was a white girl (not to mention how difficult the music is to sing)—which is maybe fortunate because what I did was listen. I listened without thinking, "I can do better than that" or "I want to do…" I listened, and I heard everybody: Sarah Vaughan and Betty Carter, Ella Fitzgerald and all the horn players and all the piano players.

In school, I did "Bye-Bye Birdie" with an all-Black cast which was hot, but I was in too deep with my students. I didn't do anything but teach, and when I wasn't teaching I would take them into the city to plays. I didn't have a life, and it was a dangerous thing, so I went off to Cornell to graduate school and got my Masters degree in acting.

Then I went on the road to dinner theaters and went to New York and did cattle calls. I wasn't involved in the women's movement at the time, and I was in plays that were directed by men who hurt my feelings a lot. I was cast totally by my size and shape; I got told "no" a lot, and I lived through it. I got an offer to be in street theater in Chicago and I left my apartment in New York, put everything in the street, took my cat and left in about a week for this street theater where we acted and sang and danced.

It was a multi-cultural troupe and we were in all kinds of neighborhoods, rich to poor with all different ethnic groups; we were half-Black and half-white, and we mixed and mingled. I started singing, and people said to me, "Why aren't you singing? You can really sing."

When I moved to California, I was cast in a man's role in the theater. I had to do all these aggressive things, and I thought, "Something's wrong here." I was starting to come out as a lesbian—I think the male director believed that my manner was too forward for women's parts—so I put an ad in the paper looking for a band. I found these guys who loved my music and were great to work with.

One time we shared the stage with The Deadly Nightshade. The audience was filled with dykes, and here I come with my band of guys. I sang this song about coming out to my mother, and the audience gave me tremendous support.

The summer after, in 1975, I found a ride to Champaign, Illinois with these two women—they lay in the back while I drove and made love the whole way; it was a great adventure, and I'll never forget them for that—to the first National Women's Music Festival. I didn't have a gig, but there were more Round Robins in those days, and I just went and sang. A lot of women—Ginni Clemmens, Betsy Rose—encouraged me.

When I got back to California I went to the Women on Wheels shows with Holly [Near], Cris [Williamson], and Margie [Adam]. I shaved my head that summer and hitched a ride to the Michigan Womyn's Music Festival. In Michigan I changed my name to Rhiannon. When I got back to California that time, I put another ad in the paper and said to the guys in the band, "I'm sorry, I've got to write music differently."

I went to a women-in-jazz workshop and met Carolyn [Brandy] and Suzanne

[Vincenza] the first night. We fell in musical love and started rehearsing within a week. Without really intending to perform, we named ourselves Alive! within a month. I played piano and sang; Carolyn played congas and violin, and Suzanne played cello and bass.

We played a gig at the old Women's Coffee House in San Francisco, then I called Ginni Clemmons and she got us a gig at the National Women's Music Festival. Then we got a gig at the Michigan Womyn's Music Festival, and it went on like that for ten years.

We were pretty much supported, in the early years especially, by women, even though we were a jazz band and weren't necessarily playing all women's lyrics. We were pushing the boundaries of the women's movement, which was very important to us. We hired two other players—Janet Small and Barbara Borden—and became a quintet. We hired a manager who was going to get us out into the mainstream. I thought I was already in the mainstream: I was going so fast, in my 30s, that I could hardly breathe.

We played all the major jazz clubs in the country and got reviewed by the big jazz critics. All the time, we were pushing against this barrier: they were always asking us which of us were lesbians and why we were playing with all women. "It's because the music is good, and because we want to," we'd say. Sometimes, we'd say, "Would you please ask Miles Davis why he plays with guys all the time," but that didn't work, they didn't care about that. Now they might—there are more women in jazz; it's been a quietly-growing stream—it's still a big deal.

We never were all lesbians in the band: sometimes the lesbians would come out; sometimes the straight women would come out at lesbian festivals and say, "Hey, let's get over this." It was real important for us to walk that line between jazz and Women's Music, between straight and gay. Our gift was that we stood in the middle and we made a political statement by the way we played.

We'd have these reviewers at clubs—I know they wanted to hate us—and a lot of times they would be taken by surprise because we played well. The band had this love affair going on onstage; I think that kind of playing is really what jazz is about. It's that intimacy of improvisation where if you're not linked close with the other players, I don't think the improvisation happens so well.

I saw men jazz players, and when it wasn't their song, they'd leave the stage and have a cigarette in the corner. Everybody was used to that. To see an ensemble all standing onstage when somebody was soloing—we would face that player and be talking to her and urging her on—that was exciting. The reviewers got it, and the audience got it, and we turned people's heads around.

Then we came to a place where we couldn't go any further. We couldn't get out of the country, we couldn't get to the European jazz festivals which are important if you're going to make the big time in jazz. What began to happen was this lateral movement: we were being produced by women who wanted more women's lyrics. We needed to get off the fence, and we let the band go.

I love the way we did it: we had a lot of talks, and we had a therapist. We'd go once every two months, and it saved us from fighting. We're all still good friends.

Post: What did you do after Alive!?

Rhiannon: It took me a couple of years; I did some solo things, I worked with Mimi Fox, I did teaching. When I started hiring guys for a new band, I would always make sure that there was at least one other woman in the band so I wouldn't be the only woman onstage.

I inserted myself into the musical community. I got hired to teach at jazz camp and I found other ways to belong. I found the two worlds—the women's community and the jazz community—far apart. jazz is still a male-dominated kind of music, and there's homophobia. I think it was easier for me than for the other members of Alive! because I'm a singer.

One of things that had happened to me during Alive! is that I wanted more room—we were very much of an ensemble, there wasn't even a leader—and when I started to get room as a solo artist, I started to tell stories.

Taking on that leadership role is something that happens to singers; when I work with singers, I tell them to go near the instrument when you're soloing with another player—don't stand and look at the audience—feel the vibration coming off the horn or the piano. That's what I was taught, that's what I learned to do, that's the way Betty Carter did it when I watched her sing.

Some storytelling is formal—the stories are old and you tell them in a certain way—and I have respect for that but that's not the way I do it. I tell stories the way I would scat sing. I let a word come out and see what's on my mind and try to go with it. Over these six years what's happened is that I have some stories that are free of improvisation, and I've finally allowed myself to structure a show so that there are certain pieces where I know what's going to happen. I never thought that was all right—as an improviser I thought I should never, ever repeat—but I'm letting myself do it, and it makes my shows more consistent.

Post: How is a 'mainstream' musical life different from that in Women's Music?

Rhiannon: In those days women's communities around the country were so hungry for the music, for us as cultural messengers, that we were always taken care of. We were fed, we were housed, we were told the local politics so I got a sense of the whole country. You don't get that when you stay in hotels, though I'm grateful for a wonderful, fancy, elegant hotel where I have my own room.

There were the times when we would get horrible rooms, like with dirty sheets, or we would be picked up in a car full of dog hair. We taught each other to get it together, and we learned to laugh, and we learned that when you go into someone's home to be respectful, to spend a little time.

Alive! didn't have as many bookings as Voicestra: we would play the weekends and then stay put in town during the week to do a workshop or do interviews. We had more time-luxury. Also, we were driving so that slowed our whole tempo down, and we didn't have the money to stay in motels so we'd drive all night.

There wasn't as much of a need to make money: there were five of us. Voicestra has twenty people—it's a huge budget, it cost $40,000 to put on one show —so it's a different deal. We'd do a show, go back to the hotel and sleep, then get on a plane the next morning, go to the next town, do the next gig.

Post: What has happened to Women's Music?

Photo: Jan E. Watson

Rhiannon: A lot of the women who kept us in their homes got tired of doing that or don't have room any more or are too busy now. It was too hard; a lot of the producers went out of business. I think it's harder for the women touring now; they don't have quite the same circuit we did.

Post: How did *Toward Home* come together for you?

Rhiannon: It was part of my progress to come to the next step. It was brought on by the facts that my lover of eight and a half years left and, with her, our child; then my mother died of cancer, and my eighteen year-old cat too, all of this within one year. I left the city [Berkeley] and moved out here [more rural northern California, near the ocean]. I experienced such a sad, terrified grown-up place; I did the piece because I looked death in the face—I was with my mother when she died—and wanted to talk about real stuff. When my mom got sick, the important things really counted. She and I had been through so many situations—my Black lovers, my lesbianism, my birth control pills way back when, my vegetarianism—it all worked her nerves. At the end none of it mattered except that I needed to be there when she died. People tell me that because the show is personal and specific, it's universal.

Post: Do you think you'll continue solo work?

Rhiannon: It's what I've always wanted: to fit in and stand out at the same time. I can't imagine getting tired of it, though, at some point, I'll probably put the autobiographical piece to rest.

Post: Will you get another cat?

Rhiannon: I've thought about it a million times. I really miss a pet a lot—it's been since my early twenties that I didn't have somebody to take care of, either a child or a cat or a lover that I was living with—it's really good though. One of the gifts of my mother dying is that I'm a whole person and when I come home at night, I'm enough.

DISCOGRAPHY

With Alive!: *Alive!* (Ladyslipper, 1979); *Call It Jazz* (Ladyslipper, 1981); *City Life* (Ladyslipper, 1982).

Solo: *Loosen Up And Improvise* (Rhiannon Music, 1986); *Finding Your Voice* (Rhiannon Music, 1987); *Toward Home* (Ladyslipper, 1991); *Live At Tomales Bay* (Rhiannon Music, 1996); *World Jazz A Cappella*, featuring Rhiannon with SoVoSo (Primarily A Cappella, 1997).

ROBIN FLOWER & LIBBY McLAREN
angels of change

Robin Flower and Libby McLaren are breaking ground with their novel fusion of Irish, Cajun, bluegrass, and folk; progressive folk, they call it. In their songs they yearn for connection with kindred spirits in diverse forms: she-wolves, faraway women, grandmothers, conscientious interveners in cycles of abuse and in larger political drama.

Flower's career began with auspicious laudatory reviews from *The Village Voice*, *Frets*, and *Billboard*. Since the late 1980s Flower has teamed with equally committed and talented musician, Libby McLaren, whose pop view has softened Flower's sophisticated, technical approach. Before Flower, McLaren had applied her rich keyboards, clear voice and ear for instrumental interplay to recording, arrangement, and accompaniment for peers such as The Roches, Ronnie Gilbert, Holly Near.

Between the two of them, Flower and McLaren play seven instruments: guitar, fiddle, accordion, banjo, mandolin (Flower), and piano, keyboards, accordion (McLaren). They have appeared at many folk and feminist music festivals, coffeehouses, and clubs throughout the English-speaking world.

Robin Flower got into music through her family; she and her sister sang along with their parents' harmonicas before they fell asleep at night. When she was ten Flower took up an instrument. Flower is glad that her parents encouraged her to pursue violin and saved money for her lessons though she bemoaned the classical emphasis and wished for more dance tunes, ear training, and person-to-person teaching.

At twelve, Flower stopped the violin; two years later, she found her instrument.

Robin Flower: I got a guitar, the best because it was the 60s, it was folk music, everybody was protesting; I loved it, it was home.

(Post) After that, all that Flower wanted for Christmas was records to learn from.

Flower: I didn't care if I was a singer, I wanted to be the guitar player. I knew, at seven, that I was not going to have a regular job or kids.

(Post) When Flower started gigging at sixteen, she was so serious that she made her sister sign contracts saying that she would practice for their shows together. After a year at art school, Flower acquired a motorcycle and took an "Easy Rider" trip to the west coast.

Flower: I fell in love with a banjo player and started flat picking, then playing mandolin, even picked up the fiddle again.

(Post) Stints with several bands resulted, as did learning jazz guitar.

Flower: During that era I had one of my best musical experiences. I got to be backup player for Hazel Dickens and Alice Gerrard; Elizabeth Cotton was on the bill. Hearing Hazel sing was mind-blowing; Elizabeth Cotton, who loved to play so much, was totally inspiring.

(Post) Teaming with flatpicker Nancy Vogl, Flower released her first album, *More Than Friends* (1979). In 1982 came *Green Sneakers*, then *First Dibs* (1984—awarded Best String Band Jazz Album by N.A.I.R.D.) and *Babies With Glasses* (Flying Fish, 1987—awarded Best Women's Music Album by N.A.I.R.D.). After several years of touring with her band, Flower tired of the financial struggle of road life.

It was at this juncture that Flower, needing a bass player for a short tour, tried out Libby McLaren, who could play bass lines on her keyboards. The musical connection was immediate; Flower and McLaren decided to continue as a duo.

McLaren's path to working with Flower centered on the piano.

Libby McLaren: I started playing when I was five. The person I wanted to study with wouldn't let me take lessons until I was in first grade. My first piano lesson was the first week of first grade. I had been waiting a year.

(Post) Despite all the piano training, McLaren attended San Francisco State thinking of herself as a singer.

McLaren: As a person who had always played piano, I had never thought of myself as a piano player. I wanted to sing like Joni Mitchell or Aretha Franklin.

(Post) After falling in love with a piano player, with whom she was in a band and in a romantic relationship for five years, McLaren assumed the role of singer. The band experience proved useful.

McLaren: For a year we played at an Oakland club every Friday night, then graduated to every Saturday. It was a great band, very fusion-oriented. We were so popular that we moved to New York in 1977.

(Post) The band split after the record deal soured; McLaren wondered about money.

McLaren: I realized I could go back to playing the piano; then be able to sing and do lots of solo gigs at all these wonderful New York-type places like the Empire Diner. I played there for years, every Thursday night. That was great because it got my piano chops back together and as a singer it was also really great.

(Post) Stints with other bands ensued, as did an introduction to the synthesizer.

McLaren: It was hard because it was electronic and technical, tricky to make the transition from the acoustic piano. But, I learned to play.

(Post) Proficiency on keyboards led to work with The Roches, lasting several years.

McLaren: It was time for me to leave New York. Soon after I moved back to California, I got a call from Robin. She was doing an album and wanted help with the vocal arranging. The first time I went over to her house, I thought, with relief, "I'm not going to starve—I will work again." We immediately fit, musically. We were very comfortable. We had fun, we laughed at the same jokes.

(Post) Flower and McLaren found that they worked the same way: very focused, intent upon hard practice, and unquestioning about the need to collectively arrange and assign instrumental and vocal parts. Several talented Bay Area women musicians have accompanied them: fiddler-vocalist Crystal Reeves, harpist Michelle Sell, guitarist-singer Teresa Chandler.

Despite the rapidity and solidity of the musical bond between Flower and McLaren, there were difficulties, among which was McLaren's struggle to play keyboard in an essentially unfamiliar style.

McLaren: Though The Roches were folk, they were more rock-oriented than Robin, who not only did folk music but very difficult folk music. I was greatly challenged by what Robin had me doing bass-wise.

Flower: My music, though folk-based, has a lot of time changes and is not easy to learn.

(Post) Other early difficulties with the pairing involved divergent conceptualizations of vocal format.

Flower: My idea of singing with another person is to take parts. Libby's idea comes from the lead-backup style.

(Post) Dealing with such differences has led to clearer communication.

Flower: We try not to say, "That's the stupidest idea I've ever heard," We say, "Would you consider this way?"

(Post) An initial project was a demo tape, with Side A featuring new studio tracks and B-Side drawing from Flower's previous recordings. In operating the drum machine and sequencer for the demo, McLaren discovered that she preferred a more natural sound.

Flower: To this day, Libby prefers to play an acoustic piano than keyboard.

(Post) For the first few years, at the end of the 80s, Flower and McLaren played for diverse audiences: folk—though they were oftimes labeled too progressive or electric for folk purists—general mainstream, and Women's Music. McLaren's learning the accordion in order to be able to play on Pete Seeger's Clearwater sloop ("There

Photo: Irene Young

Robin Flower & Libby McLaren

was no electricity on the boat, so I knew I wouldn't be able to plug in and play my keyboard.") provided a new avenue for instrumental experimentation.

McLaren: We were driving across Iowa, the windows down. Robin would be driving and I'd be trying to work this squeak box with a cassette of all these tunes blasting so I could still hear myself. Robin, of course, wore earplugs.

(Post) McLaren's new goal is learning to frail the banjo.

McLaren: Robin and I eventually will be able to add it to the songs we do, and I won't need to bring my keyboard and amp on tour.

(Post) Flower is equally exuberant about the possibilities for banjo.

Flower: I know how to arrange for strings. So, for me, it opens another thing that Libby and I can do.

(Post) Talking about strings reminds McLaren of her connections with some stringed traditions.

McLaren: I love getting more in touch with my roots music, the Scottish tunes. Flower elaborates on the theme of roots.

Flower: My mom comes from Kentucky, and her father was very musical. My mother used to say, "Your grandfather would be so proud of you. You're playing that music that he loved to play. Occasionally, she'd used the word "hillbilly"—if you're southern, you can say it. She said, "Your grandfather'd be proud of you playing that hillbilly music." That mountain music. I, too, feel rooted by what Libby and I do.

Tunes are your friends. Once you learn a tune, it is your friend. And it will remain your friend for the rest of your life. Sometimes, it's your best friend, and it will be your best friend for two or three months at a time because you can't not play that tune five times a day. Tunes are made to be played over and over again. And, sometimes, if it's an old friend, you can not play it for six months or two years, and can pick it up emotionally, later, and you haven't skipped a beat.

(Post) Flower and McLaren develop the complex arrangements of their songs following a simple guideline:

McLaren: It's the old 'IYS'—it's your song. The person who writes it has the final say.

Flower: Hopefully, it's a good idea.

McLaren: We go our own way, and return with—ideally—completed parts. Most of the time, they mesh. Part of what Teresa Trull [producer of *Angel of Change*] did was to help us to balance our parts.

(Post) Flower and McLaren are pleased with their debut duo recording, but they harbor broader visions, such as doing a wholly instrumental album. Also doing an album more purely folk styled, perhaps even recorded live in the studio, not overdubbed. Finally, they want to tour as much as possible; play as many festivals as possible; make a living performing and not have to teach; have time to fish and hike and play with their cats. Even success is less important than continuing to play.

McLaren: We're not ever going to stop playing. It's so much fun to perform for people who really appreciate what we're doing.

Flower: Sometimes, I'll stay up late at night and play my fiddle, tune after tune after tune. By the time I'm done, I am centered. I am so lucky and blessed to have that center in me nourished day after day, year after year. Because bear in mind that we are musicians before we are performers.

McLaren: Music is who I am. It's a powerful connection between the two of us. We will never stop. We will be old women playing music.

DISCOGRAPHY

Robin Flower: *More Than Friends* (Spaniel, 1979); *Green Sneakers* (Flying Fish, 1992); *First Dibs* (Flying Fish, 1984); *Babies With Glasses* (Flying Fish, 1987).

Robin Flower and Libby McLaren: *Robin Flower And Libby McLaren* (self-produced, 1988); *Angel of Change* (Little Cat, 1993).

RONNIE GILBERT
face to face with the most dangerous woman in america

"Mother Jones and I became the catalysts for bringing together as an audience two groups that usually have a hard time finding one another, the labor and women's communities," states Ronnie Gilbert in her acknowledgments to the book *Ronnie Gilbert on Mother Jones; Face To Face With The Most Dangerous Woman in America*.

Ronnie Gilbert, renowned folk singer and actor, has brought the complexities of Mother Jones to the stage in her one-woman play, "Mother Jones," her first attempt at writing for the musical stage.

Mary Harris "Mother" Jones (1833?-1930) participated in labor strikes from about the age of forty-five and spent the next forty years as a union activist for mill hands and other industrial workers. Bright, witty, and audacious, she was a powerful orator and dauntless fighter for human rights, at the forefront of the movement for safe and humane working conditions, the eight-hour work day, and child labor laws.

Ronnie Gilbert: Like Mother Jones, my mother was a unionist and a socialist. In her way, Sarah Gilbert shaped her life as Mother Jones had—actively, around dearly-held political principles: unionism, anti-racism, economic justice for all. As a child I understood my mother's example this way: Brushing your teeth twice a day and working for social justice are necessary for good personal hygiene.

(Post) Ronnie Gilbert grew up in a household in which both parents also enjoyed and encouraged music.

Gilbert: My mom had a lovely voice, and she enjoyed opera. My father loved to hear me sing the little pop songs of the time.

(Post) By the time Gilbert was sixteen, she had sung in a Gilbert and Sullivan group, learned the Wobblies' songs of the day, appeared on a radio program, and taken serious music lessons.

Young Ronnie was gifted and she applied the principles that she had been taught to her own life. In high school she refused to appear in a white-kids-in-blackface minstrel show put on by her music class.

Gilbert: It was not exactly my idea of a good thing to do. I told the teacher that, and I cited Paul Robeson. The teacher said that I would have to be in the production or I wouldn't graduate. I had to fight it out, and they finally gave in. I was not in the minstrel show, and I graduated.

(Post) Ronnie Gilbert's name first appeared in the public eye forty-five years ago when she, along with Pete Seeger, Lee Hays, and Fred Hellerman established the seminal singing group, the Weavers. In two years the Weavers exploded onto the charts, did multitudes of concerts, and sold over four million of their Decca 78rpm records (Leadbelly's "Goodnight Irene," Woody Guthrie's "So Long, It's Been Good to Know Yuh," the South African "Wimoweh" among them).

By the end of 1952 however, amid charges of subversiveness and un-Americanism, the Weavers' voices had been stilled on radio and television and their career cut short by the McCarthy-era blacklist: a chilling connection between politics and music. Yet neither the Weavers' message nor Ronnie Gilbert's spirit could be silenced.

In 1963 Gilbert was beginning to build a solo singing career when she met Joseph Chaikin, then a young actor/director with a fledgling experimental troupe, The Open Theater, and joined the group at his invitation. She has continued to act until the present time.

In the 1970s Gilbert's career turned again, when she earned a M.A. in Clinical Psychology and worked as a therapist.

The 1980s saw Gilbert meet, be inspired by, and sing with Holly Near, recording *Lifeline* (1983) and *Singing With You* (1986); and *Harp* (1985) with Near, Arlo Guthrie, and her old friend Pete Seeger. Gilbert's solo album, *The Spirit Is Free* (1985) was released on Redwood; the live *Love Will Find A Way* followed (1989), self-produced, in collaboration with new manager/life partner Donna Korones.

All of Ronnie Gilbert's knowledge, experience, triple talents (actor, writer, singer), psychological insight, intellectual analysis, solo experience, and lifelong politics contributed to "Mother Jones: The Most Dangerous Woman in America." The play succeeds both as an historical narrative and as a gripping view of the life and struggles of a union reformer from the last century, an activist who happened to be a woman.

From the first scene Gilbert takes a stance, portraying Mother Jones as spunky and sarcastic, fearless and opinionated. There are the moments in which we are confronted with Mother Jones' distaste for the upper class, and with her unflagging support of men. At other times we glimpse those wrenching life experiences (mostly involving children) which sharpened and fueled her perspective. Unusually thoughtful for a musical, the songs, mostly written by Gilbert, give insights into the Knights of Labor, Mrs. O'Leary's cow, and J.D. Rockefeller such that the personal aspects of those events and figures became indelibly stamped.

Through her story, Mother Jones' rhetoric grows, as do her questions; in watching her, we connect with one of the unsung heroes of the modern era, also with our own hope and power. In fact, one of Jones' best lines, albeit too far ahead of her time to have been much appreciated then, is "Women have such a power, but they don't know how to use it." As the play's velocity accelerates, the audience claps at the content of Mother Jones' speeches, having forgotten, for the moment, the artistry and vision that brought Jones to the stage.

In her book, Gilbert brings the Mother Jones' principles into the current era.

Gilbert: When I read her words and imagine her, I think of the African-American mothers and grandmothers of today battling to raise responsible, healthy children up out of the hell of the inner cities; I think of single mothers —Welfare Warriors, some

Photo: J.A. Rubino

call themselves —learning to wring blood from a stony system, fighting with any means possible to keep their children with them, under one roof, and decently fed; I think of lesbian mothers battling tooth and nail against a homophobic society that would rip their children from them; I think of my own mother and her contemporaries in the 1930s and 1940s, all day bending over the roaring power sewing machines, rushing home at night to cook and clean and oversee children. Immigrant women, they were, Yiddish-and Italian-speaking—nowadays they're Asians and Haitians and Latinas— pushing their children past the road blocks—a bigoted teacher, an indifferent administration, a flawed curriculum.

As we move toward the 21st century we dare to work away at the terrible knots of race, class, privilege and power (everyone's heritage from the Kingdom of the Fathers) that stop the threads between our many networks. We are questioning the Kingdom of the Fathers and challenging it with our votes, the gift of our suffragist mothers, and with our presence in the arena, the example of such as Mother Jones.

DISCOGRAPHY

Weavers: *The Best Of The Weavers* (Decca, 1950-52); *Weavers Gold* (Decca, 1950-52); *Folk Songs Around The World* (Decca, 1950-52); *The Weavers At Carnegie Hall* (Vanguard 1957); *At Home* (Vanguard 1958); *Travelin' On* (Vanguard 1959); *Carnegie Hall II* (Vanguard 1960); *Reunion At Carnegie Hall* (Vanguard 1961); *Almanac* (Vanguard 1962); *15th Reunion* (Vanguard 1963); *Greatest Hits* (Vanguard 1972); *The Weavers: Together Again* (Loom 1981); *Wasn't That A Time* 4-CD boxed set (Vanguard, 1994).

Ronnie Gilbert and Holly Near: *Lifeline* (Redwood Records, 1983); *Harp* with Arlo Guthrie and Pete Seeger (Redwood Records, 1985); *Singing With You* (Redwood Records, 1986); *This Train Still Runs* (Redwood, 1996).

Ronnie Gilbert: *The Legend Of Bessie Smith* (RCA Victor, 1959); *Come And Go With Me* (Vanguard, 1962); *Along With Ronnie Gilbert* (Mercury, 1963); *The Spirit Is Free* (Redwood Records, 1985); *Love Will Find A Way* (Abbe Alice, 1989).

SAFFIRE
uppity blues that sparkles

Gaye Adegbalola and Ann Rabson have revised the acoustic blues into a frisky, feminist, modern, multicultural musical orgy. Since their debut recording, Saffire's originals have grown more personal, their covers more passionate. Adegbalola does a lot of the writing, sings, and plays rhythm guitar and harmonica; Rabson writes, sings, plays piano and guitar. Newest member Andra Faye McIntosh contributes mandolin, fiddle, bass, as well as a clean and strikingly powerful soprano.

The story of Saffire/The Uppity Blues Women is one of personal dreams and risks. Adegbalola, a Virginia Baptist, came to music through her family. Her father was a drummer in a jazz combo; through her youth, Adegbalola heard Count Basie, Duke Ellington, and the other Big Bands her parents listened to. Adegbalola's sense of voice was shaped by the vocalists whose recordings were played in her home: Ella Fitzgerald, Sarah Vaughan.

In high school Adegbalola played flute and piccolo and loved to dance. In college she found herself fooling with the guitar and later played anti-Vietnam and Black Power protest music on the streets of New York. Her then-husband managed a group, The Last Poets, who have been cited as the forefathers of rap. Following her divorce, Adegbalola moved back to Virginia with her small son.

Ann Rabson, who is Jewish, was born in New York and raised in the Midwest. She fell in love with the blues after she heard Big Bill Broonzy on the radio. At eighteen she began to play music semi-professionally and continued playing into her adult life. In the early 1970s she moved herself and her daughter to Fredericksburg, Virginia, where she worked as a computer analyst by day.

In 1975, Adegbalola heard Ann Rabson's solo guitar act and wanted more.

Gaye Adegbalola: I followed her around for years.

(Post) Rabson agreed to give Adegbalola guitar lessons; Adegbalola learned some basic chords and fingerpicking and was hooked, though she is a rhythm player not a lead guitarist.

Adegbalola: I spent a couple of years fiercely practicing, because at the time I had a real broken heart. As a matter of fact I call my guitar Baby. That's all I held for a good while.

(Post) In 1984, Adegbalola was asked to play a room that she realized was too large for her own music: one woman and one guitar. She asked Rabson to join her at the gig.

By that time, Rabson had added piano to her musical repertoire, though she did not have a piano at her disposal.

Adegbalola: We used to sneak into the college here to rehearse. At the time, Ann was working as a computer programmer full-time while sending her daughter to school. At night she taught a class, and one of the students had a make-up test. Ann negotiated with that student to use her piano for practice while the student took the make-up.

(Post) That student was Earlene Lewis, an Okie with a bluegrass background.

Adegbalola: Earlene took the test while we were practicing. Then she came down and joined us on bass. The next week she joined us at an ongoing gig. In June 1984, Saffire, with Ann, Earlene, and me, was born.

(Post) In 1985 the three women borrowed money to buy better equipment. As a fundraiser, to pay their sources back, they manufactured and sold T-shirts proclaiming "I Love Uppity Blues Women," a tag appended to their name to avoid confusion with a Latina rapper named Sa-Fire. With their earnings the women of Saffire/The Uppity Blues Women did a ten-cut tape, *Middle Aged Blues* (1987). This early recording is currently carried by Ladyslipper. Despite the rawness the recording did well.

Adegbalola: I'm embarrassed at the harmonica I play.

(Post) In 1989, the three women were able to record their next album at King Snake Studio in Florida, a well-known blues venue.

In the meantime Rabson's daughter graduated from college, and suddenly, Rabson's situation exploded with possibilities.

Adegbalola: Ann always used to make her living playing guitar, but to raise her daughter, she had to get a more-money job. Ann had always said that the day her daughter graduated from college would be the day she would go back to playing music full-time. So came June 1988, and Ann said, "I'm going to do it. Do you all want to do it too?" We did!

My son was just going into college, but I had saved up for a year's college tuition, and I was exhausted with teaching, so I took a year's leave of absence.

(Post) The growth of Saffire convinced Adegbalola—Teacher of the Year in Virginia, 1982, for teaching eighth grade science—to stay with music full-time. On April 1, 1989, she turned in her resignation. Not many people in their mid-forties are willing to give up the security of jobs and everyday life to follow a dream. Yet, since music was their first love, Adegbalola, Lewis, and Rabson were willing to take a chance in order to join their souls and musical styles (jazz/R&B, classical/roadhouse, blues/swing, country/bluegrass) in a band. Since one is African-American (Gaye), one Jewish (Ann), one part Cherokee (Earlene); since two were raising children; since the three represented both polarities of sexual orientation, they offered hope for political harmony as well as for musical innovation.

When the president of King Snake Studio went to Bruce Iglauer at Alligator Records with the new recording the women had made, Iglauer was impressed with the writing, with the personality, and with Rabson's piano. In 1990, *Saffire/The Uppity Blues Women* was released on the Alligator label.

In 1990, that album was Alligator's second best-seller. The lead-off tune of *The Uppity Blues Women*, "The Middle Aged Blues Boogie," earned Adegbalola a W.C. Handy award for writing the "Song of the Year." Saffire/The Uppity Blues Women quickly went from performing in small Fredericksburg clubs to doing two hundred shows a year internationally and sharing the stage with artists such as B.B. King, Taj Mahal, and Etta James.

By the following year, with the release of *Hot Flash*, the group began to carve its niche. With lyrics as salacious as their titles—"Two in the Bush Is Better Than One in the Hand," "(No Need) Pissin' on a Skunk"—it became eminently clear that Saffire's material invited body movements other than just toe-tapping. Adegbalola's insinuating, field holler-style vocal, backed by Rabson's loose boogie-woogie/roadhouse piano, underscored by simple, tight bass and guitar, lay the groundwork for the group's musical appeal.

Saffire/The Uppity Blues Women, which has been profiled in *Playboy*, *The Village Voice*, the *New York Times*, *People*, *Interview*, and *Downbeat* as a novelty act, began to receive serious consideration in blues and jazz publications. In fact, after *Hot Flash* the group won first place in *Downbeat*'s Editor's Poll as Talent Deserving Wider Recognition in the Blues category.

Subsequently, Earlene Lewis left the group in 1992. Fortunately, Rabson and Adegbalola met Andra Faye McIntosh at a blues camp and jammed together.

Adegbalola: When we got ready to record the next album, I knew I wanted a fiddle on one tune. I remembered Andra and called her up. She protested that she wasn't good enough, but I told her, "I played with you enough to know. We want you."

(Post) Like her Saffire sisters, McIntosh had a respectable day job, as a registered nurse; after guesting on *Broadcasting*, McIntosh joined Saffire full-time for touring in 1992. (Faye bills herself an "Anglo-Saxon hillbilly," following the aforementioned convention of cultural self-description).

Broadcasting may be the group's most profound original album, partially because of Adegbalola's songwriting. During 1992, she was diagnosed with cancer. Flat on her back for several months, she felt helpless and increasingly angry watching media coverage of the Rodney King beating and subsequent trial. Her song, "If It Had Been A Dog," pleads for a just verdict in the trials of King's police assailants.

At another time, during that period Adegbalola was musing on the affirmation "I'm a man/I'm a hoochy coochy man."

Adegbalola: That's what the new song was going to be about, how Miss Thing was a hoochy coochy woman. But, as I lay there pissing and moaning, it occurred to me that I needed some of that Miss Thing attitude to deal with my illness. Instead of being about Miss Thing who could get anybody, the song turned out to be about Miss Thing who could fight illness. I needed some of that power, and I wrote "Miz Thang" as an invocation to make me stronger.

Ann Rabson
Photo: Marc Norberg

Andra Faye McIntosh

Gaye Adegbalola

(Post) Not only does the tune have a catchy bite all its own, but perhaps it did work as an invocation also; Adegbalola's cancer is in remission.

Saffire/The Uppity Blues Women have come into their own. *Old, New, Borrowed, Blue,* their fourth recording on Alligator, has sold over 25,000 copies, an immense number for an independent label. Here the women are so comfortable with their musical status that they return to the roots of blues and to their own influences, with covers like Ma Rainey's "Yonder Come The Blues" and Jelly Roll Morton's "Sweet Substitute." Originals like Adegbalola's "Bitch With A Bad Attitude" maintain their uppity reputation.

Gaye Adegbalola is pleased with what Saffire has done, and delighted with the reality of continuing to collaborate with Rabson and McIntosh. Her hopes?

Adegbalola: I would love for somebody like Koko Taylor to cover one of my songs. That would be a dream. That's totally from the satisfaction as a writer, aside from the fact that I would make money. I would love for somebody like Anita Baker to cover "Silent Thunder," or Dolly Parton to cover "Middle Aged Blues."

Financially, I really would like to send out for a pizza any night of the week and not have to worry about money. I would like to be more financially secure. I would love to have a little more creative space. I feel like my house is just getting in order. I've spent a lot of time dealing with health problems. My mother's eighty-one, my son is twenty-five, and I've just gotten them situated. I'm looking to do more writing and to sitting in with electric blues bands.

DISCOGRAPHY

Middle Age Blues (Saffire 1987); *The Uppity Blues Women* (Alligator, 1990); *Hot Flash* (Alligator, 1991); *Broadcasting* (Alligator, 1992); *Old, New, Borrowed, Blue* (Alligator, 1994);. *Cleanin' House* (Alligator, 1996).

For further recordings see Saffire's web page at
http://www.onewdesign.com/saffire/

SUE FINK
certified outrageous

She co-wrote one of Women's Music's all-time favorite songs, "Leaping Lesbians." She continues to write memorable songs in various styles from R&B to pop. She sparkles on keyboards and piano. She contributes musically to her peers' work (Alix Dobkin, Diane Lindsay, Margie Adam). And she is a fabulous emcee, with a quick wit, playful political astuteness, and willingness to target herself for gentle teasing. She is Sue Fink, and she remains one of the most under appreciated treasures of our feminist cultural network.

Outside of Women's Music & Culture, Sue Fink's talents are more appropriately acknowledged: she graduated magna cum laude from UCLA's music school; sang at Nixon's inauguration; performed on a State Department-sponsored, 13-nation tour of Asia with the California Chamber Singers; and sang on tour of Europe, Israel, Canada, Hawaii, and the continental U.S. with the Roger Wagner Chorale.

Brian Wilson (of the Beach Boys) and back-up singers for Aretha Franklin and Marvin Gaye have come to her to study voice. The National Association of Independent Record Distributors rewarded *Big Promise* (1985), Sue's solo debut, with an award of excellence. *True Life Adventure* (1989), her second release, featured tunes which freshly and candidly explored the age-old battle of the sexes ("I Want to Kill in A Popular War," "Letters to Marie").

Sue grew up in Beverly Hills studying piano and even a little guitar.

Sue Fink: When I was eight, and my brother John was eleven and my brother Barry was fourteen, I took a year of guitar lessons because they did. Listening to such folk artists as Peter, Paul, and Mary, the children played together as the "Finkston Trio."

(Post) From her first piano lessons at age eight, when her teacher Daisy Kaufman strapped on those rubber balls to keep her hands high, Sue knew the piano was for her.

Fink: The piano was my love; it spoke to me.

(Post)Sue also knew that she wanted to pursue music seriously.

Fink: I wanted to have The Susie Fink Show. You know, like the Perry Como Show.

(Post) Early experiences reinforced this ambition; though no one in her family was a performer, and only her grandmother played an instrument. Sue's father was an entertainment lawyer.

Fink: I spent my adolescence answering calls from Liberace (Mrs. Kaufman had been his first piano teacher) and Frank Zappa, and talking Jim Morrison through crises. [His] *Light My Fire* put me through college.

(Post) Sue spent the early 1970s teaching music in junior high schools. In 1977, she founded and conducted the L.A. Women's Community Chorus, a group which performed the music of women artists.

Along a parallel course, Sue met and collaborated with Joelyn Grippo, and together they wrote "Leaping Lesbians." In 1976 they put on a show called Bicentennial Review, with thirty-five women musicians. It was Sue's first active involvement in the burgeoning Women's Culture community.

Fink: Meg Christian was in the audience of my first performance, and she loved "Leaping Lesbians." She came up to me afterwards and asked if she could sing it.

(Post) Meg's interest, and that of other Women's Culture foremothers like editor Toni Armstrong, Jr., led to Sue's gig at the 1978 National Women's Music Festival, to her first tours, and eventually, to leaving teaching.

Fink: My lives were starting to overlap; it was getting dangerous for me to teach. There were women's events where former students had recognized me. After I got the chorus started, a parent at the school at which I was teaching found out I was a lesbian and tried to have me fired.

(Post) Sue's performing career ended prematurely due to stage fright; she played her last gig in December 1979, and returned to the chorus and to school. At the Grove Music Institute, Sue learned to arrange and compose. At the same time, she taught herself synthesizer technology because she sought a full orchestral sound for her music.

Subsequently, Sue began to address her stage fright through self-hypnosis. Realizing that she missed performing, she started a band with Diane Lindsay (keyboards), Carrie Barton (bass), and Marilyn Donadt (drums). When Diane (then on bass) went on tour with Meg, Meg asked Sue to play keyboards on the tour.

Thanks to Meg's spontaneous grace, Sue was unwittingly catapulted back into the spotlight.

Fink: Meg was singing a song, and I was playing my keyboard. Meg asked for me to do a keyboard solo. I felt paralyzed, and the only sounds that I could make with my fingers were tiny bleeps on the keys. Finally, Meg said, "Next keyboardist, please." Instead of cowering, I took a big bow, and the audience gave me an ovation. Then I relaxed. I got that if you're having fun, it's catching, and I found that if I didn't take myself so seriously, I could play freely.

I started the Certified Outrageous campaign as an antidote to the feelings of many women of being devalued and depressed. I playfully hypnotized the audience and certified the audience "outrageous." I was overcoming my fear, and I wanted to share that if it was OK for me to be who I was on stage, then it was OK for everyone to accept themselves and go for their dreams.

(Post) Soon following that tour, Meg left the women's network to pursue her spirituality. Diane asked Sue to play keyboards on Diane's tour. Sue suggested a double bill with each backing the other. Diane, who was recording her first album at the time, insisted that Sue would need an album to tour.

As it happened, Sue had little difficulty getting a recording. Due in part, to the wide audience to which her playing on Meg's tour had exposed her and, in part, to her own forthright, undaunted approach, Sue amassed $20,000 in five months.

Sue's experience with Ladyslipper, on whose label *Big Promise* was recorded, was a positive one, but Sue learned quickly that marketing her work would be challenging. Her big voice, eclectic musical style, energetic and fun-filled stage presence, and strong pro-woman and political themes did not fit readily into any established musical genre.

Though *Big Promise* reached the top thirty of college stations across the U.S.—remarkable for any debut release, even more remarkable for an independently-produced one—the college students didn't know to go to women's bookstores to buy the album and sales lagged disappointingly behind airplay.

Sue released *True Life Adventures* (1989) on her own Frostfire label. Most recently, she collaborated with Jamie Anderson on *A Family Of Friends*, the Women's Music compilation album, which features a "We are the World" chorus of women's music on the title track. The album has raised funds to fight the conservative "family values" crusade.

Fink: A group of us, including June Millington and Jamie, wrote the title track together. The song is about the idea of friends as family, and also about the fact that Women's Music can still be a community.

DISCOGRAPHY:

Big Promise (Ladyslipper, 1985); *True Life Adventure* (Frostfire, 1989).

SWEET HONEY IN THE ROCK
a community voice, singing from their soul

Bernice Johnson Reagon has been singing most of her fiftysomething years, the last twenty-one of them with Sweet Honey in The Rock. Though she may not know where they are going (Reagon states that she had no original vision for the group, only an intention), the five vocalists and one ASL (American Sign Language) interpreter are in touch with where they have come from: Africa, life, humanism. Through their harmonious voices—joyous and celebratory, contemplative and respectful, strident and angry—audiences connect with our own voices, our own selves.

Sweet Honey's audiences are a diverse and complex group of selves: gay, straight; of African, Hispanic, Asian, First Nations, and European cultures; able-bodied and disabled; hearing and deaf; male and female; children and elders. The gift of Sweet Honey is that she draws us all in, urges us to rise up in song, and forces us to look at each other as possible allies and certainly not strangers.

A Sweet Honey concert is a delicious ritual celebrating life changes, it is a challenging political baptism, it is a call to power through wonderful song. The semicircle of radiant sisters pulls from deep within the heart's wisdom to comment on contemporary exploitations and imbalances in the world. The ancestral framework of memory holds the structure together; the compelling tight choral forms weave together the individual and the community.

In 1971, Bernice Johnson moved from her hometown of Albany, Georgia to Washington, D.C. to attend graduate school at Howard University. As the vocal director of the Black Repertory Company in the nation's capitol, Reagon's job was to instruct the participants in the production of songs that covered the full range of Black life.

Bernice Johnson Reagon: Whether it was a children's song, or a work song, or a train whistle, or doo-wop, or gospel, or a spiritual, whatever was called for, I was supposed to help make sure that the actors could do it. I taught them things I knew from my particular song repertoire and when necessary, even made up songs.

(Post) Things that Reagon knew included songs in congregational style that she learned at the Black Baptist Church where her father was the minister. Reagon also knew spirituals from school choirs; the power of singing in jails and at rallies; the power of singing what you believe. Reagon's professional singing career had begun with the 1960s group, The Freedom Singers, the singing voice of the Student Non-Violent Coordinating Committee (SNCC), the radical students' wing of the Civil Rights Movement (Bernice Johnson later married and divorced the group's organizer, Cordell Reagon).

Reagon infused her theater group teaching with the passion that had inflamed

Photo: Sharon Farmer

her as a member of the NAACP and SNCC. She was asked to start a singing group based on the theater's repertoire. Reagon's first response to the request was considered uncertainty.

Reagon: I was concerned about whether or not that was a concert concept. I thought about whether it would make sense from the stage.

(Post) Deciding that such a singing group could be done, and that she would do it, Reagon began to conceptualize the structure.

Reagon: I wanted to try for a complex approach in terms of what issues we covered and in terms of what song forms we used. The first concert of the quintet Sweet Honey in the Rock—named for the fluid stability of women in the Black community—was November 23, 1973.

(Post) Reagon is quick to add that the complexity of song forms and stylistic approaches has developed as the group's personnel has changed. Carol Maillard, the only other original Sweet Honey member still performing in the group, brought dramatic experience. Ysaye Barnwell, who joined in 1979 and who commonly sings bass, initiated the processes which made Sweet Honey's concerts accessible to the deaf community. In 1980, ASL interpreter Shirley Childress Johnson became the sixth member of the group when it became apparent that Barnwell could not simultaneously sing and interpret.

A year later Aisha Kahlil brought the ensemble to a new level of improvisation; in 1985, Kahlil's sister, Nitanju Bolade Casel added her knowledge of jazz and traditional African music to Sweet Honey's capacity.

Reagon reports that she felt surprised at the broad and positive response to Sweet Honey. Her initial explanation is that people like the sound of strong Black choral singing. A moment later, she adds that there is power in the music itself, noting that Sweet Honey's first repertoire was based in the Black experience.

Reagon: In that repertoire were songs from Africa. In that repertoire were political songs that took positions on contemporary issues. I think people found the range of messages very attractive.

(Post) Reagon has learned, over the years, that the political issues addressed by Sweet Honey could be very specific and still have a universal reach; that people didn't have to agree with everything Sweet Honey said. In fact what Reagon has heard most, in terms of feedback, has been "Thank you for the work that you have done for all of these years." Reagon understands this appreciation to refer to Sweet Honey's being a particular kind of group operating in contemporary society; open and precise about their roots; and expressing an inclusive vision.

Reagon: People hear their own voice, through us, as a Black voice.

(Post) Part of Reagon's current vision includes coalition work. Though Reagon espouses harmony when it comes to Sweet Honey's music, she does not believe that the ultimate result of coalition work must be harmonious agreement. In fact, her test as to how the actual work is going measures whether you have to work hard to listen to other people; to get them to listen to you. She imagines that Sweet Honey brings together a complex community and defines Sweet Honey as the singing voice for that community, just as The Freedom Singers were a kind of singing voice of the Civil Rights movement.

Reagon: The world is so full of anxiety over the fact that people from different groups live next to each other. I like that Sweet Honey tries to lower that level of anxiety, tries to make it all right.

(Post) Reagon is clear, however, that Sweet Honey is not a collective. Though audiences may perceive the group as a homogeneous entity, the artists are as different from each other as they are similar. In other words, the challenging work of coalition has a place within the ensemble itself.

The women of Sweet Honey may seem to audiences like African queens and American legends, but Reagon treats them like women living full lives in the world and expects that they will take care of themselves so that Sweet Honey gets what she needs.

I want to know how Reagon defines the essence of Sweet Honey in the Rock. She begins by reiterating the qualities which made Sweet Honey appealing in the first place: exquisite harmonies; irresistible, traditional African songs; motion; color; political opinions and themes that hit home and to which people can genuinely relate. She adds that improvisation has played an increasingly large role and states that she is pleased and gratified to witness the spawning of so many similar groups which draw from strong vocal singing (Toshi Reagon, Zap Mama, and other community groups).

Reagon: When people say they love Sweet Honey in the Rock, they're talking about more than what I did.

(Post) Sweet Honey in the Rock has performed all over the world, has recorded more than ten albums, has received NAIRD (gospel, women's) and Grammy (traditional folk) awards, has appeared on the Oprah Winfrey Show and on the Arsenio Hall Show. I end by asking what has been a highlight for Reagon?

Reagon: That we have been able to keep on going for twenty-one years is an amazing and humbling thing to me; I'm proud. Walking on stage and feeling that a Sweet Honey concert is a safe place is one of the highest things for me.

DISCOGRAPHY

Sweet Honey In The Rock (Flying Fish, 1976); *B'lieve I'll Run On...See What The End's Gonna Be* (Redwood Records, 1978); *Good News* (Flying Fish, 1982); *We All...Every One of Us* (Flying Fish, 1983); *Feel Something Drawing Me On* (Flying Fish, 1985); *The Other Side* (Flying Fish, 1985); *Live At Carnegie Hall* (Flying Fish, 1988); *Breaths—The Best Of Sweet Honey In The Rock* (Cooking Vinyl, 1989); *All For Freedom* (Music for Little People, 1989); *I Got Shoes* (Music for Little People, 1994); *In This Land* (EarthBeat!, 1992); *Still On The Journey* (EarthBeat!, 1993); *Sacred Ground* (EarthBeat!, 1995).

TERESA TRULL
educated feminist redneck sings with soul and integrity

She burst onto the Women's Music scene with a convincing pop-soul voice, a feminist bent, and an animal near her heart (check out the hound on the jacket of her debut disc). Like many of the other pioneers of early Women's Music, Trull was simply a woman writing songs from a woman's point of view; her sensitive approach and forceful singing made her a welcomed ally to other women trying to be heard.

I heard Trull sing live many times before fully appreciating the impact of her playful voice. At the Michigan Womyn's Music Festival, mid-1980s, Trull faced a crowd of thousands from a small stage in the wilderness. Mostly she sang miked, but for a startling moment or two she would remove the electronic amplification and project, voice-only, into the crowd and beyond, into the hills and trees. What emerged from her slight form was enough to echo from miles away; to fill the glen; to resonate deeply.

After years of gospel and R&B-based singing, garnering a primarily lesbian audience (with *The Ways a Woman Can Be* and *Let It Be Known*), Trull shifted gears and embarked upon a stint doing more folk-based work with Windham Hill artist, Barbara Higbie. Their collaborative album, *Unexpected*, was highly ranked on numerous commercial listings (*Billboard*, *CashBox*).

When Trull released her fourth album, *A Step Away*, she received equally positive acclaim from reviewers and performers alike. That supporting tour featured such Bay Area luminaries as singer-keyboardist Bonnie Hayes and singer-percussionist Vicki Randle.

More recently, Trull released *Country Blessed*, a duet album with Cris Williamson, which marked a notable foray into producing. The producing idea originated with Trull—the concept of a duet album was from Williamson—and may be responsible for re-igniting Williamson's prodigious career and also for coaxing Williamson's normally exquisite voice into previously unexplored heavenly ranges.

Throughout her career Teresa Trull has produced cuts and albums for several artists (Ron Romanovsky, Hunter Davis, Romanovsky & Phillips, Deidre McCalla, Lucie Blue Tremblay, Washington Sisters, Holly Near, Ferron, Cris Williamson & Tret Fure) as well as performed with the likes of Sheila E., Joan Baez, Alex DiGrassi, and Tracy Nelson.

Of late, Trull has returned to her roots in rural northern California, working with horses—the first horse she owned was a gift from a grateful woman whose mute child Trull had inspired to sing.

Post: Tell me about your background and musical origins.

Photo: Irene Young

Teresa Trull: I was raised partially on a chicken farm and partially in Durham, NC. What actually got me into music was church. We used to sing in choir, and the choir director used to give candy bars to people who could do the best. I was highly motivated. I grew up singing, but, to be honest, I was determined to be a behavioral biologist. I wanted to work with animals. I got a chemistry scholarship to Duke University and went there planning to come out of it being a researcher. When I went to school and saw the heinous things that went on in research labs, I lost my spirit for it.

At the time I was singing for fun. This rock and roll group came to a talent show; after hearing me, one guy said, "There's something behind that voice," and asked me to join their group. He told me they would pay me. A light bulb went off in my head: "You mean I can make a living singing?"

Post: What kind of music were you doing?

Trull: Rock and roll. I, of course, grew up completely on soul and gospel, which led to conflicts in the band. They were doing original material and covering Grateful Dead and Rolling Stones; I had literally never heard of those groups. I was always asking, "Why not some Aretha songs or Sam and Dave?" I was only sixteen, and everyone else in the band was in their late 20s, so, in a multitude of ways, it was an education.

Post: Then what?

Trull: I didn't have any money. I'm from a working class family; my father lived in a trailer at the corner of two freeways, and I hadn't lived at home since I was sixteen, when my mother died and I moved out. So I was waiting tables and working the Duke grounds crew, doing all kinds of jobs to make ends meet which was part of the hard thing about school. Eventually, the band was touring and making money, I decided to go. The very last gig, we show up and it's a topless club; I was horrified. They paid us $1000 to leave!

I didn't know what to do after that. I decided that I needed to move anywhere just to try and make a living in music because I couldn't make a living in music in Durham because it's too small. I thought, "How am I going to move? I don't know anyone anywhere, I've never left this town."

I went to a feminist summer school in Vermont with some friends. At nineteen my consciousness was basically that of an educated redneck. I used to write songs about my relationships, which I thought wasn't weird at all, but women would hand me books like *The Second Sex*. I got involved in karate—which helped my discipline and presence— and met a writer who was going to Canada to write a screenplay and needed someone to housesit in Manhattan. I went right from the chicken farm to the Big Apple.

I grew up loving the country and I had thought the last two places in the world I ever wanted to go were Manhattan and Los Angeles. They were the first two places I ever lived away from Durham! What happened was: the writer got fired in two weeks, so she came back and I had to go. I was ready to put my tail between my legs and go home until I met this street woman named Frances. She turned me on to an apartment on the Lower East Side that I rented for eighty dollars a month and lived in for a year. That's when I first met Olivia Records.

Friends of mine, who ran a radio show, had recorded some of my songs and sent them to Olivia, then in California. They had heard about Olivia when they were in D.C. and tried to get me to write, but I was too bashful and felt too raw. Olivia wrote me in New York and asked if, when Meg Christian came to New York to play, I could meet with her. She came, and I played a couple of songs at her show.

Then Olivia and I were corresponding; they said that they would like to do a record with me, but it would be a year or so before they could get to it. The first warm day in New York, a woman got raped in my courtyard, and my apartment got ripped off. I wrote this to Olivia like they were inconsequential facts, and they wrote back and said, "Pack your stuff up and move out here. You can work in packing and shipping until your record happens." I got a drive-away car and moved to L.A.

Post: Were you beginning to consider a career in music?

Trull: I was making money at the time by playing on the street, but there's a weird part of me that's always been practical about money. I come from a poor family: my father's family were all hillbillies, lived in the mountains, and my parents were always struggling financially. My father had an easygoing nature about money, and I inherited it. For me it was the philosophy of using one charge card to pay off another, that money in and of itself isn't enough to make anyone happy. By that time, I was pretty proud of myself; I've been working making money doing music; I didn't need to make too much.

Post: Were you making enough to live on?

Trull: You have to understand my overhead was very slight. This sounds so silly, but this is not an 'Oh, poor me' story; I enjoyed myself. I would go down to 11th Avenue where they had these factories where you could by five pounds of chicken livers or gizzards for $1.00. I would go buy that and—I swear to God this was before I moved to California and understood nutrition—buy livers or gizzards, a half gallon of peach ice cream, a gallon of milk, and English muffins. I would make a stew with the gizzards and rice, eat peach milk shakes, and stew and English muffins every day. To this day, I still have that same kind of habit. I can eat the same meal for weeks in a row and never get tired of it.

Post: And now?

Trull: My low-stress attitude about money totally prepared me for the hand-to-mouth lifestyle of musicians. I'm still living that kind of life, elevated a couple of plateaus. I'm getting to the age, now, where I wish I had a little more security; I don't have savings or anything like that. I'm getting by, and I still have this undisturbed faith about it.

Post: Is the low financial status of musicians in Women's Music only?

Trull: No, it happens in music at large. In Women's Music what is true is that I—and maybe every musician—spend time trying to attach and detach simultaneously from the concept. For me, I've always understood Women's Music to be a temporary means to an end in the same way you'd have Black separatism in a civil rights situation and eventually hope that everyone would be equal with each other.

Hopefully, as women gain more of a foothold in the music industry, which they certainly have begun to do, what will happen is that more types of music that project different images of women will become available.

Post: Do you think that Women's Music doesn't need to be anymore?

Trull: We are definitely at a level where there is not as much demand for it. There are new generations of women who have more available to them. With Olivia, the hard thing was that they were starting a business whose purpose was to raise money for a political end. We thought that people would buy records simply because they were put out by Olivia, that people would think more politically about wanting to support something than about whether they wanted to hear the music. But, after the initial couple of records, people started to have more musical discretion.

Post: How did you deal with those changes?

Trull: I had a parting of the ways with Olivia around 1981 because I've always had politics by default. Not to demean myself because I've always had integrity—I got into situations because I don't believe in lying and I believe in being who I am, and I have my own grassroots politics which extends into the politics of the world—but the thing of it is that, with Olivia, even with my lack of worldliness about understanding politics, I brought a working class perspective to the collective. My own interest was based in my desire for security; I joined Olivia thinking that I should be part of a record company in lieu of my performing career failing.

Post: How did the parting of the ways happen?

Trull: Difference in philosophy. The people that were more philosophically united with me, got burned out, and left. All that was left was myself, Judy [Dlugacz], and Meg [Christian]. Meg was on her way out, didn't want anything to do with the record company. At that point, I was a pain in the butt because I didn't agree with where Judy wanted to go.

I wanted to make Olivia more of a record company and was willing to take risks to make it more technically viable. Judy wanted to be on the safe route, to depend on the markets that we always had used. I wanted a high technicianship and was willing to involve men on the records; Judy wanted to stay separatist. I did the record with Barbara [Higbie] on Second Wave and then told Judy what I wanted to do: to go down to Los Angeles and do a record in the most technically competitive way; I was a budding producer. I said that Olivia's records weren't cutting it, as far as fidelity was concerned. They could cut it politically and musically, but, if you put them out there with bigger industry records, they wouldn't keep up.

I went to L.A., and Olivia wasn't interested. But Redwood was interested. Then, after *A Step Away*, I got more involved in producing and with horses.

Post: Why horses?

Trull: I grew up with horses and the riding; it's a part of my own growing-up mythology; horses and birds have always been important to me. The biggest love of my life; from age three, I would just about do anything to be on a horse. As a kid, my mother had this friend who would let me stay whole weekends in her stable, where I would work for lessons. Until seventh grade, I rode at that place. Then, I rode near the chicken farm. Even when I was first working at Olivia, I was going riding up in the Berkeley hills.

Post: So, *Country Blessed* was a natural project for you?

Trull: After I did *A Step Away*, I was severely disillusioned. At the time, I was also working with Bonnie Hayes, in her band, and we toured with Huey Lewis off and on for a year. Her new record never hit the shelf, and Redwood never delivered the support for *A Step Away* that they had promised.

All my life, I'd had this big ambition to make it in music. What that meant to me was not fame and power but I wanted to be able to financially support myself. Then, I went on this tour and saw what it was really like to live that life. I had a monitor that was my very own, my own mix, but it was the worst. I have never seen more miserable people; I never saw people more slaves to what they do. The music was completely lost once they had made that change from being musicians to having a marketable product. Businessmen took over their lives. I came to a realization: This is not what I want to do. My interest is music. Then and there, I made the decision that all future decisions that I would make would have to do with my self-expression and contentment.

I went on sabbatical. I wasn't playing; I was producing. *Country Blessed* was supposed to be a Cris Williamson record: Cris singing, me producing. I had convinced Cris to do the project, and Olivia was willing. I'm sure that, from a business standpoint, they were hoping to revive the success of *Changer*.

My focus was—Cris is my best friend, Cris is an enormous talent—that one of the problems was that she had a voice that's so beautiful and amazing, nobody wanted to push her. I thought that she could sing all day—for her, a mediocre performance—yet people would be falling over backwards. I had always wanted to produce Cris, partially for selfish reasons: I had never produced a vocalist, someone whose identity was a vocalist, except for maybe myself.

Cris and I had done a ton of tours, and I knew that it would be hard for her to see me as a producer. I was producing a Hunter Davis record, and Hunter needed something to help publicize herself. What could be better than to do a duet with a famous artist? I told Hunter that I would get Cris to do the duet with her, and she was thrilled. My own agenda was to produce a great track with Cris in it, and see if I could make her enthusiastic about doing something else with my producing. And it worked.

Post: What have been some of the highlights so far in your career?

Trull: Other than *Country Blessed*, was—you'll probably laugh yourself sick—when I sang the national anthem at a Golden State Warriors' game. They were playing the Utah State jazz, and it was sold out; there were sixteen thousand people there. Somebody knew my singing and kept calling Olivia to have me sing the anthem at a game—I guess they have a hard time finding someone—but I worried that it was too tacky.

I'm a total sports junkie. I would probably sit my whole life glued in front of the TV set if I didn't have friends. After they asked me two years in a row I began to think, "Everyone says how hard the national anthem is to sing." When I showed up the sound guy looked at me and thought I was petite, with a teeny voice, so he cranked it.

I thought: I've been to a million games. What's going to happen is it's not going to be a big deal. They're going to drag a mike onto the corner of the court and everybody is going to be talking and yelling, and all they want is to get done so they can watch the game. No pressure.

Then, they cut out all the lights, put a spotlight in center court, and announced me. I was thinking, Fuck me to tears; this is serious. I distinctly remember deciding that all musicians should be in this situation—as a recording artist, you get spoiled knowing that, if you are playing a concert, people have actually paid money to come see you—because this was not secure.

The first line I was mumbling, then something clicked in my head. The fright of it all poured into me, and by the time I started the bridge I was going for it, and I had a standing ovation. I was so proud; they gave me seven tickets for the game, and I got to sit right behind the bench!

Post: What would you like in your future?

Trull: I want to be producing. The last two years I've been making my first connections outside of the women's community. Fantasy Records now recommends me. I love getting something out of people, and getting great performances, and taking care of people in the studio, and building those relations.

I'd love to do another record but the problem is that, between having a full time training business with horses and producing, I barely have time to breathe or eat. Also, I know that all kinds of people are out there struggling trying to get a record deal. I'm in a rock and roll band right now, and I am performing, but I don't have any big tours because in order to book tours, I need a new record. I've written some songs and I'd like very much to record them, but it's hard to get up the initiative to want to raise money for it. I am busy, and happy, but I wish I had more time to do my own music.

DISCOGRAPHY

The Ways A Woman Can Be (Olivia, 1977); *Let It Be Known* (Olivia, 1980); *Unexpected* with Barbara Higbie (Second Wave, 1983); *A Step Away* (Redwood, 1986); *Country Blessed* with Cris Williamson (Second Wave/Olivia 1989).

THE TOPP TWINS
one has bungee-jumped, the other hasn't

Lynda and Jools Topp, identical twins with that eerie twin kinship and an irresistible propensity for finishing each other's sentences, are as different from each other as they are from stereotypical Kiwi country/western lesbian political theatrical humorists. Physically solid, Lynda has the magnificent yodel. Jools, sparer in size and in conversation, sports a dry sense of humor, and comes alive onstage, pacing their musical sets with her guitar. Lynda is the one who fastened herself to an elastic cord, New Zealand-style, and dove, terrified, off a high place. She did it twice and proudly tells the tale; Jools wouldn't think of it.

Raised on a dairy farm on the North Island of New Zealand, Lynda and Jools milked cows from the ages of five to fifteen and obtained the "educational certificates that we needed in order to leave school." The egalitarian example of their home life set the path upon which they travel.

Lynda Topp: Home was open.

Jools Topp: Very open. It was like there were no stereotypes in the family.

Lynda: If the hay had to be picked up, everybody picked up hay. If the dishes had to be done, everybody did the dishes.

(Post) Taking inspiration from their mother, who sang, they were given a guitar when they were eleven. Because it was considered rude to have the record player going for guests, the Topp Twins got their chance to play and sing at a yearly local shindig.

Jools: The beauty of that is that we have no formal training. We taught ourselves to sing. We taught ourselves to play guitar. What we've done is we've created our own style from the background we've come from. It seems to work for us back home. We've always had an extremely good following back home.

(Post) Home is not the only place where the Topp Twins have drawn fans. In response to their unselfconscious charm and sense of fun, audiences have swelled around them; across tiny New Zealand and the broader expanses of Australia, Canada, the UK, and the United States. At a recent National Women's Music Festival, the audience liked the Topp Twins yodeling so much that, following a main stage appearance, the Topps drew a standing-room-only crowd for an after-hours coffeehouse set.

Like her down-to-earth manner, Lynda's yodel is come by honestly.

Lynda: The neighbors lived up the road from us, about twenty-five minutes on horseback. They used to have an old wind-up gramophone and old yodel records. I listened to three particular yodelers. One was a woman called Patsy Montana, the first woman to sell a million records in America. And two Australian yodelers, Shirley Thoms and June Holmes. They were my inspiration, when I was a little kid. I used to listen to the wind-up gramophone, jump on my horse, race home, get the guitar out and try desperately to remember what I heard up the road. It took three years to learn yodeling.

Jools: Because by the time she'd gotten on the horse and come home, she'd forgotten the music and had to go up the road again.

Lynda: Then I was banished to the back of the farm for a year while I was learning. We have this joke now. You know people say, "How do you learn to yodel?" and we say, "Well, have you got three years? And a farm?"

Jools: And a mother who's not going to let you in the house until you do it properly?

(Post) Jools and Lynda Topp learned community-building skills in a situation surprising for women pacifists hailing from a nuclear-free country: the territorial army. They joined in order to venture to New Zealand's South Island, and realizing that they felt different from the other enlisted women, went AWOL after coming out as lesbians.

Lynda and Jools ended up in Christchurch, the biggest city on the South Island. Supporting themselves with blue-collar jobs, they hung out, met some professional musicians and were intrigued with the thought of singing in front of a microphone. Their first gig drew three hundred people; Lynda and Jools pulled out their guitars and had a party.

A women's fundraiser followed, as did skits and theatre bits for their debut tour in 1979. Touring with Helen Caldicott in New Zealand, and with Billy Bragg in England, brought them an eclectic, loyal following. They ended up back home in 1988.

Jools: The world was coming at us

(Post) Voted New Zealand's Entertainers of the Year in 1987, their commissioned theatre show was voted Best TV Performance the same year. Their political humor expanded with their audience; they allowed their dog, River to wander onto their set during gigs.

Lynda: She's a semi-famous dog back home.

(Post) Perhaps the most resounding tribute to the talents of Lynda and Jools Topp is that their successes haven't spoiled them.

Lynda: Maybe one of the most exciting things for us is that we have had such a wonderful response from our own home.

Jools: We've established a circuit that allows us to play in all sorts of venues. We play in small towns, we play in two thousand-seat theatres in Wellington for two nights running. We've been accepted by middle New Zealanders because we're honest about our sexuality. You've got to be honest, tell the truth, say who you are first, then you can give a much stronger performance.

Lynda: There's this whole energy going on for us.

Jools: A lot of energy.

Lynda: Our audience has to be part of the show. Don't just come and watch and then walk out the door. When we do our live shows in New Zealand the audience is up on stage. We do games with them. It's like we've broken down the barriers of traditional theatre as well.

Lynda: There's a running gag in New Zealand that you never sit in the front row at one of our shows, just in case.

Jools: We tell them that no seat is safe. But I think that the beauty of a Topp Twins show is that you don't know what's going to happen. We don't know what's going to happen because seventy-five percent of the show is scripted, but the rest isn't. People come to see that twenty-five percent.

Lynda: That's what makes it magic. There's something quite beautiful about it for the performer who's prepared to be spontaneous.

(Post) The Topp Twins have never committed any of their four theatre shows to paper. They incorporate current political issues in a flexible and ever-changing way, aware of political similarities across national borderlines. They break character to do impromptu ad-libs and songs, and claim that audiences remember those moments because they are so different from the rest of the show.

Lynda and Jools feel compelled to be political performers, to function as role models, to be consistently out on stage. Their formula works because their audiences span age groups sexual orientations, urban and rural cultures, classes.

Lynda: We are raging lesbians who sing country & western and yodel, sing political songs, as well as do theatre. The diversity of our performances is the thing that keeps us alive and keeps us going.

Jools: We are educating New Zealand. And we have fun too. We tour everywhere. And every tour we try to have a new concert.

Lynda: In 1989 we toured the North Island in a gypsy caravan pulled by a tractor. It took us four months to do that tour of the North Island alone because the tractor was

going fifteen miles an hour. But when we pulled into town, the women would say, "Aw, look at that, an old gypsy caravan, isn't that beautiful?" And all the farmers would say, "I had a tractor like that in 1956."

(Post) The Topp Twins have parlayed their intuitive honesty, genuine talent, and ingenious ability to engage with all kinds of people into international recognition. They are consummate professionals: knowledgeable about technical aspects, refreshingly unassuming about participating wholly in the technical set-up, entirely focused on the show. They know who they are, they are positive about who they are, and their unquestioned assumption that they will be liked and appreciated has won hearts and set examples.

Lynda & Jools in unison: We have it pretty good.

(Since this interview, the Topp Twins have appeared on the CBS television newsmagazine "60 Minutes;" have made a successful foray into country music; and are currently writing their own TV series.)

DISCOGRAPHY

Topp Twins Go Vinyl (Topp Twins, 1982); *Twinset And Pearls* (Topp Twins, 1984); *No War In My Heart* (Topp Twins, 1987); *Wear Something Sexy* (Topp Twins, 1991); *Hightime* (Topp Twins, 1992); *Twotiming* (Topp Twins, 1994).

THROWING MUSES
Kristen Hersh, her writing has been as much of a curse as a blessing

Shirley MacLaine made it socially acceptable to channel one's own inner spirit into words: for Kristen Hersh, leader of Throwing Muses, such channeling is a necessary way of life. Hersh founded Throwing Muses half a lifetime ago, when she was fourteen, though she states that her actual writing began even earlier.

Kristen Hersh: As a nine-year-old kid, I had my father teach me to play the guitar; I imitated my favorite songwriters and made up new songs. The songs started writing themselves when I was fourteen. My son is nearly nine, so I know what it's like for a nine-year-old to do anything.

(Post) The contrasts within Hersh serve as a structure for understanding the mercurial, sometimes savage music and onstage demeanor of her performance. One moment, she is laughing over how her father had written songs for no particular purpose, the next moment describing Throwing Muses as being like Neil Young with a Jungian perspective. Downright contemptuous of overt fame-seekers, Hersh explains the tortured basis of her own writing.

Hersh: I hear lots of pieces of songs banging into one another, all playing at the same time. I have to tear them apart and turn them into a song. I don't seem to express myself or make anything up, my job is to shut up and listen. I have very little to do with the process. If I don't turn ideas into songs, they can get stuck in me and make me sick. Writing songs is better than letting the feelings get stuck in me, but it doesn't feel cathartic. If I don't write, then I begin to hallucinate the images of the songs. Then, the songs take a life of their own, like Frankenstein.

(Post) At the age of fourteen Hersh had already discovered the soothing effect of marshalling the demons within into songs, and the nascent Throwing Muses became known for the emotionally abrasive, quintessentially honest style of its Hersh-generated tunes. From the beginning, when, at nineteen, Hersh and her three cohorts left Rhode Island for the Boston club scene, her songs had always been a surprising and unpredictable blend of screeching fragility, eccentric structures, guitar splatter, dark and zipless lyrics, and intentionally dissonant bass and drum parts.

Hersh formally started a band called the Muses in 1981.

Hersh: Music moved me hard, and it has never let go of my spine. I don't remember it being a conscious effort to make records, maybe because we were young. We were playing in clubs by the time I was fifteen.

(Post) Hersh was the one responsible for buying the equipment and even teach-

Photo: Steve Gulick

ing the original (pre-David Narcizo, who is billed as TM's 'original' drummer) drummer to play. While still in high school, Hersh managed and booked the band for four years. Immediately following, Hersh found herself living in her car and showering at the YMCA: breaking into the music industry was hard.

The band's name was a twisted tribute to femaleness.

Hersh: We couldn't be "goddesses" because we had a boy in the band, so I put 'Throwing' in front of "Muses!

(Post) Hersh has more to say about female styles of music:

Hersh: The rule of pop is to be masculine, solid and predictable. The feminine rules are to be sporadic, maybe not in real time, with attention to detail, stuff that sounds deviant.

(Post) Though it was the scary, sonic sounds of X and The Violent Femmes which influenced Hersh—not the gentler music of Rhode Island-based Talking Heads—Hersh glows when speaking of what she calls 'feminine musicians:' Kurt Cobain, Michael Stipe, Mary Margaret O' Hara, the Velvet Underground. It does not escape Hersh that VU had a woman drummer, Moe Tucker, and Hersh considers, warily, that the world may have to learn to respect 'feminine' approaches to music by male musicians before women musicians are widely appreciated.

Sending rough demos around garnered the Throwing Muses an offer from 4AD, a UK-based label sporting mostly grim and nihilistic music. Because Hersh, at nineteen, was pregnant, TM wasn't able to travel to Britain to record, though Hersh claims that she continued to play every night. During the making of that first album, Hersh felt that she had to tone down her vocal attack:

Hersh: I felt it was bad for the baby for me to be screaming that loud.

(Post) In 1986, Throwing Muses released their debut and self-titled record, which launched them onto the covers of *Melody Maker* and *NME* as a band levels deeper than the previous punkers, such as the Sex Pistols, who sang more about politics. Hersh, with a curiously precise awareness, pooh-poohs that adulation.

Hersh: We were really big in England because they made us a trend, but it's never been our focus to pay attention to those things. We did want to make a good record and we did that.

(Post) Later that same year, TM released *Chains Changed* and, in 1987, *The Fat Skier*, which paved their way to the US-based major label, Sire/Warner. Hersh's songs continued to come to her, though, perhaps this new batch were less jaggedly visionary and more resembling the smoothly inviting music of another early influence, R.E.M.

The next years saw the release of two albums which served to further define Throwing Muses' unusual, personal sound: *House Tornado* (1988) and *Hunkpapa* (1989). In 1990, after bassist Leslie Langston left road life to marry and settle down, they made *The Real Ramona* (1991) with Fred Abong on bass; a year later, Hersh's stepsister, Tanya Donnelly, apparently tired of playing second string in both Throwing Muses and in the Breeders, started her own outfit, Belly. A new TM lineup—featuring

Hersh, Narcizo, and bassist Bernard Georges—produced 1992's *Red Heaven* and the current album, *University*, with its spare production and enhanced accessibility.

I wonder how Hersh integrates her creativity with her home life (she is married and has two sons), and she answers that it continues to be a mighty struggle.

Hersh: My writing has been as much of a curse as a blessing. I never ask for it to happen, but it does. I adore songs, but they are my religion so it's a big deal, and it can hurt. I try to promise it a piece of my brain, let it talk when it needs to and shut it up when it's going to take a piece of my body or my house. Time is hard, just like it is for any working parent. Little sleep, live on coffee, and I have to be much more responsible than most rock musicians.

(Post) Clear about her own dislike of the rock and roll lifestyle ("There are a lot of numbing things about it"), Hersh becomes fiercely protective when contemplating exposing her young children, Dylan and Ryder, to it.

Hersh: In family life, there's nothing numbing. It's all dangerous, and it's all high, and it's great. The baby comes with me almost everywhere.

(Post) In a chummy moment, Hersh details how, after speaking with her older son's father, she had suggested that Dylan not enter Boy Scouts ("Since they disavow homosexuality and they say that there is only one Christian God") but is gratified to learn that he might be interested in music:

Hersh: He realizes that other moms don't have records; he's starting to think it's cool instead of embarrassing.

(Post) Throwing Muses has recently been in *Billboard* (12/94), *Interview* (1/95), *People* (2/27/95), and in *Rolling Stone* (3/9/95); *University*, which was released 1/17/95, has already sold over 75,000 copies. I'm curious as to Hersh's goals.

Hersh: My goals are not business-oriented. The Grammies, for example, don't have much to do with music. It's just the industry patting itself on the back. It would be great if they gave Grammies to good bands. On the other hand, I'm not asking for it because it's not a measure of success for me. Some of our tours have been amazing, and I feel really lucky to do this as a job given the way my band sounds. So far, we've been doing what we want to do, and we haven't gone too hungry.

DISCOGRAPHY

Throwing Muses:
Throwing Muses (4AD, 1986); *Chains Changed*, EP (4AD, 1986); *The Fat Skier* (4AD, 1987); *House Tornado* (Sire, 1988); *Hunkpapa* (Sire, 1989); *The Real Ramona* (Sire, 1991); *Red Heaven* (Sire, 1992); *University* (Sire, 1995).

Kristen Hersh:
Hips and Makers (1994)

VICKI RANDLE
the most watched, unknown great-voiced musician in America

The first thing that Vicki Randle consciously remembers is music. The first thing that I remember about Vicki Randle, from watching her backstage at the Michigan Womyn's Music Festival years ago, is how seriously she takes her music. She stretched and did scales, practiced the lyrics, checked in and confirmed the energy with her principal stage mate, Linda Tillery. When she finally emerged onstage she seemed relaxed, her flying soprano effortless, her percussion fluid and passionate. Yet all of us who had witnessed knew how much of her soul she poured into those privileged moments in front of the crowd of thousands. I knew, then, that I wanted to interview her.

That interview was years in the making. First, no Women's Music publication was interested in a story about her because of her relative anonymity within Women's Music. The myth persisted, despite musicians like Randle and Tillery, that the genre was started by white-women-with-guitars playing folk music—even though she had contributed enormously to Cris Williamson's seminal *The Changer And The Changed* album, and others, in the mid-1970s.

Second, Vicki Randle was busy. By the time I was doing my own book—and could include anyone I wanted—she had been hand-picked by Branford Marsalis to sing and play percussion with Jay Leno's "Tonight Show" band. Her rep as a solid player and vocalist, though apparently invisible to the Women's Music network, had transcended that industry and landed her in focus of the world.

Third, she was doubtful that anyone could tell her story with the right mix of emotions toward Women's Music and the mainstream. Though I have never met Vicki Randle, we did spend several hours in phone conversation during which I convinced her that I was the writer who understood and who could do the job.

Her insight, knowledge, and utter musicality convinced me—again, as if I needed convincing—that I wanted her story and perspective in this book. Soon thereafter Vicki Randle let me know that she wanted to be included.

I was so willing that I agreed to do the interview by email/fax—the only one in this collection to have been conducted in that manner—but it worked out. Maybe someday we will meet and, under less impersonal circumstances, I will get to hear, in her own voice, and in her presence, the sequel to the story presented here about what makes her singing so special, her history so unique, her point of view so searing.

Post: Where was music in your early life?

Vicki Randle: My father was a jazz pianist, my mother always sang. However we didn't get our first record player until I was probably eight. My father, I think, had a bit of resentment against popular music, blaming it for the demise of jazz in the '50s and '60s and mostly didn't like to listen to music. I understand that even more personally now, as I rarely listen to music as background.

The first music that I deeply loved was the choral music I sang in the choir at St. Agatha's Catholic Church. Perhaps it was the connection to the rites and mysticism of the Catholic mass, and it never failed to fill me with wonder. I have a reverence for the power of music and what it can evoke in me. I continue to chase this feeling in the music that I hear, perform and compose.

When I was ten, we got our first console record player and, besides a large classical and jazz repertoire of my mother's, the only music I ever heard or played was the Beatles. I became a bit of a fanatic and decided that I wanted to be them. I begged my mother for a guitar and finally was able to acquire a used Sears Silvertone acoustic with a huge crack in it that one of my friends was tossing out. This guitar became the bargaining chip my mother used to make me behave and, since I wasn't ever very good at fulfilling her expectations, it spent most of its time put up in a closet, and I spent most of my time plotting ways to get at it.

I think my parents' disdain for pop music, and specifically the guitar as an instrument, made it irresistible for me. They tried to give me piano lessons but I hated them and they finally gave up trying to make me learn. Now, of course, I love playing the piano and wish I was better at it.

Even today I have never received any formal instruction on any of the instruments I play, have attended only months of college, and the only instruction I've received has been voice, even that long after I had become a professional musician.

Though I was decidedly discouraged from considering a musical career, my mother was a bit of a stage mom, finding ways to get me on a stage at every opportunity and encouraging me to perform for friends, church, school and almost any occasion. I had clearly shown a particular talent for singing and reportedly there are tapes in existence of me at age three doing so.

I am the oldest of seven kids, the next four after me were boys. We were no more than a year and a half apart so we operated essentially as a unit. My siblings and I seemed to have been blessed with an abundance of talent and skills in the arts, academics and sports. All of us played instruments, sang, acted, drew, played sports, got straight A's, etc. We all engaged in these activities together, encouraging each other. There was very little competition, as each one of us seemed to choose an arena to specialize in naturally, drawn by an affinity for it rather than being arbitrarily assigned one based on socialization, gender specifics or expectations. Even if my folks wanted to try and treat me differently because I was a girl, there really wasn't any realistic way of doing that. I learned everything the same way they did, at the same time and never heard anything about the differences between girls and boys, except possibly in the anatomy department.

Most of my brothers and sisters also became very active musically and most of us still engage regularly in the medium, even if it's not the way we support ourselves. My oldest brother and his wife have a reggae band, my third brother has a very successful career as an opera singer and has lived in England for the past eight years, my oldest sister does local civic light opera productions and the occasional club gig.

Vicki Randle

I realize now that this was a fairly utopian upbringing. It wasn't until high school that reality descended upon me and I was suddenly faced with such mysterious concepts as, "Girls don't play guitar, girls are supposed to sing" and "Let the boys think they are smarter, otherwise you'll never get a boyfriend" and the like. Really threw me and I never learned the fine art of acquiescing very well.

Post: How did you get started playing yourself?

Randle: I started playing in bands, usually metal, rock, pop and playing acoustic traditional Irish and English music with another guitar player and at the Renaissance Faire. I began to listen to jazz and Bossa Nova (which were my parents' favorite music) and discovered that I could sing solos like I heard the horns playing, while my picking style emulated the rest of the band: drums, bass and the rest of the rhythm section.

When I heard Ella Fitzgerald and other scat singers, the last piece fell into place for me, and I began to develop a style of work that couldn't really be categorized, therefore wasn't in direct competition with the guys I was playing with at the time. Eventually, though, I realized that my musical style was so eclectic that finding people to play with was a bother, so I mostly performed, and still do, solo.

Now all this would make perfect sense if I was a white girl, but I do happen to be black; well mixed-race, truth be told. If it sounds like I was pretty much raised like a white person, devoid of much contact with an African-American cultural context, you are correct. My mother is white, and since she and my father were divorced when I was nine, my exposure to anything having to do with the black culture was severely limited. My mother didn't like contemporary black music or gospel, the only music I heard in church were the baroque style compositions sung in the Catholic mass. I did not even hear Aretha Franklin, Otis Redding, Etta James or Stevie Wonder (who are my biggest influences in R&B) until I was in high school, and then very sparingly.

By the time I was fifteen, we had moved to the Redneck bastion of Southern California, Orange County, and I became the only black girl most of my peers had ever seen. I began to encounter a rather confusing scenario, where I would show up with my acoustic guitar at gigs to sing folk-country-rock type and people would ask me if I knew any Diana Ross or Aretha tunes.

I'm not sure when I began to consider myself a professional musician, but by the time I was eighteen or so it was the primary way I made my living, meager and sparse as it was. I moved to Los Angeles and began singing in clubs, mostly jazz and cabaret style music, while alternately growing a following in clubs that featured original music as a singer/songwriter. One of those clubs was the late Bla-Bla Cafe, a showcase club that was dedicated to featuring and launched many out of the mainstream singer/songwriters, where I had a regular night for several years.

When I was twenty-three, I relocated to San Francisco Bay area (I was born in San Francisco and my family is originally from there) and there I met and continued to work with many creative musicians (like Bonnie Hayes, Linda Tillery, Teresa Trull, Ray Obiedo, Narada Michael Walden) who continued to emphasize for me the fact that being a musician was the only real choice that I could make. I spent way too many years being close to destitute but for some reason I never considered another avenue or career. I just knew this was what I needed and wanted to do with my life and was willing to make the sacrifices to accommodate it.

Post: Who were your idols, mentors and peers, and how did you connect with them?

Randle: Originally, as I mentioned, there were the Beatles. Soon after that I began to listen to Folk/Rock type artists and most admired and wanted to emulate composer/singers like James Taylor, Joni Mitchell, Kenny Rankin, and other acoustic guitar-oriented songwriters. I fell in love with the power that songwriting had to invoke emotions not as easily clarified through language or music separately.

There were many people who helped and guided me along the way, mostly people I was playing with like Margie Adam and Diane Lindsay, both songwriters who partnered with me to sing their songs. I had always felt confident as a singer and musician but didn't yet consider myself a songwriter, so I often worked with other songwriters who felt less adequate as performers than I did.

I remember working with Cris Williamson, rehearsing one afternoon and reluctantly and with great trepidation worked up the courage to ask her to listen to a song I was writing. The song was "What Good Does It Do Me, Now," which Cris liked so much she included it on her next album, *Blue Rider*. It was her encouragement that particularly helped me find my voice as a songwriter.

Working with Linda Tillery really opened my eyes to the music of my African-American heritage that I had never really explored. Rather than denigrating my experience in acoustic music, she introduced me to Aretha, Otis, Etta and all the great R&B and jazz vocal greats and encouraged me to explore and learn. Linda has been one of my greatest supporters. She is enormously talented and I consider her to be one of the greats of contemporary music.

Post: How would you define Women's Music, and what do you think has happened to it?

Randle: Ah, one of my ongoing pet-peeves rearing its head again. First of all, I feel the term "Women's Music" is, and always was a thinly disguised euphemism. It is and always has been a bogus term for "lesbian music," that I've always felt, by its very existence and persistent usage, underscores the fear and homophobia we, as lesbians harbor towards ourselves.

"Women's Music" is truly a meaningless term given the definition commonly accepted by those of us who even try to understand its meaning: music by and for women. This is clearly not true. The women this music is by and for are lesbians, and the designation is supposed to be a radical declaration of pride and strength. How, then, can it be, when it dare not even speak its own name?

The artists who have operated under the umbrella of this category have always represented themselves as outlaws, revolutionaries. How revolutionary can one be spending your career preaching to the choir, while deftly sidestepping the real issues in the real world? (You can probably imagine how this opinion endears me to the Women's Music community at large).

There is a huge network of lesbians around the country and the world, complete with encoded language, largely invisible to the heterosexual population, but completely plain to each other. How was this ever designed to be anything other than the most submerged of subcultures, so inbred and insulated that the standards and practices of the world outside don't even apply?

When I began working with the originators of this musical movement there was a need to define what we were trying to do and say with this new musical adventure. Instead of defining "Women's Music" in the most obvious, confrontive and controversial way: as music by lesbians for lesbians, which would have been the most honest at the time, the spokeswomen for this movement tried to sidestep this overt declaration by attempting instead to define what "female-oriented" and "male-oriented" music was.

To the embarrassment and shock of many of us musicians, particularly those of us who did not fall under these categories, the definitions began by classifying types of music, instrumentation, lyrical content, and performance style as being specifically female or male-oriented! Incredibly enough, the original agreed-upon definition of "women-oriented" instrumentation included basically, anything acoustic and non-amplified: acoustic guitar, piano, flutes, and some hand percussion.

Types of music designated were generally anything soft and quiet: classical, folk music, a cappella vocals. Electric instruments, trap drums, horn sections, jazz, Rock, Funk, Soul, Gospel (with the notable exception of Sweet Honey in the Rock) were all considered male-oriented!

Since the primary proponents of this new genre were white, it took some time to consider that besides being nonsensical and arbitrary, these denotations were also intrinsically racist, as well as essentially contradictory. This was supposed to be a step in the direction of musical freedom for women, and yet women who had already broken through the stereotypes by playing electric bass, guitar, keyboards, horns, trap drums, playing loud dance music and rock, experimental jazz, were initially being told that their music was not affirming to women.

Fortunately, this particular set of constraints didn't last long. The definition of "Women's Music" began to be based on primary lyrical content, rather than musical form, however this was a bit constrictive in the early days. It took a long time before honest songs about the range of emotional experiences we live through as women were encouraged within this genre.

In the early days we were all encouraged to be "cheerleaders," singing songs that were affirming and uplifting and talked about women's power and strength. I remember getting into discussions with other, more sophisticated musicians about some songs I liked to perform: like "Chain of Fools" by Aretha Franklin. They felt that the lyrics weren't encouraging a powerful image of women. Now, of course, I realize that all these discussions were academic, as if singing and chanting that we were mighty and capable creatures would somehow exempt us from ever making mistakes, falling hopelessly in love with someone who treated us badly, staying at a job out of fear, not speaking up for ourselves.

The search to come up with a working definition of "Women's Music" adopted an even more insidious influence that I feel continues today, to the detriment of serious musicianship and technical expertise in all arenas of the music field. One of the basic tenets of "Women's Music" has been the very notion of nurturing and encouraging women to play and learn in a non-competitive environment.

This began, I feel, as a very good idea, encouraging women who would never had had the courage to confront the formidable obstacles erected against them, without the sense of community support backing them up. But this support quickly degenerated into the notion that to criticize or critique, to rate or judge another woman's work was equal to the kinds of meritless discrimination women had received in the music business at large.

The effect this implied gag order has made on the quality of women's work in all areas of the business cannot be dismissed. Without a basis for quality, without the impetus to assess and evaluate our own and each other's skills, we have settled for a standard that inspired women to designate themselves musicians, producers, sound engineers, record companies, without ever learning the basic and critical skills necessary to actually do the job well. The listeners were lulled into complacency, bombarded with an endless array of mediocre productions, both live and recorded, and made excuses for the poor quality based on the mere fact that women were making these records, and putting on these productions for other women. I believe lesbians who bought the records and came to shows stopped listening to the musical content and focused on the lyrical content, and the fact that this was a production that was specifically aimed at other lesbians.

For example: my first few women's music festivals were the first few festivals and the complete lack of preparation, skill, and the many people with not a whole lot of clues left me somewhat depressed rather than uplifted. Those experiences, coupled with "the battle lines:" several countrywide tours with June Millington, Linda Tillery, and Cris Williamson left me almost without hope.

Every new encounter was a repeat of the one I'd just left: a group of women who wanted to produce a concert, never having done so before, a lot of enthusiasm (at first), very little practical proficiency, and marked reluctance to obtain the needed information. For several years we, the acts that were being presented, were more responsible for actually providing the expertise necessary to produce a concert than most of the women who were in charge of the event. It was relentless and exhausting; and at first we thought we were helping these women to gain the experience they needed, but the next year a brand new group of women would replace them. It felt like running real fast just to stay in the same place.

One instance in particular, with Cris Williamson, was so laughable it's become a bit of a legend: We'd requested a sound system with two mics and two onstage monitors [speakers]. When we arrived at the auditorium, we didn't see any equipment onstage and Cris called out to the producers, "Where are the monitors?" Two women in party hats who'd been sitting in the audience jumped up and ran toward the stage exclaiming "Here we are!"

In situations like this, Cris would patiently explain to me that part of why we were here was to help educate women to get to know how to eventually become capable of staging these events. We knew that we were part of something revolutionary, that lesbians were actually crawling out of the bars and closets to congregate and become more and more visible. A few began to take real pride in the art and craft of making music work and their skill and talent began to set a new standard for all of us.

Back then what I, and I think I speak for many of my cohorts, really wanted, though, was a sense that this revolution was one of self-respect, dignity and power. Eventually we were able to see that in many arenas, women were becoming more skilled in every aspect of the music business, people like Lenny Swendinger: lights; Myrna Johnston: sound; Lisa Vogel and the Michigan women's music festival production staff; and Jeannie Rizzo Bradshaw of the Great American Music Hall in San Francisco.

I hadn't been back to any festivals and had virtually stopped performing on the women's music circuit, when I got a call from Lisa Vogel of the Michigan Womyn's Music Festival asking me if I would come and participate. Apprehensive at first, I decided to go, and was rewarded with one of the best music festival experiences I have ever had, including many of the well known and long produced jazz and Folk festivals around the world that I have performed at. It is an exemplary, ambitious, well-produced, and entirely professional event that I continued to return to for the next five years.

The production value is among the best I have ever seen, and because of this I was able to revel in the life changing experience of being surrounded by only women for days, experiencing a sense of personal safety and kinship that I had never been able to realize before. It was inspiring and encouraging and continues to be so for me. I feel that women artists, if a "should" can be applied here, should strive to be the best, most self-realized, completely honest, diligent, disciplined, and skilled artists they can be. What we have lacked in the past is access to the information, the tools and the arena to fulfill our highest purpose.

It has alternately made my life worth living and made me want to dash my brains out, pretty nearly on a daily basis since I made the choice to pursue this path, more than 30 years ago. Dealing with the grave doubts about my abilities, honestly assessing them and challenging myself to continually strive for greater knowledge and to expand my skills, is a daily struggle. It requires so much labor and focus and the courage to face my own fears, to look squarely at myself and take responsibility for my life and life's work, that the occasional conflicts I have encountered from the world outside pale by comparison.

It is so easy to blame conditions outside of ourselves for our inability to move forward, for the discrimination and bias most of us women musicians have experienced in so many forms. However I've discovered, having challenged and surmounted external barriers, I was still left with one that no amount of support or opportunity would budge: the constraints I impose upon myself. I prefer to acknowledge that the potential for discrimination exists, but to focus, not on the possibilities for failure that lurk ahead, but instead on the myriad ways I have constructed to tempt me to stray from my chosen path.

As an artist, my main concern is my creativity and what I can do to encourage it in myself as well as others. I have received much support and encouragement along the way from women, especially other musicians and have always gravitated towards people and situations that would result in my having learned something new, stretched and grown as an artist. Unfortunately, what I have seen passing for "support" among women musicians, especially in the early days of the movement, has been perverted into a kind of insular collusion based on fear of challenging the traditional bias of the music industry. The women's music movement, while it encouraged many women to try new arenas and learn skills previously unimaginable, didn't simultaneously advocate or promulgate a standard of excellence that would truly have resulted in women having increased access to this business.

Post: How did you make the transitions that led you to "The Tonight Show?"

Randle: From 1978 on I began to get hired as a backline musician and singer in various touring bands. I never actually intended it to become my career choice, I was just trying to make some money and stay in the music business, since supporting myself as a singer/songwriter was proving to be a challenge, especially in the making-a-living department.

I had begun playing percussion as an addition to playing the guitar, and somehow, I believe largely because of the magnificent and undeniable talents of Sheila (E) Escovido, the category of "female percussionist" was invented and the position suddenly was one that many bands desired to fill. I was hired often because of my dual abilities as vocalist and percussionist, and continued to work on the road in different bands until 1992, when I began working at "The Tonight Show."

At first, working as a female musician was a real challenge. I hardly ever, unless I was working with "Women's Music" artists, worked with another woman in the band. Since I was a musician rather than "just a vocalist," I was a bit of an enigma to most of the guys that I began playing with.

There was always the initial test to pass: "Can she play? Can she play as well as a man?" Once my competence was established, I was usually adopted as an honorary "Cat." The guys in the band, having never worked with women before, often had no idea how to treat me as a woman AND a musician at the same time. One reason was their lack of contact with (and habitual lack of respect for) women created confusion: either I was a woman, therefore designated "prey" or "mom," or I was a musician, and the only references applicable had to do with other male musicians.

They usually opted for the latter, and I was routinely bombarded with sexist jokes and comments about other women, to which I would feel duty-bound to rebut, reminding them that I was in fact a member of the group they were "dissing." I remember one of my first tours with George Benson was full of silly episodes. The management company asked if I would be willing to wear evening gowns to perform in, as they were trying to class up George's image. I explained that it was a little difficult to play percussion in an evening gown. The idea fizzled out primarily because the band refused to wear tuxes, either.

The guys in the band largely ignored me the first week or so, not having any idea how to relate to me, except for one of the first nights in the hotel, when the sax player knocked on my door to ask me if I could sew a button on his shirt. Incredulous, I told him that it was a safe bet that his dog could probably do better at sewing on buttons, as I'd never learned the first thing about sewing; I was a musician.

Eventually the guys warmed up to me and after about two weeks on the road, they heard that the salary that I had been hired at was less than half of what they were making. I had no idea what to ask for when I was hired, so I picked a figure that was $100 a week more than the last road gig I'd done. The management, of course, were delighted. The guys in the band, to their everlasting credit, marched me into the manager's office and demanded that my salary be equalized with theirs.

Clearly, this never would have happened had I done it on my own and I was finally able to learn, through other's valuing of my abilities and worth, that I was definitely on par with any male musician and deserved to be paid just as well, if not more, since often I was doing the job of two people: singing and playing. I never made that mistake again.

It was often a completely new concept for the road management to consider that I would require separate dressing facilities, more time than the others before the gig for dressing and make-up, etc. I've changed clothes in more makeshift dressing rooms: closets, sheets hung up, even a freight elevator once.

I also learned that I will most often be treated with the same amount of respect, courtesy and consideration that I carry myself with and treat others with. I've made lasting friendships with the guys I've played with, especially on the Tonight Show. It's a very rare occasion to be able to work with musicians closely for nearly four years, much less five days a week, forty-eight weeks a year, and still have the same respect and admiration for them as I did when I started. Familiarity often breeds contempt in a business as arbitrary and volatile as this one, but Jay and the band are fun, open-minded human beings, highly talented artists and with integrity and decency, and it's still a privilege to work with them.

Post: What are you hopes, dreams, and plans as far as your music and your career?

Randle: I would like to spend much more time than I have devoted so far to recording and performing my own compositions. I would like to work composing for other mediums than pop music, such as the little bits of composing I have done for dance companies and independent films. I am awfully pleased with the blessings that I have been shown, to be able to work doing what I love, and love doing what I need to do to make a living. I understand how rare and fortunate an occurrence this is. I don't ever see myself "retiring" or coming to a place in my life where I would want to stop.

I have other interests and aspirations that have nothing to do with music: I would like to return to college and continue my education, perhaps get a few degrees. I am interested in computers (read: obsessed by them) and never tire of trying new things. There are hundreds of books yet to read and I have a great desire to write, something that is becoming more and more of an enticement for me.

DISCOGRAPHY

Who Do We Think We Are (Windham Hill, 1994); *By the Fireside* Turtle Island Quartet (Windham Hill, 1995); *From the Vaults of Boomtown* (Close Enough, 1996).

For a complete list of Vicki Randle recordings visit her web site at http://www.primenet.com/~vrandle/factsheet.html